MIRACLE MOMENTS
IN
MONTREAL CANADIENS
HISTORY

THE TURNING POINTS,
THE MEMORABLE GAMES,
THE INCREDIBLE RECORDS

BY JIM HYNES

SPORTS
PUBLISHING

Sports Publishing books may be purchased in bulk at special discounts for sales promotion, corporate gifts, fund-raising, or educational purposes. Special editions can also be created to specifications. For details, contact the Special Sales Department, Sports Publishing, 307 West 36th Street, 11th Floor, New York, NY 10018 or sportspubbooks@skyhorsepublishing.com.

Sports Publishing® is a registered trademark of Skyhorse Publishing, Inc.®, a Delaware corporation.

Visit our website at www.sportspubbooks.com.

10 9 8 7 6 5 4 3 2 1

Library of Congress Cataloging-in-Publication Data is available on file.

Cover design by Tom Lau
Cover photo credit AP Images

ISBN: 978-1-61321-982-9
Ebook ISBN: 978-1-61321-983-6

Printed in China

AP Photo/Ron Frehm

Contents

INTRODUCTION

Montreal Canadiens supporters and many other hockey fans will understand the significance of the number of essays in this book—24, as in the number of Stanley Cups that
the team has won. When I started writing early in the 2015–16 season, the Canadiens
had just come off the greatest start in their 107-year history by winning their first nine
games. On December 1, 2015, they had a record of 19–4–3 and sat atop the NHL standings, and I started wondering if I shouldn't plan for a 25th essay . . . just in case. Later, after
the wheels came off, I considered making room for a 25th called, "The Great Collapse
of 2015–16," but thought better of it. So 24 it is.

Habs fans love a good hockey debate, so I won't be at all surprised if some don't
agree with what I consider to be the team's 24 most essential moments. With a team as
old and successful as the Canadiens, there were certainly many to choose from. In particular, I regret not paying greater tribute to the great Canadiens teams of the mid- to
late-1960s, who won four Stanley Cups in five years. But they had such stiff competition
from the dynasties that preceded and followed them.

If there was one important, joyful, hilarious, touching, tearjerker moment I wish I
could have shared with you, but could not, it would be the unveiling of the Canadiens'
Dream Team at the Montreal Forum on January 12, 1985, when the greatest legends in
team history were honored during celebrations of its 75th anniversary. So I will now.

The elected members of the Dream Team were Larry Robinson and Doug Har-
vey on defense, Jean Béliveau at center, Dickie Moore at left wing, Maurice "Rocket"
Richard at right wing, and in goal, Jacques Plante. Hector "Toe" Blake was the coach.
All, except for Blake, wearing his usual fedora, were in full uniform. The Canadiens'
opponents that night, by the way, were the Buffalo Sabres, coached by none other than
Scotty Bowman.

As a special treat, the team included the oldest surviving Canadiens player at the time,
eighty-three-year-old Hall of Famer Aurèle Joliat, a star of the 1920s and '30s and the last
survivor of the very first game played at the Forum 60 years before (he scored two goals).

As part of the ceremony, each player was to skate in alone on Jacques Plante and
shoot on goal. I don't know whose idea it was to suit Joliat up, perhaps the stubborn
"Little Giant" himself, but it was a risky move indeed.

Joliat, a favorite of my late father, was a comical sight in his modern hockey equipment, with the same little black cap he had worn as a player. But the real tragicomedy

began when he jauntily hopped out onto the Forum ice, and, about four strides in to his journey, lost his balance and fell. Helped to his feet by a Sabres player, Joliat resumed his rush up ice. The crowd cheered wildly as he began to stick-handle and dance about on his skates, but the cheers turned to a groan of horror after Joliat tripped over the red carpet the others were standing on at center ice. It's a miracle he didn't break a hip. But he regained his feet, adjusted his cap, and continued on his way. About ten feet from the net, he fired a low shot that eluded a flopping Plante. A loud roar went up and Joliat simultaneously slammed his stick and doffed his cap in celebration. Then, waving his cap at the crowd, he broke from the script and went for a little skate, successfully hopping over a section of red carpet the second time around. My friends and I, watching on TV at age nineteen or so, simultaneously laughed our heads off and cried our eyes out.

So there's your 25th moment, if you need one. It's on YouTube. Seriously, check it out.

In writing this book, I came to realize how fortunate I have been to see some of the team's greatest moments in person. I was at the Forum with my best pals on March 11, 1996 to witness the closing of the legendary rink, and at the then-Molson Centre on April 9, 2002 with my colleague and friend Jim McRae to see Saku Koivu's courageous return from cancer. Incredible nights, both.

I also saw Guy Lafleur and Ken Dryden in their rookie seasons of 1971, the Canadiens win a Stanley Cup Finals game against the Boston Bruins in 1978, and Wayne Gretzky and the Edmonton Oilers beat them in a first-round playoff game in 1981. Not bad for someone who had limited access to those hard-to-get Habs tickets.

The others I watched on TV, like the incredible Game 7 comeback against Boston in 1979, the notorious Good Friday Massacre of 1984, the Stanley Cups playoffs of 1986 and 1993, and the Centennial celebrations of 2009, with family or friends. In the case of the Centennial celebrations, I watched the events unfold with my two sons Jason and Sam, who have grown up to be big Canadiens fans, too. I wonder why?

Now I follow the Canadiens from my new home in Ithaca, NY, where I was happy to find a number of fellow Habs fans. When I left Montreal in 2013 after living there my whole life, my friends didn't ask me why, or anything about where I was moving . . . they wanted to know how I would be able to follow the Habs.

I've managed just fine. But please, no more Great Collapses.

Enjoy the moments.

Go Habs Go!

—Jim Hynes
April 2016
Ithaca, NY

1ST
PERIOD
THE REGULAR SEASON

Five for the Phantom in Canadiens' NHL debut

1

The top professional hockey league in the world is getting ready to celebrate its 100th anniversary in 2017, but it almost didn't survive its inaugural season. And the same can be said of its most iconic franchise, the Montreal Canadiens.

In 1909, the owners of Eastern Canada's top professional hockey circuit tried to rid themselves of a troublesome owner by dissolving their league and founding a new one without him (*see 1909: The Creation of Habs Nation, page 143*). But that strategy back-fired when the scorned team found new partners and founded the even better National Hockey Association (NHA). In 1917, the NHA employed the same tactic itself to dump the Toronto Blueshirts litigious owner, Eddie Livingstone, and successfully created the NHL in the process.

The eighth and final season of the NHA was a tumultuous one. The league had managed to survive, and at times thrive, during the first two years of World War I, but as Canada intensified its troops' contribution, several top players left their teams to enlist. The Ottawa Senators even proposed suspending league operations for one season, but were outvoted by the other five teams.

Then there was Eddie Livingstone, whom author D'Arcy Jenish, in his book, *The NHL: A Centennial History*, described as "a slight bespectacled man who had the gen-tle demeanour of a pastor but the fastidious personality of a tax collector or a customs inspector." The former junior player and Ontario Hockey Association referee turned hockey impresario had been a thorn in the side of his fellow NHA owners since he purchased the Toronto Ontarios (soon renamed the Shamrocks) in 1914. In 1914–15, he feuded with the league and Montreal Wanderers owner Sam Lichtenhein over a forfeited game. In 1915, Livingstone purchased the Toronto Blueshirts and transferred his Shamrocks players to his new squad. The empty Shamrocks franchise was seized by the league and kept dormant for one season. Livingstone also bickered with the owners

3

of the Blueshirts' home rink, the Arena Gardens, and at various times threatened to move the Blueshirts to Boston or start a rival league if he didn't get his way in some dispute or other.

Before the 1916–17 season, the NHA and the Canadian military came up with a unique way to deal with the exodus of talent caused by the newly enlisted players. The dormant Shamrocks franchise was handed over to the Canadian military, which then stocked its 228th Battalion, a.k.a. The Northern Fusiliers, with a number of the recently enlisted stars. The Toronto-based "Army Team," as it came to be known, featured a number of ex-Blueshirts, including star goaltender Percy LeSueur and stalwarts George and Howard McNamara. To make matters worse, from Livingstone's point of view anyhow, the new team would also play in Arena Gardens.

The idea of adding a military team to the league in the middle of a war proved to be an ill-fated one for the NHA when the 228th Battalion was ordered overseas on February 8, 1917. Fed up with Livingstone, who had continually argued with and repeatedly threatened to sue his fellow owners, and to keep the number of its teams even for scheduling purposes, the NHA unilaterally suspended the Blueshirts at a February 11 meeting. The Toronto players were dispersed among the four remaining teams. Three games into the second half of what they'd planned to be a split season anyway, the NHA simply started over with four teams: The Ottawa Senators, the Quebec Bulldogs, the Montreal Wanderers, and the Montreal Canadiens.

The defending Stanley Cup champion Canadiens (*see Canadiens Win Their First Stanley Cup, page 61*), winners of the first half with a record of 7–3, had a complete reversal of fortunes, and finished the second half, won by Ottawa, with three wins and seven losses.

Coached by the still-playing Newsy Lalonde, and led by its veteran core of Lalonde, Didier Pitre, Jack Laviolette, and star goaltender Georges Vezina, the Canadiens captured the two-game total goals series to determine an NHA champion by a score of 7–6, but were badly outplayed in the 1917 Stanley Cup Finals by the powerful Seattle Metropolitans, who became the first US team to claim the Cup. After winning Game 1 by a score of 8–4, the Canadiens lost the three following games: 6–1, 4–1 and 9–1.

What's in a name?

More turmoil marked the off-season, not the least of which was a lawsuit against the league by the spurned Livingstone, who was once again making noise about starting a rival league. The war in Europe also raged on. In September, when it was time to start preparing for the 1917–18 NHA season, the Ottawa Senators announced they would sit out a year, while the Quebec Bulldogs contemplated doing the same. NHA President Frank Robinson also resigned.

By November, a number of developments saved the upcoming season. The Senators changed their minds and decided to play, and the Toronto Arena Company, desperate to draw crowds to their Arena Gardens, announced that they would back an NHA team.

The Eddie Livingstone problem, however, remained. At a meeting on November 22, representatives of all four teams, including Quebec, simply decided to fold the NHA. Four days later, the same group got together, again at Montreal's Windsor Hotel, and founded the National Hockey League, a brand-new entity that a now livid Livingstone was simply not invited to join. As the NHL's first president, the owners chose Frank Calder, who had served as the NHA's Secretary-Treasurer since 1914.

The Quebec Bulldogs finally passed on the NHL, which meant that the league would consist of only four teams in 1917–18. The Bulldogs players were dispersed among the remaining teams, with the provincial rival Montreal Canadiens reaping the greatest benefits. "Bad" Joe Hall (*see Up Close: "Bad" Joe Hall, page 9*) was a thirty-five-year-old defenseman from Brandon, Manitoba, who earned his simple but accurate moniker with his rugged style of play and fiery temper. But the true prize was twenty-seven-year-old "Phantom" Joe Malone (*see Up Close: "Gentleman" Joe Malone, page 7*), a high-scoring, swift-skating center who had notched 41 goals in 19 games the previous season.

The Montreal Wanderers almost joined the Bulldogs on the sidelines. Complaining that they'd been losing money and couldn't ice a competitive squad unless other teams shared more players with them, the once-powerful Wanderers threatened to sit out the season as well. But when the schedule was drawn up, they were slated to host the new Toronto entry on opening night, December 19, at Westmount Arena. The Canadiens would also make their NHL debut that night, facing the Senators at Ottawa's Dey Arena.

Like the rest of the topsy-turvy season that would follow, the NHL's opening night went less than smoothly, at least in Ottawa. A December 20, 1917 *Ottawa Journal* article, under the headline "Ottawa's Disorganized Team is Beaten by Canadiens in Opening Game," spends almost as much time discussing NHL labor relations as it does describing the action on the ice.

With little else in the way of bargaining power, it was fairly common for players back in the early days of pro hockey to hold out for more money at the very last minute. Six Senators players, including regulars Hamby Shore and Jack Darragh, employed this tactic not long before the puck was set to drop on the NHL's first season.

The packed crowd waited impatiently as these last-minute negotiations delayed the game by fifteen minutes. Meanwhile, back in Montreal, Wanderers defenseman Dave Ritchie was busy scoring the first goal in NHL history before a meager crowd of 700.

When the puck finally dropped in Ottawa, the Canadiens pounced quickly, jumping out to a 3–0 lead on Joe Malone's natural hat trick. With both Shore and Darragh eventually joining the game after settling their financial affairs, the Senators rallied, but solid goaltending by Vezina, two more goals by Malone, and singles by Hall and Pitre gave the Canadiens a 7–4 win.

"The Ottawas, if they had gone on the ice at full strength and under different conditions, might have played better hockey than they did, and it would be hardly fair to judge them on last night's showing," the *Ottawa Journal* reported. But the paper also conceded "[Canadiens owner] Kennedy's team will take some beating again this season for the championship."

And then there were three

Despite the Canadiens being the defending Cup champions, the Wanderers were still English Montreal's team. The December 20, 1917 *Montreal Gazette* devoted most of its hockey section to the Wanderers' 10–9 defeat of Toronto. But the win was the last bit of good news for the Wanderers and their followers, and the Canadiens would soon be the only team for whom Montreal hockey fans could cheer.

The Canadiens followed their opening night victory with an 11–2 pasting of the Wanderers three nights later, then split a home and away series with Toronto. They were scheduled to take on the Wanderers again on January 2, 1918, when the Westmount Arena, home to both Montreal teams, was destroyed by fire that very day. Both teams lost almost all of their equipment and uniforms. It was the last straw for Wanderers owner Sam Lichtenhein, who had been ready to throw in the towel before the season began. On January 4, he announced that the team was pulling out of the remainder of the season.

Had Canadiens owner George Kennedy followed Lichtenhein's lead, the NHL would have been dead in the water less than three weeks after it started play, and hockey history may have unfolded completely differently. But there was no quit in the former wrestler and dynamic entrepreneur. The game against the Wanderers was scratched from the schedule, but three days later, back in the Jubilee Rink that was their first home, with borrowed equipment and uniforms, the Canadiens hosted and defeated the Ottawa Senators by a score of 6–5 after 27 minutes of overtime. They won four more times in January to win the first half of the split season.

The second half of the Canadiens' season was less convincing, with the team managing only three wins in eight games. They played second-half winners Toronto in a two-game, total goals playoff to determine the NHL's first champion and its representative in the Stanley Cup Finals. Toronto prevailed on the strength of a 7–3 home ice, opening game win, then defeated the PCHA Champion Vancouver Millionaires 3 games to 2.

The Canadiens were champions of the three-team NHL's 1918–19 season and went west to play the Seattle Metropolitans for the Stanley Cup in the midst of a Spanish Flu epidemic. The series was tied 2–2 when the fifth and deciding game was canceled after a number of players from each team fell ill. Nobody won the Stanley Cup in 1919, the only time except for the NHL lockout year of 2004–05 the trophy was not awarded.

Up Close: "Gentleman" Joe Malone

Born Maurice Joseph Cletus Malone in Sillery, just outside of Quebec City, in 1890, Joe Malone was one of hockey's first great pure goal-scorers. Malone earned the nickname "Phantom" for his easy skating style and uncanny ability to make his way through enemy defenses. He was also sometimes called "Gentleman Joe" for his sportsmanship in a time of physical, even violent, hockey.

An all-around athlete who also excelled at lacrosse, Malone made his pro hockey debut with his hometown Quebec Bulldogs at the age of nineteen, scoring eight goals in 12 games in 1907–08. The unpredictable nature of early pro hockey forced him to leave Quebec City on a number of occasions, but he almost always returned to play in "La Vielle Capitale." And it was there, in the period between 1910 and 1917, playing for the Bulldogs in the NHA, that Malone achieved many of his greatest successes. In 1911–12, he scored 21 goals in 18 games and led the Bulldogs to a Stanley Cup, scoring a combined five goals in two Cup challenge games. The following season, Malone exploded for an incredible 43 goals in 20 games as the Bulldogs repeated as Cup champs.

After scoring 41 goals in the 1916–17 season, Malone found himself without a team as the Bulldogs opted to sit out the first two NHL seasons. Quebec's loss was Montreal's gain, as Malone, playing on a line with Canadiens stars Newsy Lalonde and Didier Pitre, scored 44 goals in 20 games in 1917–18, a single-season record that would stand until 1945, when Maurice "Rocket" Richard" scored 50 goals in 50 games (*see page 10*).

Back with the Bulldogs for the 1919–20 season, Malone scored 39 goals in 24 games, including an NHL record seven-goal performance against the Toronto St. Patricks on January 31, 1920 that still stands. He also had a six-goal game that year to go with his three five-goal games in 1917–18. (Malone had another seven goal-game, in 1913, as well as an eight-goal game, in 1917, both in the NHA. And he scored nine goals in a 1913 Stanley Cup game.)

Malone retired after the 1923–24 season with 322 goals in a combined 249 NHA/NHL games and was inducted to the Hockey Hall of Fame in 1950. In 1998, seventy-four

Joe Malone scored 44 goals in 20 games for the Canadiens in 1917–18, a single-season record until 1944–45 (Hockey Hall of Fame).

years after he played his last game, *The Hockey News* magazine ranked him 39th on its list of the Top 100 NHL Players of All Time.

Up Close: "Bad" Joe Hall:

Kind and well-mannered off the ice according to the many friends, and even rivals, he made over a 17-year career in hockey, on the ice Joseph Henry Hall was one of hockey's original bad boys, thus his simple nickname.

The words "rough" and "tumble" crop up regularly in descriptions of the Manitoba-born defenseman's playing style. And while his run-ins with opposing players, which often earned him suspensions and fines, are legendary, and his penalty minutes grew with every passing season, Hall also had a reputation as a skilled and much sought-after game changer who could score big goals in big games.

Hall was also, plain and simple, a winner. After scoring 15 goals with his hometown Brandon Hockey Club in 1906–07, he was lent to the Kenora Thistles and helped them to a Stanley Cup win over the Montreal Wanderers.

Playing with the Joe Malone–led Quebec Bulldogs, where he toiled for seven seasons, Hall was part of two more Stanley Cup winners in 1912 and 1913. Together with Malone, he joined the Montreal Canadiens for the NHL's inaugural 1917–18 season, scoring eight goals (and totaling 100 penalty minutes) in 21 games.

In the spring of 1919, at the age of thirty-seven, Hall was still a member of the NHL champion Canadiens when they traveled to Seattle to face the PCHA champion Seattle Metropolitans to play for the Stanley Cup. The best-of-five series, played amidst the Spanish Flu epidemic of 1918–1919, was tied 2–2 after a 4–3 Canadiens win on March 30 when Hall and four other Montreal players as well as owner/manager George Kennedy were felled by the flu. Game 5 was never played, and the Cup was never awarded that year.

In an April 3 telegram PCHA President Frank Patrick wrote NHL President Frank Calder with an update about the stricken Canadiens:

" ALL BOYS EXCEPT HALL ARE DOING NICELY—LALONDE BERLANQUETTE (SIC) COUTURE HAVE BEEN NORMAL FOR TWO DAYS—THEY WILL GET OUT SATURDAY—KENNEDY HAS A SLIGHT TEMPERATURE YET BUT CONSIDER HIM DOING WELL AND NO DANGER—HALL DEVELOPED PNEUMONIA TODAY HE IS EASILY WORST CASE BUT ARE HOPING FOR THE BEST. "

Joe Hall passed away two days later in a Seattle sanitarium. In 1961, he was inducted into the Hockey Hall of Fame.

The Rocket Scores 50 in 50

2

After his breakthrough season of 1943–44, which culminated in a record-breaking play-off performance that helped bring the Montreal Canadiens their fifth Stanley Cup (*see Rocket Richard 5, Leafs 1, page 68*), twenty-three-year-old Maurice "Rocket" Richard wasn't about to rest on his accomplishments.

With his critics dismissing him as a wartime player in a watered-down, wartime league, Richard attacked the 1944–45 season and the NHL record books with vigor, often displaying his soon to be legendary bad temper at the same time.

Richard and his colleagues on the legendary Punch Line, Elmer Lach (*see Up Close: Elmer Lach, page 15*) and Hector "Toe" Blake (*see Up Close: Hector "Toe" Blake, page 92*), claimed the top three spots in the NHL's scoring race early and hung on to them for much of the year. In the fifth game of the Canadiens' season, a 9–2 victory over Chicago on November 9, Richard scored three goals and the Punch Line combined for an incredible 17 points.

Richard's consistent scoring did not go unnoticed by the Canadiens' opponents. Many players would resort to illegal tactics, like holding and tripping, to slow down the Montreal star. Others would take advantage of the frustrated Rocket's increasingly fiery temper, physically and verbally assaulting him until he retaliated. After all, the one place Richard had shown he could not score from was the inside of the penalty box.

In New York's Madison Square Garden, on December 17, after Richard's two-goal performance in an 8–5 win over Boston the previous night, New York Rangers defenseman Bob "Killer" Dill took it upon himself to get Richard off his game. While the incident has been mythologized to include two knockout punches, the truth is somewhat less dramatic. Nevertheless, newspaper accounts of the game describe a quick end to the first encounter between the two, who came together behind the New York net after a Richard scoring chance. Before Dill could throw even a single punch, Richard dropped him to the ice with a right hand to the jaw. Dill, the nephew of boxing champions Mike and Tom Gibbons (and played by widely disliked NHLer Sean Avery in Richard's film biography), was helped to his feet, cursing and threatening Richard, who awaited him in the penalty box. Dill's tirade continued until an irate Richard crossed over to the New York side of the shared sin bin and confronted the raging Ranger. Dill swung first, and Richard swung last, cutting the red-faced Blueshirt over the left eye. New York sportswriters were enthused by the boxing match within a hockey game, and one even talked of organizing a Dill-Richard rematch inside a real boxing ring. Richard scored the first Canadiens goal that night in a 4–1 win.

Moving day

By the Christmas break, Richard had scored at a steady, if not breakneck, pace. But nobody was talking about breaking records, yet. What happened on December 28 changed all that.

Accounts differ, with many saying he begged not to play that night and others claiming the exact opposite, but one thing that is known is that Maurice Richard and his family moved into a new home earlier that day, with the Rocket himself personally hauling much of the furniture up and down tenement staircases. Some versions of the story even include a piano!

An exhausted Richard showed up at the Montreal Forum as usual that night, donning his number 9 jersey for a game against the Detroit Red Wings. Canadiens coach Dick Irvin wasn't expecting much out of the pooped Rocket, but that didn't stop him from sending him out onto the ice early in the proceedings. One minute and 17 seconds into the game, Richard pounced on a Leo Lamoureux rebound and knocked it past Detroit netminder Harry Lumley. Before the game was over, Richard would score four more times and add three assists to set a new NHL single-game scoring record with eight points.

In the December 29 edition of the *Montreal Gazette*, sportswriter Dink Carroll wrote that:

> " RICHARD HAD ONE OF THOSE NIGHTS THAT HE COMES UP WITH EVERY ONCE IN A WHILE WHEN HE SEEMS TO BE TOUCHED WITH HOCKEY GENIUS. HE MADE HAIR-RAISING PLAYS LAST NIGHT THAT HE ALONE OF ALL THE PLAYERS IN THE LEAGUE AT PRESENT TIME IS PROBABLY CAPABLE OF MAKING. IN THE FINAL PERIOD THE 12,744 FANS WHO PACKED THE FORUM LIKE A SARDINE CAN, AWARE THAT HE WAS ON THE WAY TO A NEW RECORD, ROSE AS A MAN AND ROARED WITH EXCITEMENT EVERY TIME HE TOUCHED THE PUCK. "

Richard's record-setting performance even spawned a "Heritage Minute," a series of 60-second television spots highlighting famous moments in Canadian history.

If fans and sportswriters hadn't yet clued in that some existing scoring records were at risk, they did on January 20, 1945, when Richard scored goals number 30, 31, and 32 in the 30th game of the season, a 5–2 defeat of New York. Former Canadien Joe Malone's 1918 record of 44 goals in a single season suddenly seemed within reach. In a nine-game span between that game and a February 10 win against Detroit, Richard would score at least one goal per game for a total of 14 goals. He woke up on the morning of February 11 with 43 goals and 12 more games to play.

Richard's quest had now captivated hockey fans in Montreal and across North America. Canadiens fans headed to the Forum in droves, with some 5,000 people reportedly turned away from one game. When it became clear that his record would fall, the press even began hounding the long-retired Malone, who had set his single season scoring record in only 20 games, for his thoughts on the Canadiens' new scoring star. But fifty-four-year-old "Phantom Joe," not wanting to distract the young Rocket, kept them at bay.

A flair for the dramatic

The record was tied in Toronto on February 17, when the Canadiens stretched their unbeaten streak to 16 games with a 4–3 win. After they played the Blackhawks to a scoreless tie in Chicago the next day, all eyes turned to the Forum, where the Canadiens were hosting the Leafs again on Saturday, February 25. As it had in the 1944 playoffs, Toronto once again turned to forward Bob Davidson, aided this time by fellow defensive specialist Nick Metz, to cover Richard.

Referee King Clancy had his hands full from the start. Davidson took a penalty in each period, with Richard joining him once in the second frame. The game was a fight-filled one, with an over-exuberant fan even joining the fray at one point. Although they had tried valiantly to set him up for a goal, Richard's teammates also took advantage of Toronto's obsession with stopping him, and Lach scored midway through the third to give Montreal a 4–2 lead. The 13,961 fans that squeezed into the Forum, however, grew restless as the seconds ticked away. They had not gotten what they came for. And with Richard showing clear signs of fatigue, it seemed the quest for 45 would be put on hold. Furthermore, the Canadiens' next two games would be on the road.

A face-off in the Toronto end late in the third gave Irvin a chance to keep an exhausted Richard on for one last crack at the record. He jumped on his chance seconds later, collecting a loose puck in front of the Toronto goal and firing it past Leafs goalie Frank "Ulcers" McCool. The Forum faithful went wild, littering the ice with debris and cheering raucously. Joe Malone appeared on the chaotic scene and presented Richard with the puck he'd just put past McCool.

The next target was 50, but it would prove more difficult to achieve than most people thought. Aware of what Richard was trying to do, his opponents doubled their efforts and spared no defensive tactics, legal or illegal. But in game number 47 on March 11, with 46 goals then to his credit, a two-goal performance got Richard to number 48. He struck again on March 15, notching the only Montreal goal in a rare 2–1 loss in Detroit. He needed only one more goal and had two more games in which to score it, and game number 49 would see the Canadiens play the Blackhawks at home.

The game was a wild one. Chicago struck three times in the first 12 minutes and jumped out to a 3–0 lead. Blake had the lone goal in the second period before Bobby Fillion, twice, scored three minutes apart in the middle of the third and Lach followed with one of his own to give the Canadiens another win. In between, Richard had the chance to break the record in the most dramatic of fashions when he was awarded a penalty shot in the second period. But his shot was blocked by Chicago substitute goalie Doug Stevenson. Later, Richard appeared to have scored his 50th of the year, but remained stuck at 49 when referee King Clancy disallowed the goal, nearly setting off a riot in the process. If Richard were to reach the 50-goal mark, he would have to do it the following night, March 18, in the Boston Garden.

The first-place Canadiens headed for Boston to play the fourth-place Bruins in the final game of the 1944–45 season, with both teams having already clinched playoff spots. A crowd of more than 12,000 was on hand to witness a wide-open game that nevertheless featured a scoreless first period. The second frame ended knotted 1–1 on goals by Boston's Herb Cain and Montreal's Dutch Hiller. With Richard still seeking his elusive 50th, Jack McGill put the Bruins ahead 2–1 with than less five minutes to play in the third.

Richard was running out of time. But McGill's tally seemed to wake him and the slumbering Canadiens. Suddenly, as they had done all season long, the members of Montreal's Punch Line took over the game and its scoresheet.

With 2:15 left to play, Richard took a pass from Lach and fired it past Bruins goaltender Harvey Bennett. A milestone once thought unattainable had been reached. Maurice Richard had scored 50 goals in 50 games. It would be 36 years before another NHLer could lay claim to the same feat.

With the score tied, the Punch Line got back to work. Fifty-seven seconds later it was Blake's turn, on a pass from Richard. And 18 seconds after that, it was Lach, unassisted. Minutes from a 2–1 defeat, the Canadiens had rallied to win, 4–2.

When it was all over Elmer Lach (who was later named NHL MVP), not Richard, sat atop the NHL's list of scoring leaders with 80 points. His 54 assists were also a new

Maurice "Rocket" Richard storms the opposing goal during the epic "50 in 50" season of 1944–45 (Le Studio du Hockey/Hockey Hall of Fame).

NHL record. Richard, with 23 assists to go along with his incredible 50 goals, was second with 73 points, while Blake's 67 gave him third place.

The Canadiens, who had enjoyed an 80-point season, losing only eight of 50 games, dropped their first-round playoff series to Toronto in six. All four Leafs wins were by one goal, with one coming in overtime. Richard, who had 10 multiple-goal games during the regular season, scored four goals in Game 5 alone, and finished the playoffs with six goals and two assists.

THE 50-GOAL CLUB

Nobody scored 50 goals in an NHL season again until after Maurice Richard retired in 1960, despite the fact that the schedule was lengthened to 60 games in 1946 and 70 games in 1949. The next player to score 50 goals in a season was Richard's former teammate, Bernard "Boom-Boom" Geoffrion, who had 50 in 64 games in 1960–61. The following year, Chicago's Bobby Hull scored exactly 50 goals in 70 games. Hull had four more seasons of 50 or more goals, playing between 65 and 78 games.

The next player to score 50 goals in 50 games was Mike Bossy of the New York Islanders, who tallied twice in the dying minutes of the 50th game of the 1980–81 season to reach the 50-goal mark. Ironically, Richard had urged the Canadiens to choose Bossy, who grew up near Richard's own home in Montreal's Ahuntsic neighborhood, in the 1977 amateur draft. They passed, and Bossy went on to score 573 NHL goals (more than Richard) and enjoy nine straight 50-goal seasons.

Less than a year later, Wayne Gretzky would take the goal-scoring milestone to another place entirely when he scored his 50th goal of 1981–82 in less than half a season. On December 30, 1981, in his 39th game of the season, he scored five times to reach the 50-goal mark.

Since Maurice Richard reached the 50-goal mark in March 1945, the milestone has been reached 185 more times by 89 different players.

Up Close: Elmer Lach

Elmer James Lach joined the Canadiens in 1940–41 at the age of twenty-two and was soon considered one of the NHL's premiere centermen. He retired after the 1954 season as one of the greatest playmakers in NHL history.

Nicknamed the Nokomis Flash after his Saskatchewan hometown, Lach enjoyed his greatest successes as a member of the Canadiens' fabled Punch Line from 1943–44 to 1947–48. He led the NHL in assists in 1944–45, 1945–46, and again in 1951–52 and was the league's top scorer twice, making him the first-ever Art Ross Trophy recipient, in 1947–48. Lach won the NHL's Hart Trophy as the league's most valuable player in 1945.

A three-time Stanley Cup champion, Lach scored the winning goal in the Cup-clinching fifth game in overtime against Boston in the 1953 Stanley Cup Finals. After the goal, Maurice Richard leapt into his outstretched arms with such force that Lach suffered a broken nose.

Lach's tenacious style of play won him the hearts of Canadiens fans, but almost certainly shortened his career due to the many serious injuries he incurred. He missed almost all of 1941–42, his sophomore season, after dislocating his shoulder and fracturing his wrist in the first game of the year. Lach is believed to have broken his nose seven times and his jaw three times. In February of 1947, he fractured his skull.

Elmer Lach was inducted into the Hockey Hall of Fame in 1966. In 1998, *The Hockey News* magazine ranked him at number 68 on its list of the Top 100 NHL Players of All Time. Lach was the oldest living Canadiens player prior to his death in Montreal at age ninety-seven on April 4, 2015.

Jacques Plante Debuts the Goalie Mask

3

It wasn't a milestone goal, miraculous save, or even a particularly good game. In fact, it was just a small part of another regular season matchup in an era where the same six teams played each other over and over again. But in 2007, 48 years after the event took place, *The Hockey News* magazine ranked it fourth in its special edition chronicling "Sixty Moments That Changed the Game." And it occurred on one of the biggest stages in the sporting world, just a short stroll from Broadway, in New York City's iconic Madison Square Garden. On November 1, 1959, Jacques Plante of the Montreal Canadiens became the first goaltender to wear a goalie mask in a hockey game.

Goalies had worn masks in hockey games before, but they were borrowed from other sports. Montreal Maroons netminder and future Hall of Famer Clint Benedict, nicknamed "Praying Benny" and "Tumbling Clint" for his once illegal habit of flopping to the ice to make saves, was the first goalie to wear a mask in an NHL game. It just wasn't a goalie mask, though. On February 20, 1930, also at Madison Square Garden, and after suffering severe facial injuries six weeks prior, Benedict returned to action sporting a strange-looking mask when the Maroons took to the ice against the New York Americans. An article in the February 23, 1930 edition of the *New York Times* noted: "Benedict, the Maroons goalie, played his first game since his injuries over a month ago, wearing a huge mask to protect his injured nose."

If the mask looked nothing like the goalie masks that appeared nearly 30 years later, it's because it was never intended for hockey. Manufactured by a Boston sporting goods company, it has been described as both a football face guard and a boxer's sparring mask. Made of leather supported by wire, it covered the forehead, nose, and lower face, but not the eyes. The large nosepiece obscured Benedict's vision, but, in the short-term, it was better than nothing. The game against the Americans ended in a 3–3 tie, and it is unclear how long Benedict continued to use the mask, but he wore it for the last time in a defeat he blamed directly on his bulky face protector.

Before and after Benedict, other goalies also looked to other sports for facial protection. Some have suggested that the first goaltender to wear a mask was a woman. In 1927, Elizabeth Graham of the Queen's University women's hockey team took to the ice wearing a fencing mask to protect her teeth. Others wore masks designed for lacrosse. But the mask most popular with amateur goalies for decades, years before Elizabeth Graham, was the baseball catcher's mask, invented by Harvard's Fred Thayer in 1877 . . . 52 years before Jacques Plante was born.

So, with a decent sports mask available since 1877, albeit one featuring vision-obscuring metal bars, why did it take another 82 or more years for professional hockey goalies to start wearing them? The answer lies in both the equipment and rules of early hockey, and even more, as time wore on, in the attitudes of the members of the hockey establishment.

Early hockey sticks were thick, heavy pieces of wood with flat, uncurved blades. And in the game's first years, many leagues, including the NHL, forbade goaltenders from throwing themselves to the ice to make saves. To do so was to incur a two-minute penalty. Back then, most goals were scored by whipping shots along the ice, or just a few inches above its surface. Goalies simply didn't need masks in hockey's early days. But, thanks mostly to the clever Clint Benedict, the NHL lifted its ban on sprawling goalies in 1918, and after sticks improved and ever-stronger players began lifting their shots, the profession of goaltender became a dangerous one indeed, with gruesome facial injuries of all kinds, including eye injuries leading to blindness, becoming increasingly common.

As mad as it seems today, though, hockey coaches, mangers, fans, and even some netminders themselves resisted the idea of offering facial protection to goalies as late as the 1950s. The idea of goalies wearing masks was attacked from all sides, with arguments both technical and psychological. Some said they would be too heavy and too hot to wear. Others questioned the courage of the wearer, suggesting that a real man would never hide his face from his opponents. Muzz Patrick, the general manager of the New York Rangers, even invoked a dubious at best financial argument: "The goaltenders in our organization will never wear a mask," he said. Why? "Because women who like hockey want to see the players' faces." Even badly scarred ones, it seems.

It takes a trailblazer

That someone would eventually introduce the goalie mask to pro hockey, however, was inevitable, and that Jacques Plante would be that the person made a lot of sense. Plante was an innovator with a mind of his own. Though it earned him scorn at the time, he was the first goaltender to regularly wander away from his net to play the puck. Plante also pioneered the stand-up style of goaltending that emphasized cutting down angles and "squaring-up" to the shooter. He later authored some of the first, and finest, books on goaltending.

Off the ice, Plante was known as both a hypochondriac and all-around oddball, to his coaches and teammates, at least. He liked to read and paint landscapes in his spare time, and on road trips, while his teammates whiled away the hours in trains and hotel rooms smoking cigars and playing cards, Plante would put his time to good use, knitting long underwear, undershirts, scarves, and wool hats for himself, his family, and friends.

Debuting for the Canadiens in 1952–53, Plante took over the netminder's job full-time in 1954–55. The following season, he helped lead the powerful Canadiens to the first of what would be five consecutive Stanley Cup championships (*see Five Consecutive Cups, page 84*). By 1959–60, he was a star, with four Vezina trophies as the NHL's best goaltender under his belt.

At the same time he was collecting trophies and accolades, however, Plante had also acquired a frightening number of injuries—four broken noses, a broken jaw, fractured cheekbones, and a hairline fracture of his skull to go along with the approximately 200 stitches required to close gashes in his face and head.

Plante began toying with the idea of wearing a protective mask almost from the moment he became a full-time NHLer, and he openly talked about his desire to do so. He reportedly tried a plastic one sent to him by a Granby, Quebec man as early as 1954, and old photos show him with a variety of other kinds of facial protection, including a catcher's mask.

That same year, Plante tested a clear plastic, full-face shield that a St. Mary's, Ontario inventor by the name of Delbert Louch had sent to each of the NHL's six starting goaltenders. One by one, they tried to cast aside Louch's "shatterproof face protector for all sports," complaining about heat, fog, and glare. All except the pioneering Plante, who cut a large eye opening and added padding to the interior of the one he was given. Though Plante never wore his modified Louch mask in a game, he used it regularly in practices.

By the late 1950s, the only truly logical argument against goalies wearing masks was the complaint that they would not be able to see properly when wearing one, thereby impairing their ability to make saves. Without the mask sitting flush against his face, it was difficult for a goaltender to see well to the side, and especially, down to his feet, where blocked pucks often collected. Jacques Plante needed a better mask.

Enter the mask

Everyone who had ever read a Montreal newspaper sports section knew about Jacques Plante and his quest for finding facial protection. In the spring of 1959, shortly after backstopping the Canadiens to their fourth straight Cup, Plante received a letter from a man

Goaltending pioneer Jacques Plante shows off the mask he debuted on November 1, 1959 (Studio Alain Brouillard/Hockey Hall of Fame).

with an idea for a better goalie mask. His name was Bill Burchmore, a thirty-six-year-old Montrealer and the sales manager for a company called Fibreglass Canada Ltd. A youth hockey coach and longtime Canadiens fan, Burchmore had seen Plante injured by a shot to the face the previous season. At work the next day, he came across what he thought might be the answer to the conundrum of poor mask fit in the "person" of a fiberglass mannequin. The answer, he believed, lay in creating a fiberglass mask from a plaster mold of the intended wearer's face. The result, in theory, would fit like a second skin.

Plante was both skeptical and reluctant at first. He knew he'd have to persuade his coach, ornery Canadiens legend Hector "Toe" Blake, to let him wear one in games. Although Blake was allowing Plante to experiment with masks in practices, he believed, among other things, that they made goalies complacent. The idea of having a plaster mold of his face didn't exactly appeal to Plante either, but he was eventually persuaded to make his way to the Montreal General Hospital to have his face slathered with plaster of Paris.

From the face mold made that day, Bill Burchmore built a simple mask, layering sheets of fiberglass cloth saturated with resin over each other until he'd created 14-ounce, 1.8-inch-thick shield that could withstand the force of a fiercely fired hockey puck. Burchmore padded the inside with strips of rubber and attached leather straps to its sides. He painted it, perhaps to hide its presence, a so-called flesh tone.

The new mask was a hit . . . with Plante, anyway. He used it during training camp and claimed he could follow the puck perfectly well while wearing it. And he felt more confident rather than complacent. But Plante failed to convince coach Blake to allow him to wear it in games, and when the 1959–60 NHL season got under way, Plante stood before his goal bare-faced once again.

It didn't help the cause of the mask that the powerhouse Canadiens got off to a terrific start that season. When they pulled into Madison Square Garden on November 1 to take on the Rangers, who were led by star forward Andy Bathgate, the NHL's reigning Hart Trophy winner as league MVP and the third-leading scorer in 1958–59, the defending champion Canadiens were in the midst of an eight-game unbeaten streak. Why mess with a good thing?

As with many great legends, the details sometimes differ according to who's doing the telling, and how long after the event actually occurred. But one thing is certain—what happened that night helped change the game of hockey forever.

For years, the shot in question was said to be an accidental backhand. In more recent times, however, Andy Bathgate has confessed that there was nothing accidental about it. Angry over what he perceived to be an intentional trip by Plante that sent him headlong into the boards in a game earlier that season, the Rangers' star was looking for some measure of revenge. Three minutes and sixteen seconds into the game, he seized his opportunity and purposely lifted a quick, rising shot that struck the Canadiens net-minder in the face, opening a ragged cut along his nose.

"I just gave him a fairly good wrist shot," Bathgate told Canadian television sports network TSN on the 50th anniversary of the event in 2009. "And I was trying to hit him somewhere where he would remember me, and I nailed him. It wasn't a hard shot. If I'd really wanted to shoot it hard I could have broken his jaw. But he bled good."

Plante fell to the ice in pain, then was helped to his feet and escorted to the Garden clinic where Rangers team physician Kazuo Yanagisawa used seven stitches to close the gash in his face. As the crowd waited impatiently for action to resume, Plante and Toe Blake had a heated exchange behind the scenes. Plante would keep playing, he said, but not without his new mask. Blake fumed, but he had little choice. In a time before official backup goaltenders, his only alternative would have been an emergency amateur back-stop of questionable ability pulled from the stands, so he eventually relented.

When Plante finally skated back onto the ice more than 20 minutes after being hit, a hush fell over the 15,925 Garden faithful as they took in the strange, and historic, scene. The comedians in the press box, meanwhile, had a field day describing the spec-tacle before them. The following day's newspapers told of a goaltender that looked like "something out of a Hollywood horror show" or a "man dead from the neck up" who "startles elderly women and children." One reporter, perhaps a theater critic filling in for a sportswriter colleague, described Plante as looking like "a character in a Japanese Noh play."

When the final buzzer sounded, the Garden scoreboard read Montreal 3, Rangers 1. Plante had surrendered but one goal wearing Bill Burchmore's creation, while Rangers goalie Lorne "Gump" Worsley, who would later go down in history as one of the great-est mask resisters of all time, gave up three. Plante stuck around after the game to pose for photographers, his uniform stained with his own blood, holding up his new mask for the world to see. He left the Garden that night after striking a deal with Coach Blake. He could continue wearing the mask until his injury healed. Later on they agreed that he could keep wearing it as long as the team kept winning. And win they did, extending their streak to 18 games and not suffering a loss until early December.

Despite the success he and the team had after he first donned the mask, it wasn't all smooth sailing for Plante and his mask mission. The strange new piece of equipment was the talk of the hockey world, and while some expressed admiration, many more ques-tioned the courage of the man behind the mask. And then there was the cantankerous Toe Blake, still unconvinced of the mask's effectiveness.

In fact, while the story is often told that Plante heroically donned the mask that night and never again played without one, he actually played one more maskless game. With the Canadiens slumping near season's end, Blake urged Plante to leave his mask in the locker room for a March 8, 1960 contest against the Detroit Red Wings. The Canadiens lost by a 3–0 score and the much-maligned mask returned the following night. Five weeks later the Canadiens swept the Toronto Maple Leafs in four straight games to claim a record fifth consecutive Stanley Cup. At the NHL's annual awards banquet, Plante collected a fifth straight Vezina Trophy as the league's best goaltender.

While the reception it received wasn't exactly a warm one, the goalie mask may have taken much longer to be accepted had Jacques Plante not won hockey games while wearing his. Mere months after Plante, Boston Bruins netminder Don Simmons became the second NHL goalie to don a mask, and many minor league goaltenders followed suit. Goaltending legend Terry Sawchuk, his face and psyche damaged by years of playing without one, adopted the mask in 1962.

It's often believed that the aforementioned Gump Worsley was the last of the barefaced goalies. The rotund, buzz-cut wearing "Gumper" liked to joke that "my face is my mask" and that it would be unfair to deprive hockey fans of his "beautiful face." But after playing 855 games without a mask, he wore one for the final six of his career, which ended in 1974. The last brave face in hockey actually belongs to the little known Andy Brown. Mostly a backup netminder who played in only 62 games with Detroit and Pittsburgh, Brown defended the Pittsburgh goal without a mask in a 6–3 loss to the Atlanta Flames on April 7, 1974. The 1974–75 season began with every single NHL goaltender sporting a mask. Brown, however, moved to the World Hockey Association, where he played another 86 games, all without a mask, over three seasons with the Indianapolis Racers before retiring in 1977.

BURCHMORE AND PLANTE LEAD THE MASK REVOLUTION

Jacques Plante is often incorrectly referred to as the inventor of the goalie mask. More precisely, Plante championed the mask's cause, pushing for its acceptance and wearing the first mask made for hockey in a game. The true title of goalie mask inventor belongs to Montrealer Bill Burchmore, the man who imagined, designed, and made Plante's first three masks.

Following its debut on November 1, 1959, the goalie mask was soon big news, and so was its creator. On December 12, Burchmore was the subject of a *Montreal Gazette* article under the headline "Mount Royal Inventor Comes to Goalies' Aid." The report, penned by reporter Pat Curran, recounts how other goalies were ordering masks at a cost of $300 each, and also offered the intriguing news that "Burchmore has also been contacted by the Russian Embassy."

Plante only wore Burchmore's first creation for a few months. By January of 1960, he had come up with a better, but even weirder looking mask. Called the "pretzel mask" for reasons obvious to anyone who's ever seen one, it consisted of caramel-colored fiberglass bars contoured to the face. Almost four ounces lighter, it was also much cooler than the original mask, thanks to improved airflow. Plante wore a second and larger Burchmore-made pretzel mask for the 1961–62 season, in which he played all 70 of his team's games and became the first ever goaltender to win the Hart Trophy as NHL MVP.

Plante later worked with other mask designers, and in 1970 founded his own mask-making company, Fibrosport. Numerous NHL goaltenders wore Fibrosport masks throughout the decade.

THE CASE OF THE MISSING MASK

The off-Broadway stage where the goalie mask made its debut in 1959 was also the scene of one of the most bizarre incidents in hockey history, and Jacques Plante, through no fault of his own, found himself thrust front and center once again.

On April 8, 1971, during Game 2 of the first-round playoff series between the Maple Leafs and the New York Rangers, Toronto goalie Bernie Parent lost his mask after wading into a late-game brawl. During the ensuing chaos, Rangers star Vic Hadfield picked up the mask and flung it high into the Madison Square Garden stands. Despite pleas for its return, and a thorough search of the area by a number of police officers, the mask was never located.

Today's NHL goalies have several masks, but Parent in 1971 owned but one, and wisely chose to watch the rest of the game from the safety of the Leafs' bench. It is somehow fitting, however, that the game had to be completed by Toronto's forty-two-year-old backup goalie, Jacques Plante, the mask pioneer who was the first to wear one in a game more than a decade earlier.

The missing mask resurfaced at a sports memorabilia show in 2012. Its exact whereabouts for the intervening 41 years remain shrouded in mystery.

1976–77:
The Greatest Season

4

Of all the record-setting numbers posted by the Montreal Canadiens in 1976–77, the most impressive was humble number eight. That's eight, as in eight losses for the entire year, the fewest ever recorded in a minimum 70-game NHL season, or one loss about every month or so, give or take. The closest team to the Canadiens in league standings that year was the Philadelphia Flyers and they lost twice as many games, 16, a number any team would be thrilled to claim, then or now. Instead, the benchmark is eight, unlikely ever to be matched.

The Canadiens were in a league by themselves in 1976–77, finishing with a record 60 wins, eight losses, and 12 ties. With a still-record 132 points they were 20 points north of the Flyers (112) in the overall standings, and outscored the opposition by 216 goals (another record). Individually, they led just about every key offensive and defensive category, including: goals (Steve Shutt, 60), assists (Guy Lafleur, 80), points (Lafleur, 136), plus/minus (Larry Robinson, 120), shutouts (Dryden, 10), and goaltender wins (Dryden, 41). They also claimed four out of six First Team All-Star positions and most of the league awards, including the Hart Trophy for the NHL's Most Valuable Player (Lafleur).

The only team to come close to matching the Canadiens' sterling regular-season performance that year was Montreal itself during its Stanley Cup playoff run. The Canadiens went 12–2 in the postseason, giving up just 23 goals, or 1.64 per game, en route to a second straight championship.

The 1976–77 Canadiens were the 1927 "Murderers' Row" New York Yankees. They had no weakness up and down the bench, or behind it. Hall of Fame coach Scotty Bowman ruled the team with an iron fist, always demanding more from his players regardless of their team or individual successes, this on a squad that would eventually send nine players to the Hockey Hall of Fame alongside their famous coach. From start—a 10–1 destruction of the Pittsburgh Penguins—to finish—an 11–0 annihilation of the Washington Capitals in the second-to-last game of the season—the Canadiens would show

24

few chinks in their red, white, and blue armor. When they did slip slightly, losing two games in five days at one point, they quickly got their act back together and ran off a string of 21 undefeated games. They lost only once on Montreal Forum ice all year, and that was a one-goal squeaker to their archrivals, the Boston Bruins.

Sam and Scotty

To what did the Canadiens owe so much of their success that season? For starters, they were built using a template designed by experienced hockey man and general manager, Sam Pollock, in which every player, except for center Peter Mahovlich, was drafted or developed within the team's junior and minor-league system. That system would be emulated by more than a few teams over time—although never quite matched— including in later years by the multi-Cup-winning New Jersey Devils. The Devils' architect, general manager Lou Lamoriello, would fashion his squad in the likeness of the most successful teams in sports history, including the New York Yankees, the Green Bay Packers, and the Montreal Canadiens. There could be no better company or higher praise.

Ironically, if the players themselves were looking for praise in 1976–77, the last place they would find it was coming from their coach. While it's true that Bowman had one thing on his mind and one thing only, winning—appropriate for the coach with the most wins of all time—he was equally adept at keeping his team on edge if he felt they were growing too comfortable with their own success. He ran an exceptionally tight ship and there was no mistaking who was at the helm, even among veterans like Mahovlich.

"Scotty never allowed us to get bored," the strapping center later told *The Hockey News* magazine. "Everybody talks about all the talent we had. But one of the things Scotty did very well was he knew how to manipulate that talent to make sure that talent was ready to play every night. We always had two or three extra players around who could take your spot in the lineup and the team wouldn't miss a beat. Even though we were winning all the time, even if you had bumps and bruises, you kept playing because you were scared to death of losing your spot in the lineup. When you go through the first half of the season and you've lost only four or five games, it's the coach who creates the atmosphere where everybody is on pins and needles."

If the Canadiens themselves were on pins and needles, imagine how the competition felt, especially those who rolled into the Forum during Montreal's 34-game home undefeated streak between November 1, 1976 and April 2, 1977. Imagine what it was like during the national anthem, to look down the ice, past the big "CH" logo at center and see, for starters, 6-foot-4 Dryden standing in front of the goal. Then imagine the

Two of the "Big Three": Serge Savard (left) and Larry Robinson (right). Together with fellow Hall of Famer Guy Lapointe, the famed trio dominated games at both ends of the ice (Portnoy/Hockey Hall of Fame).

virtually impenetrable defensive corps in front of him that featured "The Big Three" of Robinson, Guy Lapointe, and Serge Savard. Finally, think about having to contend with a forward lineup that boasted, according to more than a few hockey experts, four first lines, with the likes of Lafleur, Shutt, Jacques Lemaire, Yvan Cournoyer, and with only two players over the age of thirty (Cournoyer and Jimmy Roberts). On most nights, there would be no imagining the outcome.

If you wanted to try to match the Canadiens' speed, God bless. They could burn you with the likes of Lafleur and Cournoyer, nicknamed "The Roadrunner." If you wanted to try to out-gun them, you would need to get through lock-down specialists Doug Jarvis and Bob Gainey, the latter deemed the best two-way player of his generation. If you wanted to try to intimidate them with rough and tumble play—not an uncommon strategy when facing a skilled opponent especially during the 1970s NHL—good luck with that. They were essentially fearless, from the veterans to youngsters like Doug Risebrough, who led the team in penalty minutes, 132, and still managed to score 22 goals.

And did we mention Dryden?

For some, the lasting image of the 1976–77 Canadiens was Lafleur flying down the right wing, his long, light brown hair flowing in the wind, and unleashing a screaming slap shot behind a sacrificial opposing goalie, or Savard peeling away from a fore-checking forward with his signature, ballet-like "Savardian Spin-o-rama" or even Bowman, stoically behind the bench, chewing ice with his chin slightly raised from the earned confidence. The most symbolic image, however, was surely that of Dryden, standing oh-so casually during breaks in the play, leaning on the end of his goal stick, chin on gloves, elbows out to the sides, not a care in the world. It was almost like he was leaning on a rake while chatting with his neighbor over a garden hedge.

Dryden, already held in mythical regard in Montreal for having won a Stanley Cup in his first year in the league, 1970–71—even before achieving official rookie status—and "stealing" a quarterfinal series against the heavily favored Bruins (*see Dryden Debuts as Canadiens Shock Bruins, page 95*), would elevate his heroic play and image in 1976–77 by winning 41 of the 56 games he played during the regular season, and 12 of 14 in the playoffs. He would lose just 6 of the 56 games he played that year.

In his unique way of seeing the game—unique as the number 29 on his back and his cat-like nimbleness for such a large goalie—Dryden would say that he saw himself as "an extension of the Canadiens' offense" by virtue of being able to turn aside just about anything the opposition would throw at him, thereby removing any iota of confidence shooters might have mustered. The Canadiens' daunting defense would take it from there, and their finesse forwards would finish things off.

The Canadiens would win 30 games by 4 goals or more in 1976–77 and grow stronger and more dominant as the season wore on. After recording a loss in Buffalo in early March, they nearly ran the table over the final 12 games of the season, winning 10 and tying 2 and outscoring their opponents 59–12. They would finish with a second-best-ever winning percentage of .825. It was as if they were priming themselves for the playoffs.

In the postseason, Montreal swept the St. Louis Blues, 4–0, downed the gritty and up-and-coming New York Islanders, 4–2, and blanked the Bruins, 4–0, to win their second straight Cup and the 20th in team history. Lafleur led the way offensively with 26 points, and Dryden recorded 4 shutouts in just 14 games. In other words, not much had changed from the regular season.

In the end, though, it was about more than mere numbers and had everything to do with the way Montreal achieved its wonder season: Simply put, they did it with a style and panache befitting their Gallic heritage. Still widely celebrated as the "Flying Frenchmen," a moniker bestowed in earlier years when the likes of Maurice Richard and Jean Béliveau immortalized the *bleu, blanc, rouge* with effortless grace, speed, and poise. The newer cast, led by the likes of Lafleur, Lemaire, and Lapointe, were equally poised and elegant, and re-introduced a brand of hockey that would counter the rough-and-ready style being offered by teams like the two-time Cup-winning Flyers, whose "Broad Street Bullies" nickname told you all you needed to know about their preferred style of play.

Montreal had ended the Flyers' two-Cup run the previous season by sweeping them in the final, 4–0, and, if not fully ending, certainly putting a damper on the back-alley style of hockey that had crept into the game in the early-1970s (*see Good vs. Evil: The Series That Saved Hockey, page 103*). Speed and skill were back, and the Canadiens would set the pace over a four-year Cup run with the 1976–77 season being the new measure.

The true impact of the Canadiens' era-changing style of play was perhaps summed up best by their legendary defenseman, eight-time Stanley Cup winner and Hall of Famer, Savard:

"This is not only a victory for the Canadiens; it is a victory for hockey. Young people have seen that a team can play electrifying, fascinating hockey while still behaving like gentlemen."

Other NHL teams got the message. The Islanders' dynasty that followed was itself built on speed and skill, as were the 1980s Edmonton Oilers and, much later, the recent Chicago Blackhawks championship teams (managed by Bowman's son, Stan). In one way or another, they all owed a debt of gratitude to the 1976–77 Canadiens and their standard of hockey excellence.

The closest any NHL team has come to matching the Canadiens' remarkable season was Montreal's 1977–78 team. That group of slackers, with largely the same lineup as the record-setters from the year before, notched only 59 wins, 10 losses, and 11 ties in the regular season, and went 12–3 in the playoffs en route to a third-straight Cup. Amazingly, their team and individual stats were almost identical to those of the previous year. Almost. There could only be one greatest season of all time, and it belongs to the 1976–77 Montreal Canadiens—a team that lost only eight times.

Up Close: The Big Three

They joined the team at different times, but between 1974 and 1979, the Canadiens could boast having three of the NHL's six best defensemen all on one team. Savard, Lapointe, and Robinson: they called them The Big Three.

The group's elder statesman was Serge Savard, two and five years older than Guy Lapointe and Larry Robinson respectively. Savard joined the Canadiens full-time at the age of twenty-one in 1967 and won two of his eight Stanley Cups with the great Jean Béliveau–led teams of the 1960s. Strong and defensively responsible, Savard was also a smooth skater who could join the offense, and he frequently employed his patented "spin-a-rama" to shed forecheckers and lead an offensive charge.

Guy Lapointe joined Savard and the Canadiens in 1970 and combined hard checking and impeccable positioning with sharp offensive instincts in becoming a First-Team All-Star in 1972–73. An incorrigible prankster in the dressing room, Lapointe was all business on the ice, and his powerful shot was a key part of Montreal's fearsome power play. He scored more than 20 goals in three straight seasons, with the 28 he tallied in 1974–75 still a team record for defensemen.

Then there was the "Big Bird," the curly-haired 6-foot-4 Larry Robinson, who used his strength, reach, and skating to dominate hockey games. The most decorated of the Big Three, Robinson won the Conn Smythe Trophy in 1978, the Norris Trophy as the NHL's best defenseman in 1977 and 1980, and was a First-Team All-Star in 1977, 1979, and 1980. In 1998, *The Hockey News* magazine placed Robinson at number 24 on its list of the Top 100 NHL Players of All Time.

Time-on-ice was not kept track of in the time of The Big Three the way it is today, but suffice to say that, with the three future Hall of Famers in the lineup, the fifth and sixth defensemen on the Canadiens of that era often didn't break a sweat.

Guy! Guy! Guy!: Lafleur Scores Two in Forum Return

5

There's an old saying among hockey players and fans that winning always makes the postgame beer taste better. That's certainly always been the case in Montreal, especially on Saturday nights, when Canadiens games have always had a special air about them. Montreal hockey fans, especially back when the team played in the Forum, were known to dress a little more sharply for Saturday games, and perhaps even expect a bit more of a show, or at the very least a win, to send them off into the Montreal night. Goals by visiting teams, seven nights a week, have always been unwelcome, usually greeted by a derisive silence. But on Saturday February 4, 1989, with a very special guest in town, Canadiens fans roared in appreciation after two goals by the New York Rangers.

Guy Lafleur was a special player. And for most of the 14 seasons he played there as a member of the Canadiens, he could do no wrong in Montreal. Even the police were rumored to have afforded him special privileges from time to time.

After leading his Quebec Remparts team to a Memorial Cup Championship in the spring of 1971, following a 130-goal, 209-point regular season, Lafleur was a household name in Quebec when the Canadiens picked him first overall in the NHL Amateur Draft. In Montreal, he was touted as the heir-apparent to his own boyhood idol, Canadiens captain Jean Béliveau, who'd just announced his retirement after leading the team to another Stanley Cup, his tenth.

Today, a 29-goal rookie year would be considered an achievement, but Canadiens fans had high expectations for Lafleur, and after seasons of 28 and 21 goals, some considered the well-paid right-winger to be a bit of a dud.

That all changed in the fall of 1974, when the now helmetless Lafleur suddenly found his stride, scoring 53 goals in 70 games and finished fourth among the 1974–75 NHL scoring leaders. From 1975 to 1980, Lafleur produced five more 50-goal seasons and helped lead the Canadiens to four consecutive Stanley Cups, winning three straight scoring titles from 1975–76 to 1977–78, two Hart Trophies as NHL MVP, and one

Conn Smythe Trophy as the 1977 NHL playoff MVP. To his legion of French-speaking fans, he was "Le Demon Blond." In English he was "the Flower." To many others, he was simply "Guy."

A smooth, fast skater with great hands and a booming shot, Lafleur possessed excellent vision on the ice, and almost always assisted on many more goals than he scored. Perhaps most impressively, he accomplished all of this with style. Lafleur's patented dashes up the ice, long hair flowing as he weaved through enemy lines, brought the Forum faithful to their feet, eliciting a swelling roar of excitement and deafening chants of "Guy! Guy! Guy!"

Then the cheering stopped—not all at once, but gradually over a four-year period as Lafleur hit his thirties and the Canadiens went from being a dominant team to merely a good one.

Injuries didn't help Lafleur either. After scoring 50 goals in 74 games in 1979–80, a knee injury ended his season after three playoff games (in which he scored three times). Without their top scorer, the Canadiens, seeking a fifth-consecutive Stanley Cup, lost their second-round series to the inferior Minnesota North Stars in seven games.

Et tu, Coco?

More injuries and other assorted mishaps, including a late-night car accident, followed in 1980–81, when Lafleur played only 51 of the Canadiens' 80 games, still managing 27 goals. Nevertheless, it was the beginning of the end, one that was hastened by two of Lafleur's former teammates.

Lafleur still led the faltering Canadiens in scoring in both 1982–83 and 1983–84, but with less impressive totals. The latter season saw two of his old 1970s teammates return to the fold, Serge Savard as general manager, and Jacques Lemaire, his centerman for some of his most productive seasons, as assistant coach. In February of 1984, with the Canadiens slipping in the standings, Savard promoted Lemaire, "Coco" to his old teammates, to head coach. Under Lemaire, who saw a defensive system as the answer to the Canadiens' on-ice problems, Lafleur became a little-used spare part, an overpaid fourth-liner who usually played only a few minutes a game. Then, after barely making the playoffs, the Canadiens made an impressive run to the third round, where they took the first two games of their series against the New York Islanders, who were seeking a fifth-straight Stanley Cup. The Canadiens lost the series 4–2, but coach Lemaire had grown in the esteem of Canadiens fans and management, while Lafleur, who contributed a measly 3 assists in 12 playoff games, had become a highly-paid problem.

A healthy thirty-four-year-old Lafleur, who had played in all 80 of his team's games for the first time in five years in 1983–84, claimed to be optimistic about the 1984–85 season, and told reporters that he felt capable of scoring 40–50 goals. But if his spirit was willing, it wasn't for long. After scoring only twice in the first 19 games and seeing his ice time dwindle under Lemaire and his defense-first style, Lafleur's sprit was broken. The situation, he later said, was making him sick. So he asked for a trade, but was turned down by Savard, who feared the fan backlash that might trigger. So, on November 26, in a move that allowed his bosses to save face, but which he would later regret, he announced his retirement from a game that had been his whole life. The announcement shocked the hockey world and was front-page news in Quebec and across Canada. It even came up in the House of Commons in Ottawa, where Member of Parliament Lorne Nystrom paid tribute to the new retiree:

> **IT MAY BE THAT EVERYWHERE ELSE IN THE WORLD, THE ASCENDANCE OF FLOWER POWER BEGAN AND ENDED IN THE SIXTIES, MR. SPEAKER, BUT IN MONTREAL IT BEGAN IN 1971 AND ENDED YESTERDAY WHEN GUY LAFLEUR RETIRED. THIS IS THE END OF A GREAT ERA, MR. SPEAKER. I AM CERTAIN THAT THE HOUSE AND THE ENTIRE POPULATION OF CANADA WILL JOIN ME IN WISHING HIM GOOD LUCK IN THE FUTURE AND THANKING HIM FOR THE UNFORGETTABLE MOMENTS HE HAS GIVEN US.**

Lafleur himself said all the right things at the press conference announcing his departure, but to his fans and those who followed the game closely, he looked and sounded anything but happy to be hanging up his skates. And he never did get around to filing his retirement papers.

The Canadiens gave Lafleur a job as an "ambassador," and he hated it from Day One. He hung around for less than a year, long enough for the team to retire his jersey during a special tribute night on February 16, 1985. But the once shy boy from Thurso, Quebec was increasingly given to speaking his mind, and what came out of his mouth didn't always please his bosses. After some unflattering remarks about his public relations job and the salary he was being offered after his player's contract would end, his employment with the Canadiens was terminated by "mutual agreement" in September 1985. The divorce between a team and one of its legends was official.

Back in a Blueshirt

Old-timers' games aside, Lafleur stayed out of the spotlight until the spring of 1988, when it was announced that he would be inducted into the Hockey Hall of Fame (in his first year of eligibility). But in August, before he could even be inducted, word surfaced that he had the itch to play again, was working with a trainer, and was even contacting some NHL teams in search of a tryout. News of Lafleur's comeback surprised many, and most people were skeptical about the chances of a thirty-seven-year-old smoker who'd been out of the game for almost four years. But those close to him, and the more perceptive among the fans and media, knew that Lafleur's competitive fires still burned and that he'd left the game too soon.

The Los Angeles Kings and Pittsburgh Penguins expressed interest, but the New York Rangers were the first to act. After a few discussions between Lafleur and his camp and Rangers general manager Phil Esposito and coach Michel Bergeron, New York offered Lafleur a tryout. He went directly from the Hall of Fame's induction ceremony in Toronto on September 8 to Trois-Rivières, the Quebec town 90 miles northeast of Montreal where the Rangers were holding their training camp.

After working out all summer, and having cut back, but not all the way back, on cigarettes, Lafleur reported to the Rangers in shape and weighing 175 pounds, six less than his last playing weight. That he scored the first goal in the Rangers' first intra-squad game was a good sign. The word from his new teammates and those who played against him in preseason games was "Guy's still got it," and the Rangers signed him to a one-year, $400,000 contract.

Lafleur made his official return to the NHL on October 6, 1988 in a 2–2 tie with Chicago. He scored his first NHL goal in almost four years against Vancouver ten days later on a pass from thirty-seven-year-old Marcel Dionne . . . the second pick in the 1971 Amateur Draft. Lafleur was just heating up when the Canadiens visited Madison Square Garden on November 21. The Canadiens took the game, 4–2, but Lafleur scored the first Rangers goal, his fourth of the year. It was a good sign. Eight days later Lafleur scored two goals in a defeat of Winnipeg. And on December 4, he collected four assists in a 10–6 loss to Edmonton. But less than a week later, in Boston, he broke a bone in his left foot and would be out of the lineup for almost a month.

The Rangers' December 17 visit to the Forum had long been circled on many Canadiens' calendars. Before Lafleur's injury, scalpers were reportedly asking for and getting $300 per ticket for the game. The Canadiens honored Lafleur's return with a nice ceremony, and he appeared on the ice in a Rangers jersey, but in dress shoes, not skates, waving to the crowd. It was nice, but it wasn't the same.

"Guy! Guy! Guy!"

Lafleur returned to action in early January and had almost a month to get back in the swing of things before the Rangers' much-anticipated return to Montreal on February 4. When the big day finally came around, Lafleur faced a media circus, but since the formalities of celebrating his return had already been taken care of in December, he could concentrate on hockey once game time came around.

With two goals and an assist, Guy Lafleur was named the game's second star when he returned to the Montreal Forum as a New York Ranger on February 4, 1989 (Paul Bereswill/Hockey Hall of Fame).

The game was shown across the country on the Canadian Broadcast Corporation's weekly *Hockey Night in Canada* telecast. Dick Irvin Jr. handled the play-by-play while the legendary Scotty Bowman, who coached Lafleur from 1971 through 1979 on five Stanley Cup–winning teams, served as analyst.

Lafleur received his first standing ovation of the night during the pregame warm-up. His next occurred before a live television audience as the teams hit the ice minutes before the start of the game.

"Four years out of hockey, but my goodness how they love him in Montreal," Irvin said as Lafleur took the ice to the roars of the sellout Forum crowd. "Here's Lafleur coming on the ice and he is getting an immediate standing O. This is the second one he's gotten, and a familiar chant of 'Guy! Guy! Guy!' goes up. Would you have believed it, really?"

To say that the fans on hand that night were torn would not be entirely accurate. Canadiens fans do not want their team to lose a game . . . ever. But they wanted Lafleur to do well, too.

Stéphane Richer, who had become the first Canadiens player since Lafleur to score 50 goals in a season the year before, opened the scoring 3:30 into the game. The Rangers answered right back, with David Shaw putting one past Canadiens star goaltender, Patrick Roy, at the 4:19 mark on assists from Jason Lafreniere and . . . Guy Lafleur! The crowd roared their approval when the Forum house announcer called Lafleur's name. The Rangers struck again less than two minutes later, and when the first period ended with the Rangers leading 2–1, the fans weren't quite as amused.

The Rangers jumped out to a 3–1 lead 4:56 into the second, but Montreal's Bobby Smith replied 18 seconds later.

Rangers 3, Canadiens 2.

Then, midway through the period, the unexpected happened after a battle for the puck in the corner to Roy's left:

"Guy Lafleur against Gilles Thibodeau . . . Lafleur with the puck . . . good play against the boards by the 'Flower' . . . now it's Miller . . . a centering pass, here's Lafleur . . . scores!" called Irvin with an excitement in his voice usually reserved for Canadiens goals. The crowd went wild, jumping to their collective feet and roaring their approval.

While Lafleur was congratulated by his teammates, Irvin and Bowman said nothing for almost 20 seconds, letting the cheering crowd do all the talking.

Bowman finally broke the silence: "We don't have a tally, Dick, of how many times he's scored in that net, but you know it's a couple of hundred, probably. But Lafleur showing the magic in front of the net . . . he was able to take that rebound and put it right in the net . . . and what an ovation."

"Scotty, I've never heard the other team score and an ovation like this . . . ever at the Montreal Forum," Irvin said. The cheers morphed into a "Guy! Guy! Guy!" chant that continued up to and through the announcement of the goal.

Rangers 4, Canadiens 2, but not for long.

Five minutes later, after a near miss by Montreal, Lafleur got his stick on a long clearing pass by Kip Miller. Instead of playing the body, Montreal defenseman Petr Svoboda tried to play the bouncing puck. Big mistake.

Lafleur corralled the puck, and with both Canadiens defensemen closing in on him, surprised Roy with a long shot between the legs.

"And here's Lafleur, he's in all alone, shot . . . scores! What a night for the Flower!"

The fans roared again, perhaps even more loudly, as a beaming Lafleur raised an arm in celebration and was mobbed by his teammates. The camera cut between cheering Canadiens jersey–clad fans and the scowling face of Montreal coach, Pat Burns.

Rangers 5, Candiens 2.

"Well he said he was coming back to enjoy hockey, Dick," Bowman said. "He won't enjoy it any more than this moment, right now."

The Canadiens lineup had a number of Lafleur's old teammates in it, many of whom would later admit to being mesmerized by the mere sight of him.

"For a long time we were Lafleur watchers rather than playing our game," said future Hall of Famer Larry Robinson, who played with him for more than a decade.

The second period ended 5–3 in the Rangers' favor after a late goal by Montreal's Shayne Corson. Burns, an ex-policeman known for his colorful language and fiery temper, used the second intermission to wake his team from any of its remaining Lafleur-induced reverie. Sparkplug winger Claude Lemieux got the Canadiens within one only 39 seconds into the third, and speedster Russ Courtnall struck less than three minutes later to tie the game. At the 9:13 mark, Corson gave the Canadiens the lead with his second of the night. He completed his hat trick into an empty net with only 15 seconds to play.

Canadiens 7, Rangers 5.

When the siren sounded to end the game, the fans stood as one to cheer the winners and one of the losers. They had gotten exactly what they'd dreamed of, an exciting Canadiens win and another magical performance by their hero, Guy Lafleur. Who could ask for anything more?

Lafleur went on to make one more grand statement before the season's end. On February 27, at Madison Square Garden, against the Wayne Gretzky–led Los Angeles Kings, one of the teams that had passed on him, Lafleur scored three goals in a 6–4 Rangers win. It was the 17th and final hat trick of his career. Lafleur then scored his 18th goal of the season in the last game of the year. His 27 assists gave him a more than respectable 45 points in 67 games.

Yet Lafleur was not done. A free agent at season's end, he followed coach Michel Bergeron back to Quebec City, where he'd been a junior hockey hero for four years. In two seasons with the Nordiques, Lafleur scored 24 goals, the final one, his 560th, coming in his second-to last game on March 30, 1991, a 4–3 loss to . . . the Canadiens at the Montreal Forum.

IF THEY DON'T . . . WANT YOU HERE, THEY JUST MIGHT . . . TAKE YOU THERE

When the New York Rangers signed Guy Lafleur in 1988, it wasn't the first time a Canadiens legend found new life in the Big Apple. In 1966, future Hall of Famer Bernie "Boom-Boom" Geoffrion also came out of retirement to play two seasons in New York.

The two teams have also been frequent trading partners over the years, with some big names, often fading Canadiens stars, moving between the two teams.

In 1936, the Canadiens repatriated the great Howie Morenz to Montreal for cash. In 1947, they sent popular forward Buddy O'Connor to New York, where he narrowly missed winning the NHL scoring title in his first year as a Ranger. In 1961, the Canadiens traded Doug Harvey, one of the greatest players in NHL history, to the Rangers for "Leapin'" Lou Fontinato. Harvey promptly won the seventh Norris Trophy of his career as the NHL's best defenseman. And in 1963, goaltending legend Jacques Plante went to the Rangers in a seven-player blockbuster that brought Lorne "Gump" Worsley to Montreal.

Lesser player swaps have seen the likes of Montreal fan favorite Chris Nilan (1988) and Rangers star Alex (Alexi) Kovalev (2004) switch allegiances.

The most one-sided in all of the Canadiens-Rangers trades occurred in 2009, when Montreal sent Chris Higgins and prospects Doug Janik, Pavel Valentenko, and former first-round draft pick Ryan McDonagh to New York in exchange for Tom Pyatt, Michael Busto, and center Scott Gomez. The overpaid and unproductive Gomez would become one of the biggest busts in Canadiens history, while twenty-year-old McDonagh developed into one of the best defensemen in the NHL.

St. Patrick's Last Day: Roy Quits Canadiens Mid-Game

6

If not for Patrick Roy, only 22 Stanley Cup banners would hang from the rafters inside Montreal's Bell Centre. Of that there can be no argument. And if not for the events of December 2, 1995, which saw the Canadiens' star goaltender play his last game under extraordinary circumstances, 25 or more banners may hang there today. That, however, we will never know.

One of the most eventful periods in Canadiens history began shortly after the team won its 24th Stanley Cup in 1993 (*see 1993 Playoffs: Cup Full of Overtime, page 131*). In Montreal, the pressure to win is always immense, even crushing to some. And when the team broke ground on a new arena a few weeks later, a new dimension was added. To counter any backlash from fans and the media over the decision to abandon the legendary Montreal Forum, the already image-obsessed Canadiens wanted to make sure they could ice a winning team when they would move there in three years' time.

The problem was, despite their Cup win, the Canadiens weren't exactly a powerhouse. They had a number of good players, but only one real star (actually, superstar) in goaltender Patrick Roy.

With only 48 NHL games under his belt, twenty-year-old Roy played every minute of the 1986 playoffs, leading the Canadiens to a 23rd Stanley Cup and earning the Conn Smythe Trophy as playoff MVP (*see A Saint Is Born: Rookie Roy Channels Dryden, page 124*). Seven years later, with Roy refusing to cede a goal in 10 consecutive playoff overtime games, the team that finished a disappointing third in the Adams Division during the regular season captured its 24th and most unlikely Stanley Cup. Roy was once again awarded the Conn Smythe Trophy.

In between, Roy emerged as the NHL's premier netminder, winning three Vezina trophies as best goaltender and four Jennings trophies (shared) for giving up the fewest goals. He was a First-Team All-Star four times and played in five NHL All-Star Games. The Canadiens, meanwhile, had been little better than an average team since 1989, when they reached the Stanley Cup Finals before losing to the Calgary Flames.

Roy, however, was a star the team's management, and some fans, seemed to have difficulty fully embracing. Early in his career, even while posting league-leading statistics, he played fewer games than many other number-one goalies. Later, when the team struggled, he would take more than his fair share of blame from fans and the media. Before the 1993 Cup win, fans would regularly call for him to be traded. And the talk started up again a few years later. Some fans and commentators found that success, wealth, and fame had made Roy self-centered and arrogant. But he was universally embraced by his teammates, who valued his leadership and dedication to winning.

Tumultuous times

The Canadiens' problems began in the spring of 1994, not long after Roy furthered his legend by rising from his hospital bed to lead the Canadiens to a pair of improbable wins in their first-round playoff series against the archrival Boston Bruins (*see St. Patrick's Bellyache, page 43*). But the Bruins prevailed in seven games and the Canadiens literally hit the golf course early.

Some commentators called the loss an embarrassment and speculated about the heads that might roll. The first head belonged to popular team captain Guy Carbonneau, who on a golf outing with his close friend Roy and their teammate Vincent Damphousse a few days later flipped the middle finger to a tabloid newspaper photographer who had followed the trio out onto the course. Carbonneau's bird, not birdie, made the front page of the paper the next day and was illogically and incorrectly perceived by some as being directed at Canadiens fans. The thirty-four-year-old Carbonneau, a two-time Stanley Cup winner and three-time recipient of the Frank J. Selke Award given to the NHL's best defensive forward, was traded to the St. Louis Blues in August for Montreal native Jim Montgomery. The message sent by Canadiens management was clear—no individual, no matter how effective, loyal, or popular, is bigger than the team.

If losing by one goal in Game 7 of the first round was an embarrassment, what do you call missing the playoffs entirely, which the Canadiens did for the first time in 25 years in the spring of 1995? The word most freely spoken and written was "disgrace." General manager Serge Savard's attempt to add some offense to his team via a pair of blockbuster trades had failed miserably, and cost them the leadership of Carbonneau's successor Kirk Muller, who served as captain for all of 33 games. Muller's own successor, Mike Keane, didn't help matters when he ignited a media storm by declaring during an interview that he had no intention of learning French.

The Canadiens opened the 1995–96 season at home with a 7–1 loss to the Philadelphia Flyers. After they dropped the next game, 6–1 to the Florida Panthers, Canadiens fans were apoplectic. When they lost the next two, it was team president Ronald Corey's turn to burst a blood vessel, and he promptly fired Savard, head coach Jacques Demers, as well as the team's assistant general manager and head scout. How's that for rolling heads?

If the firings only four games into the new season had raised a lot of eyebrows, the announcement of the new coach and GM raised many more, including Patrick Roy's. The team was actually without a coach or GM for four days, with retained assistant coach Jacques Laperrière running practices and taking over behind the bench for one game, another loss. The next day, Corey reached into the Canadiens' past in an effort to bring back the spirit and pride that had once made the team great. He hired former players Rejean Houle, who'd been closely associated with the team through his public relations and communications functions with Molson Breweries, and Mario Tremblay, who had spent the decade after his retirement from the Canadiens analyzing the team on television and radio, as general manager and head coach, respectively. Their old teammate, Hall of Famer Yvan Cournoyer, was hired as an additional assistant coach.

As players, the three were proven winners, with 20 Stanley Cups between them. But it was their lack of experience that saw the hiring questioned, and even mocked, in some quarters.

In his column the next day, *La Presse*'s Rejean Tremblay cruelly pointed out that Houle had "spent the last ten years selling beer" and had "never managed anything other than a softball team in his life." Patrick Roy, when asked for his reaction, told reporters that he had taken a cold shower after hearing the news "to make sure I wasn't dreaming."

The Canadiens got off on the right foot under Mario Tremblay, winning six games in a row after his hiring. Unfortunately, the relationship between the new coach and his star goaltender, who had briefly been teammates and roommates in 1985–86, didn't. Tremblay was furious when Roy burst out laughing at something he'd said in English with his Lac St. Jean French accent before his first game as coach, and things went downhill from there, even though the team won 12 of the next 14 games. Tremblay, who wanted to establish that he was the boss and that all players were equal in status, installed new rules that riled the 10-year veteran. Citing an older team rule, in the midst of a three-game winning streak, he even chased Roy from a hotel bar where he was quietly sipping a beer with a teammate.

Scotty and his Wings

Ironically, a former Canadiens coach, maybe the greatest hockey coach of all-time, came to play a part in the Roy-Tremblay saga.

Scotty Bowman had been Tremblay's coach for the first five years of his career, and the new Canadiens' bench boss was still bitter about the harsh way the old one had treated him. Now Bowman was the coach of the Detroit Red Wings, one of the best teams in the NHL, and Tremblay made his feelings about him public in an interview before the two teams were to meet in Detroit on November 28.

Tremblay wanted to beat Bowman so badly he could taste it, but the superior Red Wings won the game, 3–2. A headline in the following day's *Journal de Montreal* newspaper read: "Bowman Has the Last Word."

Tremblay's mood worsened after a 5–4 road loss in St. Louis the next day, and the Canadiens flew home to prepare for the next game. As fate would have it, the team's next opponents were Scotty Bowman and his powerful Red Wings . . . on a Saturday night, at the Forum, in front of a national television audience.

December 2, 1995, a night that would go down in infamy, started badly for Roy, Tremblay, and the Canadiens even before the teams took to the ice. In his 1997 biography of Tremblay, *La Presse* reporter Mathias Brunet revealed that the coach and the goalie had a testy exchange in the locker room before the game.

Having overslept from his pregame nap, Damphousse, one of the team's best players, arrived only minutes before the warm-up, a transgression, much to Roy's irritation, Tremblay chose to overlook. But Roy, unable to hold his tongue, decided to call his coach out over the perceived double standard. "Hey Mario, if his name was [sparingly used] Yves Sarault, would he be playing tonight?"

Things went from uncomfortable to out of control in record time.

Bowman, who left the Canadiens after eight seasons and five Stanley Cups after he was overlooked for the team's general manager's job in 1979, relied heavily on his top two forward lines from the drop of the puck. It was clear he wanted to win as badly as Tremblay did. And he was better equipped to do it.

The Red Wings got on the board when Igor Larionov scored on the power play at 3:10. Slava Kozlov and Montreal's Mark Recchi exchanged goals midway through the period before Kozlov's second of the night restored the Wings' two-goal lead. Things stayed that way until Canadiens defenseman Patrice Brisebois was assessed a game misconduct and a five-minute penalty for checking from behind with just over two minutes remaining in the period. The Red Wings power play unit scored 11 seconds later, and then again with 59 seconds left to put them ahead 5–1.

Even casual hockey fans know that two things would normally have happened at this point. With such a commanding lead, Scotty Bowman would have eased off the gas pedal and rested his better players, and Mario Tremblay would have replaced Roy with his backup, Pat Jablonski. But neither did. Tremblay, who later said he thought the team still had a chance to come back, sent Roy out to start the second period. And, with Brisebois's major still on the board, Bowman sent his top power play unit out onto the ice. At 2:52, with one second left in the penalty, Kozlov completed his hat trick. After Red Wings rookie and Quebec native Mathieu Dandenault scored on a breakaway less

Patrick Roy responded with a mock gesture of his own after fans sarcastically cheered a routine save in what turned out to be his last game in a Canadiens uniform (AP Photo/Montreal La Presse-Bernard Brault).

than two minutes later, Roy looked towards the Canadiens' bench for any sign that he was being mercifully pulled. But none came, and the score climbed. At 8–1, after the crowd mockingly applauded a routine save he'd just made, Roy sarcastically raised his arms. After Sergei Fedorov scored to make it 9–1, Roy looked up to see Jablonski finally coming onto the ice to end his torment. But it was too late for Roy, who understood that he'd been purposely hung out to dry by his own coach. After handing his gloves and stick to a trainer, Roy passed Tremblay on his way to the stool reserved for the backup goalie. Tremblay looked him up and down, but said nothing. Then Roy abruptly turned around, passed his coach again, and stopped in front of Ronald Corey, seated, as always, directly behind the Canadiens' bench.

"It's my last game in Montreal," he told a confused looking Corey before making his way back to his seat. On the way, he had to pass Tremblay, who again said nothing, but with arms crossed and his chin set and arrogantly raised, looked for all the world like . . . Scotty Bowman.

"You heard what I said," the now seated Roy shouted in the coach's direction.

Most of those on hand in the Forum witnessed what had just happened, but not all of them understood. The TV audience of 1.5 million, aided by numerous replays, soon did.

When the second period finally ended, Tremblay stormed up to Roy in the team's dressing room, demanding to know what he'd said to the team's president. The two exchanged harsh words, the last they would have for each other for almost 18 years.

Detroit scored twice in the third to make the final score 11–1 . . . a total humiliation for the Canadiens, Mario Tremblay, and Patrick Roy.

After the game, Roy and his agent talked into the wee hours about what to do next. But the damage was done. Roy had broken the Canadiens' cardinal rule: no individual is bigger than the team. There was no going back.

The Canadiens suspended Roy, then traded him and captain Mike Keane to the Colorado Avalanche four days later. In return, the Canadiens received forwards Andrei Kovalenko and Martin Rucinsky as well as young goaltender Jocelyn Thibault. Six months later the Avalanche won the Stanley Cup. Scotty Bowman and the Detroit Red Wings won the next two. Roy won his fourth and final Stanley Cup and third Conn Smythe Trophy with the Avalanche in 2001.

And the Montreal Canadiens? Well, they are still waiting for their 25th.

ST. PATRICK'S BELLYACHE

The Canadiens' quest to repeat as Stanley Cup champions hit a serious roadblock in their first-round playoff series against the Boston Bruins in April of 1994. The teams had split the series' first two games, with Patrick Roy making 40 saves in the Canadiens' 3–2, Game 2 victory in Boston. A few days later, back in Montreal, the star of Montreal's 1993 Cup win felt some tenderness in his side, which progressed to a dull ache . . . which became a stabbing, unbearable pain. The diagnosis was appendicitis, which is almost always treated with an appendectomy, followed by two or three weeks' rest. The news hit Montreal like a bomb. Without Patrick, everyone conceded, the Canadiens were toast.

No one was more upset than Roy himself, who begged the Canadiens' team doctors to find a nonsurgical solution to his ferocious bellyache. Rather than perform surgery, they treated Roy in the hospital with antibiotics in hopes that he could return to action before the end of the series. And return he did, on a stretcher via an ambulance from the hospital to the rink. After missing Game 3, a 6–3 loss, Roy returned to lead the Canadiens to a 5–2 win, despite being outshot 41–15. Two days later, in a game that was completely domi-nated by the Bruins, Roy stopped 60 of the 61 shots he faced and Kirk Muller scored in overtime to give the Canadiens a 2–1 win and 3–2 series lead. Unfortunately, there was a limit to how much the Montreal General Hospital's most famous outpatient could take. He and the Canadiens ran out of gas and the Bruins won games 6 and 7 to end Montreal's season.

Shutting Down a Shrine: The Closing of the Montreal Forum

7

Few Montrealers were indifferent in 1991 when it was announced that the Canadiens would soon be leaving the Montreal Forum, the team's official home since 1926, to move into a new, state-of-the-art facility. While many accepted the explanation of economic necessity behind the move, others considered the closing of hockey's high temple sacrilegious, and wondered if a renovation wouldn't suffice. But whether they were for or against, none of the sellout crowd of 17,959 or the millions of television viewers who saw the Canadiens' final game in the Forum on March 11, 1996 were unmoved by the long ceremony that followed it. And by the end of the long, standing ovation for the team's greatest player, there were few dry eyes in the house the Canadian Arena Company had built in 1924.

The Montreal Forum was built over 159 days beginning in June 1924 at a cost of $1.5 million, not for the Canadiens, but for the expansion Montreal Hockey Club, later called the Maroons. Located at the corner of Atwater and Ste-Catherine streets, the new building and its principal occupant were the property of the Canadian Arena Company. Founded by three prominent Montrealers and financially supported by a group of other wealthy, mostly Anglophone, businessmen, the company was created to found an NHL team for the city's English-speaking fans after the demise of the once-beloved Wanderers, who folded the day after their home, the nearby Westmount Arena, was destroyed by fire six years earlier. The city's many amateur teams and leagues would also use the rink, but the professionals of the NHL were to be the main draw.

The Maroons were scheduled to open the building with their first game of the 1924–25 regular season on December 3. But with the new ice-making plant at their Mount-Royal Arena home malfunctioning, the defending Stanley Cup champion Montreal Canadiens instead inaugurated the Forum on November 29. A capacity crowd of 9,300 saw the temporary home team beat the visiting Toronto St. Patricks, 7–3. Only 55 seconds into the game, Canadiens forward Billy Boucher, on his way

45

to a hat trick, notched the first of the thousands of goals that would be scored in the Forum's 71-year history.

The Canadiens moved out of the Mount-Royal Arena and into the Forum permanently in 1926, and shared it with the Maroons until that club's demise in 1938. Of the 22 Stanley Cups the team won while calling the building home, 12 were captured on Forum ice.

Over the years, the Forum acquired shrine status as the site of some of the greatest moments in hockey history. Team Canada's 7–3 loss in Game 1 in the legendary 1972 Canada-USSR Summit Series left the Forum faithful stunned. Three years later, it was the scene of what many believe to be the greatest hockey game ever played, the 3–3, New Year's Eve 1975 exhibition game tie between the Canadiens and the Soviet Central Red Army club team (*see The Greatest Game, page 164*).

Not all of the Forum's finest moments were hockey related. Everyone from the Beatles and Rolling Stones to Frank Sinatra, Louis Armstrong, Luciano Pavarotti, the Bolshoi Ballet, and the London Symphony Orchestra graced its concert stage. During Montreal's 1976 Summer Games, the Forum was the site of a gymnastics event where fourteen-year-old Romanian gymnast Nadia Comaneci posted the first-ever perfect score of 10 in an Olympics on her way to a Gold Medal. And many Montreal-area youngsters had made their first visits to the Forum to see the Shriners' Circus, Ice Capades, or Harlem Globetrotters.

The Forum was renovated a number of times over the years. In 1946, Canadiens General Manager Frank Selke oversaw $115,000 worth of work that did away with the wire fencing that separated the more expensive seats from the sarcastically named "Millionaires Section," and saw the old brown seats painted and reorganized into red, white, and blue tiers. In 1949, a $600,000 expansion brought the Forum's seating capacity to 13,550, and $10 million of work in 1968 added another 3,000 seats as well as the building's iconic hockey stick escalators. Between 1968 and 1978, a sold-out Forum, with additional standing room, could accommodate almost 19,000 hockey fans, and for many games until its 1996 closing, it did just that. However, later renovations reduced the capacity to 18,000.

By the end of the 1980s, the economics of hockey were changing, and Canadiens management recognized it would need to adapt if the team were to remain competitive. The Forum as it was could no longer generate the revenue the team needed, and after a study concluded that further renovations were not a feasible option, the team began looking for sites in downtown Montreal on which to build a new arena. On June 22, 1993, 13 days after the Canadiens won their 24th (and last) Stanley Cup at the Forum, construction began on what would be the Molson Centre.

End of an era

The last game at the Forum was a much-anticipated one, hyped for weeks by the media and fans alike. At approximately 6:00 p.m. on Monday, March 11, 1996, the Forum doors were thrown open and the last fans to ever watch a Canadiens game with standing room tickets scrambled up the stairs to find a good spot from which to take in the game. Some 16,000 others, holding much sought-after tickets for reserved seats, followed in a more orderly fashion.

The Canadiens were coming off a March 9 win against Ottawa, but had dropped five of the six games previous to that. This would not be a good night to lose. But they had promised their fans a special evening, and they did not fail to deliver.

Maybe it was by chance that the opponents on this historic night were the Dallas Stars, who had four former Montreal players on their roster and whose general manager was Hall of Famer Bob Gainey, the captain of the Canadiens between 1981 and 1989. The choice ended up being an inspired one for more reasons than one—Dallas started the season poorly and would finish last in their division and 11th in the Western Conference, out of a playoff spot.

Maurice "Rocket" Richard got his first ovation of the evening when he and fellow Canadiens legends Jean Béliveau and Guy Lafleur performed the ceremonial opening face-off between then-team captain Pierre Turgeon and the Stars' Guy Carbonneau, who had been Gainey's successor as Canadiens captain. Dallas' starting lineup for the actual opening face-off of the game featured former Canadiens Carbonneau, Brent Gilchrist, Mike Lalor, Craig Ludwig, and Montreal-area native Benoit Hogue, who, after the night was over, probably wished he had once played for his hometown team.

The game itself could not, and would not, live up to the occasion, which Forum house announcer Michel Lacroix called "the last act of a masterpiece." The Canadiens, perhaps feeling the pressure to succeed on such a special occasion, came out slowly, and were eventually outshot 9–7 in the first period, but they struck first where it counted most, with captain Turgeon, the team's top scorer, notching his 32nd of the season at the 6:20 mark.

The Canadiens took a 1–0 lead into the first intermission. Perhaps it was the sight of the team's living legends wandering the hallways, or a fiery talk by coach and former player Mario Tremblay, but it was an inspired group that emerged for a second period that would see them outshoot Dallas 15–5. Mark Recchi put Montreal up 2–0 with his 21st of the year at 6:33. After Dallas' Derian Hatcher cut the lead to one, Canadiens rookie and future captain Saku Koivu potted his 17th of the season to restore the two-goal lead. Then, two and a half minutes later, the Russian Tank, Andrei Kovalenko, who would be traded the next off-season after only 51 games in a Canadiens uniform, scored what would prove to be the last ever goal at the Montreal Forum.

The third period was a lackluster one, with each team taking eight shots and neither scoring. With the clock winding down on 71 years of hockey history, the fans stood and began the countdown, 10–9–8–7–6–5–4–3–2–1 . . . The Canadiens won 4–1 and the Forum itself was history. But unlike most games, nobody left the building when it ended, because the best part of the night still lay ahead.

Passing the torch

At game's end, Forum workers rolled out the red carpets, forming a large square in the center of the rink. From a podium at each end, tuxedo-clad masters of ceremony Dick Irvin Jr. (in English) and Richard Garneau (in French) took turns presenting every living Canadiens Hall of Famer, each wearing the team's famous red jersey. They began with the builders, including 1970s coach Scotty Bowman, and moved on to the players. In descending order from the 1970s down through the 1940s they appeared when called— Lapointe, Shutt, Gainey, Lafleur, Dryden—each greeted with a roar of approval and love by the fans. Then it was the heroes of the '60s and '50s, Jean Beliveau, Henri Richard, Dickie Moore, and finally the great Elmer Lach and seventy-six-year-old Emile "Butch" Bouchard. Here, the ceremony's organizers played fast and loose with the chronology, purposely saving the best for last.

In French, Garneau announced, ". . . and now, Mr. Hockey. Named 14 times to an NHL All-Star team, Hart trophy winner and eight-time Stanley Cup champion. The first 50-goal scorer in NHL history, he was the symbol of an entire people, who saw themselves in his exploits and personality. He twice scored five goals in a single game and was named all three stars in one of them. Other players ended up scoring more goals than 'The Rocket,' but no one ever scored them the way he did. Captain of the Canadiens, incontestable leader of the team, inducted into the Hall of Fame in 1961, the greatest legend in hockey history, number nine, Maurice 'Rocket' Richard!"

To the cheers of the fans and his fellow Canadiens' legends, the seventy-four-year-old Rocket stepped out onto the Forum ice, waving to the crowd, and took his place on the red carpet. The cheers continued to rain down on Richard, who shyly waved and appeared uneasy at the adulation. Lach and Bouchard then appeared at his side, and raised his arms skyward. The crowd roared again and Richard wiped his eyes, once described as intense and staring, black as coal, and lighting up as he descended upon the net, striking fear into the hearts of the goaltenders that faced him. But time had dimmed the Rocket's red glare. And now they glistened with tears as the tribute continued unabated. Richard used hand gestures to try and quiet his admirers, but they carried on for several more minutes, despite Garneau's attempts to start speaking again. In all, the ovation lasted almost eight minutes.

"Ladies and gentlemen, you have before you the heart and soul of the Montreal Forum," Garneau was finally allowed to say.

Now the cameras cut to the Canadiens' dressing room, where Bouchard, the team's oldest living captain, stood gazing up at the team motto, borrowed from John McCrae's World War I poem, "In Flanders Fields," painted on the wall:

"To you from failing hands we throw the torch; be yours to hold it high."

Bouchard grabbed a lit torch from its stand and made his way back to the ice, where he passed it down the line to the team's past captains; first to Richard, on to Beliveau, then Henri Richard, Yvan Cournoyer, Serge Savard, Gainey, and the freshly showered and now Canadiens jersey–clad Carbonneau, who passed it to Turgeon. The current captain called for his teammates, who had sat on the bench in full uniform throughout the almost 45-minute ceremony, to join him, and those who had been passed the torch held it high as they skated a last lap on Forum ice.

Some fans lingered, but most made their way out of the building. Finally, the Forum went dark.

An auction was held the next day, with everything from the Stanley Cup banners that hung from the rafters to the Forum's red, white, and blue seats up for bids. More than $750,000 was raised for charity.

In with the new

Everything else was loaded onto moving trucks. It's not known if the famous Forum ghosts, who were said to help the Canadiens and torment their opponents at key moments, ever made the trip. Also unconfirmed is the fate of the grills that made the Forum's famous toasted hot dogs. Some say they made their way to the team's new home. Mustard only, please.

A parade was held later in the week to help the team transition into the $270 million Molson Centre. The Canadiens inaugurated their beautiful new home with another ceremony, and a 4–2 win over the New York Rangers the next day, Saturday, March 16.

The jury is still out on the new building, which became the Bell Centre in September 2002. With its more than 21,000 seats and 135 luxurious private loges, it has succeeded in generating the much-needed revenues it was intended to. But the team never quite managed to use the extra money to lure big-name free agents to Montreal, one of the reasons it gave for the move in the first place. More importantly, the Canadiens have failed to win a Stanley Cup in their now 20-year-old home.

The fervor of the fans, together with all of the high technology on display, from the ultra-high-definition scoreboard to the blaring sound system, has succeed in creating a dynamic atmosphere there, and the Bell Centre is regularly cited as a favorite place to play by players across the NHL. But it just isn't the Forum.

"To you from failing hands we throw the torch; be yours to hold it high." Captain Pierre Turgeon and his Canadiens teammates closed out the ceremony marking the last game at the Montreal Forum in March 1996 (Doug MacLellan/Hockey Hall of Fame).

As for the old hockey shrine, it wasn't demolished like some other famous sporting venues. It was transformed into an entertainment complex featuring shops, restaurants, and movie theatres and renamed the Pepsi Forum, a fate, to some diehards, worse than the wrecking ball.

FUNERAL FOR A FRIEND

Of all the events for which the Montreal Forum was the venue, including six-day bicycle races in the 1930s and early '40s, the most unusual was probably a funeral.

On March 11, 1937, the Forum hosted the funeral of Canadiens superstar Howie Morenz, who died three days earlier at age thirty-four from complications due to a broken leg he suffered in a game on January 28. More than fifty thousand people came to pay their respects and view Morenz's casket, which lay at center ice. Another 15,000 attended the funeral itself.

Two other public visitations for players were held at the Canadiens' next home.

After his death from abdominal cancer in 2000, a viewing for Maurice "Rocket" Richard held over two days drew 115,000 people to the Molson Centre, where he was lying in state. On May 31, a state funeral, the first in Quebec for a non-politician, was held for him at Montreal's Notre-Dame Basilica.

The same honors were bestowed posthumously on the great Jean Béliveau after his passing on December 2, 2014. Two days of visitation at the Bell Centre were followed by his state funeral at Mary, Queen of the World Cathedral on December 10. On December 9, a 15-minute tribute to Béliveau was held before the Canadiens game against the Vancouver Canucks. His regular seat, left empty for the occasion, was adorned with his number 4, and the game's attendance was officially announced as 21,286, one short of capacity, ending a streak of 422 consecutive sold-out games.

A Comeback for the Ages

8

After missing the playoffs the previous season, the 2007–08 Montreal Canadiens were a very pleasant surprise to their legion of fans. On February 19, 2008, sixty games into the 99th season in team history, the Canadiens were on a three-game winning streak and had 73 points and a share of the top spot in the NHL's Eastern Conference. But after 25 minutes of play in that evening's game, it was the visiting New York Rangers who looked like world-beaters, while the Canadiens looked a lot like their 2006–07 selves. The fans that filled the Bell Centre or tuned in to the game on television that night would have been forgiven for heading home early, or tuning out altogether. But few did. And those who stayed, or who resisted turning the channel, ended up being richly rewarded for their loyalty.

The game was a tightly contested one in the early going with neither team succeeding in putting one past Canadiens rookie netminder Carey Price or his New York counterpart, two-time Vezina Trophy finalist Henrik Lundqvist, who had signed a new six-year, $41.25 million contract with the Rangers just six days earlier.

Then the wheels came off the Canadiens' wagon. Rangers forward Brandon Dubinsky took a pass from the slumping Jaromir Jagr just outside the New York blue line and sprinted the length of the ice. With the Canadiens defensive pair of Andrei Markov and Mike Komisarek in full retreat, Dubinsky pulled the trigger on a wrist shot that eluded Price. Rangers 1, Canadiens 0.

Rangers coach Tom Renney elected to keep the Jagr-Dubinsky-Sean Avery line on the ice and Canadiens coach Guy Carbonneau responded by going back to the Markov-Komisarek pairing to counter them. The move backfired. Fourteen seconds later, Avery pounced on a Jagr rebound and fired it past Price. Rangers 2, Canadiens 0. And the camera cut to the Canadiens' other goaltender, Cristobal Huet, sitting on the Montreal bench.

Less than five minutes later, with former Rangers star Alexei Kovalev in the penalty box for high-sticking, veteran Brendan Shanahan one-timed a Jagr pass from the high slot past Price. Rangers 3, Canadiens 0, and that was it for the highly touted Montreal rookie, who allowed three goals on 11 shots. Carbonneau signaled to Huet to don his gear and take his place in the Montreal net.

The period mercifully ended for the Canadiens, who still trailed by three. Jagr, with assists on all three New York goals, passed Ray Bourque to become the tenth-leading scorer in NHL history with 1,580 points.

Any serious hopes for a Canadiens comeback were dashed 2:44 into the second frame when winger Chris Higgins was given a double minor for high-sticking. The Rangers would have a four-minute power play.

Nine seconds before the first penalty expired, Shanahan tipped in a Paul Mara shot for his 20th of the season. And 28 seconds after that, Chris Drury took a Scott Gomez pass in the slot and wristed it beyond Huet. Jagr had his fourth assist. Rangers 5, Canadiens 0, and there were still almost 35 minutes left to play. Except for a handful of people wearing Rangers jerseys, the sellout crowd of 21,273 sat in stony silence. But almost everyone stayed.

Those watching at home couldn't help but notice that the Canadiens' French language TV crew of play-by-play man Pierre Houde and analyst Yvon Pedneault, covering the game for the RDS network, seemed to abandon their posts at times, periodically discussing anything except for the action on the ice below. But they turned their attention back to the game just in time to see the Canadiens' fourth line capitalize on a bad line change by the Rangers. Mark Streit took a long pass from Andrei Markov at the Rangers' blue line, carried it to the top of the left circle, and hit the onrushing Michael Ryder with a perfect pass in the slot. Lundqvist had no chance as Ryder wristed home his 10th of the year. Rangers 5, Canadiens 1.

Four and a half minutes later, seconds after a long Canadiens shot hit the post beyond Lundqvist, and with the French TV crew admiring how the Canadiens were showing a lot of character by continuing to compete, it was once again Streit to Ryder, whose long shot through traffic found its way past the Rangers' netminder. Rangers 5, Canadiens 2.

Coming with some seven minutes left to play in the second period, the goal did more than get the Canadiens back in the game; it woke the subdued crowd, who now roared with delight. Rangers coach Tom Renney, sensing that the ice was beginning to tilt favorably in the Canadiens' direction, called a time-out to compose his troops.

The fans were now fully committed to the Canadiens' cause, and when the officials penalized the fired-up Komisarek on a dodgy call with 2:24 left in the period, they showed their displeasure by littering the ice with the souvenir "Go Habs Go" mini banners they'd been handed at the Bell Centre entrances before the game. It took several minutes to clean the ice and resume play.

The Canadiens came out for the third with a renewed sense of urgency. Their league-leading power play failed to take advantage of a Martin Straka slashing penalty three minutes into the period, but they kept chipping away, pressuring the Rangers in their zone. On one such sequence, Markov twice kept the puck in the New York end before catching a clearing attempt with his gloved hand, retrieving his own blocked shot, then hitting an open Kovalev with a pass in the circle to the left of the Rangers' goaltender. The flashy Russian sniper put everything he had into a one-timer, which Lundqvist initially appeared to stop before the puck pushed through his pads and trickled across the goal line. The crowd erupted. Rangers 5, Canadiens 3. And there was still 13:17 to go.

Carbonneau sent his fourth line out again. The fans were still loudly cheering the goal announcement when the Canadiens won the face-off and moved the puck back to their own blue line. Defenseman Ryan O'Byrne passed it to center Maxim Lapierre at the Rangers' line, and he steered it to Ryder. The Canadiens' right-winger, with two goals already under his belt, drove to the middle of the ice as Streit headed for the goalmouth. Ryder shot and the puck deflected to Lundqvist's right and into the net. More mayhem ensued. A number of fans, assuming Ryder had just completed a hat trick, now littered the ice with caps. Those who hadn't thrown their banners away earlier now danced with them above their heads. Rangers 5, Canadiens 4. And there was still 13:08 to go. The entire sequence, from center ice face-off to goal, had taken nine seconds. The goal was later credited to Streit for his third point of the night.

Now the Bell Centre was completely engulfed in noise, which grew louder when Rangers defenseman Marek Malik drew a hooking penalty with 5:38 remaining in the third. The Canadiens' vaunted power play would get another chance to have its say in this wild game.

With one minute remaining in the Canadiens' man-advantage, Gomez picked a loose puck up and fired it deep into the Canadiens' zone. Markov retrieved it behind his goal line then quickly spun and fired a long pass to Kovalev, who immediately dropped it for an onrushing Saku Koivu. The Canadiens' captain crossed into the offensive zone with speed, and attempted to take the puck to the Rangers' net himself. The play was briefly broken up, but Montreal's Andrei Kostitsyn picked up the loose puck near the left face-off circle and took it to the left boards, deep in Rangers territory. On his way, he peeked over his right shoulder, where he spotted a hard-charging and uncovered Kovalev. Kostitsyn passed the puck slightly back and to his right towards the face-off circle just as Kovalev arrived, stick already cocked for another one-timer, and his blast flew past Lundqvist and into the net. The fans leapt to their feet as one, arms raised and roaring mightily. Kovalev, meanwhile, lay on the ice, momentarily frozen in a comical pose, on his back, with his feet pointing up to the rafters, his momentum having carried him forward and almost up and over. The Bell Centre was a pulsing chamber of deafening noise. Rangers 5, Canadiens 5, with 3:22 left on the clock.

Pedneault: "Kovalev!"

Houde: "Who else? Five-five."

With the noise in the building now at an ear-piercing level, Pedneault paid tribute to the Canadiens fans: "You know what, Pierre? Hats-off to the fans here at the Bell Centre. Even at 5–0, these fans were behind their team."

The third period ended and the teams headed to sudden-death overtime, with both sides coming close to ending the game on a number of good scoring chances, each snuffed out by remarkable saves. A shootout would be needed to decide the winner.

The Canadiens elected to have New York shoot first, and the Rangers sent out Brendan Shanahan, whose second period goal had him 20 on the season for the 19th straight year, leaving him second only to the great Gordie Howe in that category. He picked up the puck with speed, then slowed as he neared the Canadiens goal and tried threading a quick shot between Huet's legs. But the Montreal netminder outwaited the Rangers veteran and the puck stayed out.

Montreal made the somewhat strange choice of defenseman Markov as their first shooter. The skilled Russian tried an unusual move, one he'd scored with before—a quick, low backhand shot. But Lundqvist read it perfectly and whipped a pad out to make the save. Shooting next for New York was Chris Drury. Unlike Shanahan, he broke in with speed and deked to his left. But Huet stayed with him all the way and blocked Drury's backhand with his right pad.

Montreal's second shooter was Koivu, who had scored on a beautiful deke on his previous shootout attempt a month earlier. He swept in from his left, cut back to the middle, and deked hard to his backhand. The move froze Lundqvist for a fraction of a second, just long enough for Koivu to swing the puck back to his forehand and slide it just inches from the netminder's outstretched pad and into the goal.

The fans leapt once again from their seats, arms raised and roaring in celebration. But the game was not over. The Rangers could still extend the shootout on their third attempt. And the shooter just happened to be one of the greatest scorers in the history of the game, Jaromir Jagr. Just four days past his thirty-sixth birthday, the Czech didn't waste any time, grabbing the puck at center ice and sweeping slightly to his left before cutting back to the middle and heading straight for Huet. Stick-handling all the way, Jagr suddenly hit the brakes at the top of the crease and made a hard, fast move to his backhand. For an instant, he appeared to have Huet beat, but he failed to control the puck, and it rolled off his stick and harmlessly away from the net. A third Montreal shooter would not be needed.

Final score: Canadiens 6, Rangers 5.

Huet leapt to his feet and into the arms of his onrushing teammates as the crowd cel-ebrated a win that not long before had seemed like a certain loss. The players skated off the ice to the sound of 21,000 people singing "olé, olé, olé, olé" at the top of their lungs.

Saku Koivu celebrates Alexei Kovalev's game-tying goal late in the third period of the Canadiens' comeback win over the New York Rangers in February 2008 (Allen McInnis/ Montreal Gazette. Reprinted by permission).

Journalists, meanwhile, scrambled for the record books, with many surprised to confirm that the Canadiens had just mounted the biggest comeback in their 99-year history. Never before had the team won a game after trailing by five goals. The Rangers, on the other hand, had never before lost a game they'd been leading by 5 goals.

Later, in their respective locker rooms, players from both teams commented that their ears were still ringing from the incredible noise the Bell Centre fans had made during the second half of the game. The mood in the Canadiens' room was euphoric. The Rangers, whose overtime loss still gave them a precious point in the standings, were more philosophical than crushed. And New York Coach Tom Renney paid a compliment to those who witnessed the historic occasion from inside the Bell Centre. "I give the Montreal fans a ton of credit," he said. "They did what you're supposed to do."

THE SECOND BIGGEST COMEBACK?

The Canadiens' comeback against the Rangers on February 19, 2008 was the numerically "biggest" in team history, but it wasn't the "greatest." That honor would have to go to the team's April 8, 1971 Game 2 Stanley Cup Quarter-finals defeat of the defending champion Boston Bruins (*see Dryden Debuts as Canadiens Shock Bruins, page 95*), in which the Canadiens rallied from an early 5–1 deficit to win 7–5.

Six years after the 2008 rally, on March 15, 2014, the Canadiens pulled off another dramatic comeback that had playoff implications for both teams involved.

In the 68th game of the regular season, the Canadiens, in the midst of a three-game losing streak, trailed the visiting Ottawa Senators 2–1 after two periods. It could have been worse. The Senators had a goal called back at 14:51 of the second period after a long and confusing video review.

The Senators struck quickly in the third, with goals by Ales Hemsky and Clarke MacArthur putting the home team in a 4–1 hole. The Canadiens, who were battling for a playoff spot, seemed headed for a sure loss. Even a goal by Montreal's Lars Eller with 3:22 to play seemed only to delay the inevitable. The Canadiens barely celebrated it, and only a smattering of the fans on hand stood to cheer. In fact, a quick look at the stands reveals that several had already left the building. Things got quite a bit livelier 1:16 later when Montreal captain Brian Gionta redirected a hard pass from P. K. Subban past a now rattled Senators goalie, Robin Lehner.

Senators 4, Canadiens 3, 2:04 left to play.

The Canadiens caught another break 16 seconds later when Ottawa's Kyle Turris was sent off for hooking. With goaltender Carey Price pulled for an extra attacker, six Canadiens swarmed the Ottawa zone. Players battled ferociously in front of the Ottawa net, and Lehner stumbled after an Ottawa defender pushed a Montreal forward into him. He got to his feet just in time to see the Canadiens' Subban, owner of one of the hardest slap shots in the NHL, take a pass at the top of the right face-off circle with two seconds left on the clock. But Subban resisted letting a slapper fly, and spotted Canadiens center David Desharnais uncovered and calling for the puck to Lehner's right. Subban's pass found him with exactly one second to play, and the diminutive D.D. shot the puck high over the diving Lehner and a sprawled Ottawa defen-seman and into the net. The crowd roared and the goal horn blared, but the red goal light did not go on, replaced instead by the green light indicating the end of a period. While Lehner had a meltdown, arguing that he'd been pushed during the mad scramble, the game announcers speculated that the goal had come too late. But a video review showed the puck had entered the net with 0.2 seconds to play.

Senators 4, Canadiens 4. And the game was headed for overtime.

What happened next still thrills Canadiens fans and infuriates Senators supporters. With 1:20 elapsed in overtime, Montreal's Max Pacioretty put a harmless-looking shot on goal. The puck came to rest against Lehner's right pad, and briefly, beneath his blocker. But the referee, perched just feet away, did not blow his whistle. Desharnais and Pacioretty jammed away at Lehner, and the puck suddenly came free. Montreal defenseman Francis Bouillon, who had started turning away from the play, quickly reversed course and the puck came directly to him. He wasted no time firing into a wide-open Ottawa net.

Lehner and his teammates went ballistic, chasing the referees to the penalty box area. Senators forward Bobby Ryan had to be physically restrained, and was given a game misconduct penalty. But the Ottawa protests would fall on deaf ears. The Canadiens had scored four times in under five minutes.

Final score: Canadiens 5, Senators 4.

2ND PERIOD

THE PLAYOFFS

Canadiens Win Their First Stanley Cup

The Montreal Canadiens are professional hockey's oldest and winningest franchise, but it took several years for the team and its fans to savor the sweet smell of success.

Playing in the National Hockey Association (NHA) since their founding in 1909 (*see 1909: The Creation of Habs Nation, page 143*), the Canadiens soon started to earn the support of Montreal's French-speaking hockey fans and newspapers. In fact, owner George Kennedy's Canadiens, officially the Club Athlétique Canadien, were the only NHA team to turn a profit in 1910–11. Fans traveled by the thousands from the French East End of Montreal to the Westmount Arena in the Anglo West End to watch them play, singing songs of encouragement throughout the games. The most popular tune was borrowed from one used to support one of the Canadiens' French predecessor teams. Substituting "Canadiens" for "Montagnards," the fans marked particularly happy moments by singing "Halte la, halte la, halte la, les Canadiens sont la!" (It translates poorly, but basically means: "Stop right there, the Canadiens are here!"). The song is still occasionally sung at Canadiens home games today.

It didn't hurt that the team had more or less exclusive access to French-speaking players, not off the ice anyhow. The team's fans started referring to it as "l'équipe des habitants" (the people's team). Soon that reference to the fans was transferred directly to the team itself, who became Les Habitants, a nickname, shortened to "Habs" in English, that they still sport over a hundred years later.

Things didn't go quite as smoothly on the ice. After briefly losing star forward Newsy Lalonde and other players to the upstart Pacific Coast Hockey Association (PCHA), the Canadiens slipped in the standings in 1911–12, posting an 8–10 record and finishing last.

Lalonde returned for the 1912–13 season, joining a team that still featured original Canadiens Didier Pitre and Jack Laviolette as well as star goaltender Georges Vezina (*see Up Close: Georges Vezina: Cool as a Cucumber, page 66*). A new rule that year allowed the

Canadiens to sign two non-French players (Fred Povey and Don Smith), while their NHA opponents were each allowed to roster two French players. That season also saw the Canadiens briefly wear the much-maligned "barber pole" jersey (*see sidebar, Bleu, Blanc, Rouge, page 66*). Vezina, who allowed the fewest goals in the league in his debut season of 1910–11 and again the following year, posted the first shutout in team history when the Canadiens blanked the Senators 6–0 in Ottawa on January 18. Unfortunately, they only won three more games that season. The Canadiens' 9–11 record left them tied with a new NHA addition, the Toronto Hockey Club, and an old foe, the Ottawa Senators, for third place behind the suddenly powerful Quebec Bulldogs and the Montreal Wanderers. Lalonde led the team with 25 goals.

The next season was the Canadiens' most successful to date. Propelled by Newsy Lalonde 22 goals and Vezina's 3.3 goals-against-average, the team finished in a tie with the Toronto HC, nicknamed the Blueshirts, atop the NHA standings with a 13–7 record.

The team began the season more or less alternating wins and losses, including an 8–2 win over the Wanderers January 10, in which Newsy Lalonde scored a record six goals. A four-game winning streak in early February got the team back in the race, but things looked grim for the Canadiens after a 6–5 loss to Ottawa on February 25 that required 30 minutes of overtime. But they rallied with a 6–5 overtime win of their own against the Wanderers on the 28th and caught Toronto by beating their new Queen City counterparts, the Toronto Tecumsehs, 5–3 on March 4, the 20th and final game of the season. With Montreal and Toronto HC finishing with identical 13–7 records, the NHA called for a two-game, total goals series to break the deadlock and determine a champion. The Canadiens were off to the playoffs for the first time.

Closing in on the Cup

As NHA champions were automatically awarded the silver bowl, no less than the Stanley Cup itself was at stake when the Canadiens and Toronto HC met in a two-game, total goals series. On March 7, with more than 6,000 fans in the sold-out Westmount Arena raucously cheering them on, the Canadiens won the first game, 2–0. But the team ran out of fuel somewhere between Montreal and Toronto, where they dropped Game 2 by a 6–0 score. It was the first Stanley Cup win for a team from Toronto.

With five new players in the lineup and Newsy Lalonde holding out for more money, the Canadiens got off to a terrible start in 1914–15, dropping their first eight games. Despite a 30-goal season for thirty-one-year-old Didier Pitre, the team never recovered and finished dead last with a 6–14 record.

The Canadiens made a number of changes prior to the 1915–16 season, bolstering their defense with the additions of veterans Howard McNamara (who was named team

Despite many changes to the lineup prior to the season, the 1915–16 edition was the first Canadiens team to capture a Stanley Cup (Hockey Hall of Fame).

captain) and George "Goldie" Prodgers and moving Jack Laviolette to forward. Newsy Lalonde replaced the retired Jimmy Gardner as player-coach.

The team, however, took some time to gel, and an increasingly impatient Kennedy let it be known that Lalonde's job was in peril if the team didn't start winning soon. He even took the unusual step of paying his players a combined $100 for every win, and charging them an equal amount for losses. For the month of January, at least, it turned out to be a break-even proposition.

A 9–5 loss to the Wanderers on February 2 left the Canadiens with a disappointing record of 5–6–1. Then they caught fire, winning 11 of 12 games, including the final 7 of the season. The season-ending 6–4 win over Toronto left Montreal with an overall record of 16–7–1, easily good enough for first place in the now five-team NHA. The team, led by Newsy Lalonde's 28, scored 104 goals while Georges Vezina allowed only 76. George Kennedy's changes had worked.

In the past, an NHA championship would have meant a Stanley Cup as well, but beginning the previous season, the Cup's trustees changed formats, now requiring the

NHA champion to face the champions of the PCHA in a best-of-five series. The Portland Rosebuds, the first US-based team to play for the Stanley Cup, were coming to town.

The Rosebuds became the first US-based team to play in a professional Canadian hockey league when the New Westminster Royals of the PCHA moved to Portland in 1914. The Rosebuds, sometimes called the Uncle Sams, won the 1916 league title by posting a 13–5 record. By winning, the Rosebuds took over possession of the Stanley Cup from the previous champions, the Cyclone Taylor–led Vancouver Millionaires, and, somewhat controversially, engraved their name on it: "Portland Ore./PCHA Champions/1915–16".

The custom of the time called for the hosting of the Cup Finals to alternate between the NHA and PCHA, so the 1916 Stanley Cup challenge series took place in Montreal between the 20th and 30th of March, on excellent ice conditions in the Westmount Arena. Games 1, 3, and 5 were played under NHA rules, which meant five skaters plus a goaltender per side (the NHA eliminated the Rover position in 1910). Games 2 and 4 were played by PCHA rules, with six skaters.

The Rosebuds arrived in Montreal by train on March 29. But if the Canadiens were expecting a travel-weary opponent, they were soon surprised. There is no record of who tallied for the visitors, but Portland goaltender Tommy Murray shut out the home team and the Rosebuds skated to a 2–0 victory. The Canadiens were badly outplayed. Only the brilliance of Montreal netminder Georges Vezina kept the score close.

Things looked grim for the Canadiens as they took to the ice for Game 2 without Lalonde, who was sick, and Laviolette, who suffered a broken nose in Game 1. But the home side bared down defensively and eked out a 2–1 win to tie the series.

Media reports of the day describe fast-paced, penalty-filled games with tight checking. Indeed, both Laviolette and Lalonde were ejected from Game 3, the latter after punching rugged Portland defenseman Ernie "Moose" Johnson, a former Wanderer and Montreal native. The incident escalated into a full-scale brawl that only broke up after the Town of Westmount's Chief of Police stepped onto the ice and threatened the participants with a night in jail unless they got back to playing hockey. The Canadiens eventually prevailed by a score of 6–3 thanks to a three-goal performance by Didier Pitre.

On the brink of elimination, Portland hit the ice in Game 4 firing on all pistons and jumped out to a 3–0 lead. But Montreal answered back with four straight goals. The Canadiens were one period away from winning the Stanley Cup, but three third-period Portland goals, two by winger Fred "Smokey" Harris, sent the series to a fifth and deciding game, and scores of fans back home in disbelief and disappointment.

The games were well attended in the early going, with many of those unable to find tickets following the action by telegraph at popular gathering places. Game 5, however, featured a number of empty seats, due, in part, to the Canadiens' dismal showing in Game 4.

Those on hand for the final and deciding game erupted in cheers when Montreal substitute Erksine "Skene" Ronan, a former NHA scoring champion acquired from Toronto mid-season, tallied at the 11:50 mark of the first period. Back and forth action for the remainder of the game left skaters on both sides drained. The Canadiens in particular were visibly faltering when Portand's Tommy Dunderdale, another former NHA star, knotted the game at 1–1 6:45 into the third.

With the clock ticking down and both teams battling desperately, the game's deciding play began, fittingly, after a Georges Vezina save. Newsy Lalonde collected the rebound and left it behind the Montreal net for defensesman Goldie Prodgers, who barrelled the length of the ice before deftly deking Tommy Murray and lobbing the puck into the empty Portland net at the 10:30 mark. Vezina and the Montreal defense then repelled an increasingly furious Portland attack until the final bell sounded to announce the first Stanley Cup in Canadiens history.

Under the headline, "Flying Frenchmen Lift Stanley Cup," the March 31, 1916 edition of the *Montreal Gazette* credited the Canadiens' crafty use of substitutes as the deciding factor in the victory.

" THE OUTSTANDING FEATURE OF THE SERIES HAS BEEN THE MAKING GOOD OF MEN WHO HAVE BEEN USED AS SUBSTITUTES THROUGHOUT THE SCHEDULED SEASON; ARBOUR, PRODGERS AND LALONDE HAVE BEEN THE OUTSTANDING STARS OF THE LOCALS, WHILE ON THE FEW OCCASIONS THAT RONAN WAS USED HE MADE GOOD. HIS GOAL OF LAST NIGHT WAS PERHAPS A FLUKEY ONE, BUT IT COUNTED AND STARTED THE FRENCH CLUB ON THEIR VICTORIOUS MARCH. "

After the game, exhausted players from both squads, team officials, and NHA executives gathered at Montreal's St. Regis Hotel for a banquet at which the Stanley Cup was presented to the new champions. Rather than take part in a raucous victory parade, as is now the custom, the Canadiens got on a Chicoutimi-bound train the next day to take part in an already scheduled exhibition game.

The Portland Rosebuds remain the only team never to win the Stanley Cup and still have their name engraved on it. The Canadiens soon added their own, along with the words: "Defeated Portland."

2nd Period

Up Close: Georges Vezina: Cool as a Cucumber

Born January 21, 1887, and nicknamed the "Chicoutimi Cucumber" after his hometown and for his legendary cool, calm demeanor, Georges Vezina was the only man to defend the Canadiens' net for 328 consecutive games over a 15-year period, a record that stood for over 30 years. Joining the team in 1910 at the age of twenty-three, he led the NHA in goals-against-average in his first two seasons. Vezina, whose netminding was a key factor in the Canadiens' first Stanley Cup victory in 1916, led the team to the Stanley Cup Finals again in 1917 and 1919 and was between the pipes for the team's second Cup win in 1924. In between, he posted the first shutout in NHL history when the Canadiens defeated the Toronto Arenas 9–0 on February 18, 1918, in the league's second season of operation.

Vezina struggled to get through the training camp that preceded the 1925–26 season, and showed up for the first game of the year looking ill and suffering from a high fever. In the dressing room after a scoreless first period, he collapsed but recovered in time to start the second. When the game resumed, he collapsed again and had to be carried from the ice. He never played again. Vezina was diagnosed with tuberculosis and returned home to Chicoutimi, where he died, four months after his final game. He was thirty-eight years old.

In 1927, the Canadiens purchased and donated to the NHL a trophy bearing his name that is still awarded annually to the league's top goaltender. And Vezina was among the 12 original inductees when the Hockey Hall of Fame was founded in 1945. He named his second child, born on March 30, 1916, the same day the Canadiens won their first Stanley Cup, Marcel Stanley Vezina, after the coveted trophy.

BLEU, BLANC, ROUGE

The Montreal Canadiens jersey is one of the most recognizable in all of sports. But the team went through a number of uniform and crest changes before finally settling on the red, white, and blue color scheme and famous CH logo, changing designs six times between 1911–12 and 1916–17.

Under the ownership of the O'Brien family in 1909–10, the team wore colors more closely identified with one of their great rivals, the Toronto Maple Leafs. The jerseys (traditionally called "sweaters" in Canada) were blue with white bars in the shape of a rectangle around the collar and a large, white "C" for "Canadiens" across the front. The team found its historic principal color the following season when it unveiled a red jersey with green and white stripes around the waist and cuffs and a crest featuring a stylized "C" and "A" for "Club Athletique Canadien," its official name from 1910 to March 1916.

The 1911–12 season saw the Canadiens finally hit on the color combination, inspired perhaps by the English Union Jack and the French "tricolore" (also a nickname for the team) for which it is known: red, white, and blue (or bleu, blanc, rouge, another French nickname for the Canadiens). This mostly white jersey featured blue and red stripes on the cuffs and a red stylized "C" in the top left corner against a white background.

The 1912–13 season saw the Canadiens debut what is easily the most controversial of their jerseys. Loved by some but reviled by many more, the "barber pole" jersey featured thick red, white, and blue horizontal bars and a crest consisting of the letters "CAC" inside a white maple leaf outline. After a protest by the Ottawa Senators, who thought the barber pole look too similar to their own red, white, and black version and confused fans when the two teams met, the Canadiens had to wear different jerseys for their matches against their old rivals from the nation's capital. The change was a significant one in that the alternate jerseys, red with a broad blue bar and white "C", would be the basis for the classic ones worn for so many years now.

The Canadiens finally stuck with a jersey design for two years in a row from 1913 to 1915. These were another step closer to the classic design: red with a broad blue bar across which a small letter "A" sat inside a large, stylized "C". A similar jersey, featuring a red "CA" logo and blue stripes on the arms, was worn in 1915–16, the year of the team's first Stanley Cup conquest.

Finally, when owner George Kennedy reorganized his sports businesses and officially renamed the team the "Club de Hockey Canadien" in March 1916, the "A" in the crest was replaced by an "H", creating the famous "CH" logo. Other slight tweaks have taken place over the years, but the Canadiens' uniforms have been essentially the same ever since. Only one major change took place, in 1924–25 when the "CH" was replaced by a globe to celebrate a world championship, the Stanley Cup win of 1924. But the "CH" was back for good the next season.

The Canadiens wore replicas of most of these designs, to mixed reviews from purists, during their centennial celebrations spanning 2009 and 2010. The team also created a special jersey for the Winter Classic game played on New Year's Day 2016. White with a distinctive red collar, it featured a large chest stripe a lighter shade of blue, similar to the original 1909 jersey color, and a globe similar to the 1924 model on the arms. The "CH" logo was larger and with inverted colors, the "C" being white and the "H" red.

2nd Period

Rocket Richard 5, Leafs, 1

10

After nearly claiming their second Stanley Cup in 1919 with the core group of players from the team's 1909 founding and 1916 championship, it was an almost entirely new group that would win another title in 1924. Newcomers Billy Boucher, Aurel Joliat, and Howie Morenz *(see Up Close: Howie Morenz: The Stratford Streak, page 74)* accounted for 44 of the team's mediocre 59 goals in 24 regular games. Luckily, veteran goalie Georges Vezina *(see Up Close: Georges Vezina: Cool as a Cucumber, page 66)* gave up a league-best 48.

Most of the 1924 team was still around for Cups two and three, in 1930 and 1931. Vezina died suddenly in 1926, and future Hall of Famer George Hainsworth subsequently stepped in. Howie Morenz had also emerged as a superstar. At the height of his powers, in 1929–30, he scored 40 goals in 44 games.

The NHL was constantly changing in the 1920s and 30s. Before and during the Great Depression, teams came and went, with as many as 10 competing in the last third of the 1920s after the addition of franchises in Chicago, Detroit, and a second one in New York. The Canadiens even lost their monopoly on the hearts of Montreal hockey fans when the Montreal Maroons *(see sidebar, The Montreal Maroons, page 75)* joined the league in 1924 (the same year as the Boston Bruins). Around this time, a number of rule changes were introduced and teams started using all of their players instead of relying on their "60-minute men." The Brooklyn Americans, who played as the New York Americans from 1925 to 1941, dropped out of the NHL following the 1941–42 season, bringing the number of teams in the league down to six. The 1942–43 season marked the start of the inaccurately named Original Six era (which lasted until 1967).

The economy wasn't the only thing that was depressed between 1933 and 1939; Canadiens fans were too, for the most part. Even when things seemed to improve, they went horribly wrong again. Morenz, who was traded to Chicago in 1934, returned for the 1936–37 season and helped the team regain its form. But he died suddenly and tragically in a Montreal hospital in March of 1937, a blood clot stopping his heart five weeks after he broke his leg during a game. After a first-place finish that season, the Canadiens lost their best-of-five playoff semifinal against Detroit, 3–2 then returned to lower rungs of the standings. In 1939–40, in what was a seven-team NHL, the team finished dead last with a record of 10–33–5. World War II would soon help end the Depression, but the suffering of Canadiens fans would last a few years longer. Luckily, help was on its way.

New blood

Although it took a few years for them to have an impact, changes made in 1940 would eventually make the Canadiens contenders again.

After years of financial losses, the consortium that owned the team, led by Ernest Savard, sold the Canadiens to the Montreal Arena Company, the owners of the Montreal Forum, the team's home since 1926. New team president Donat Raymond wasted little time righting a ship that, if not quite sinking, was listing badly. He first hired former player and Chicago and Toronto bench boss Dick Irvin to coach the team. He then hired veteran hockey man Tommy Gorman, who had served as the general manager of the Maroons from 1934 until the team folded in 1938, to run the Canadiens and the Forum, as was the custom at the time.

The team struggled for three seasons, but, through sharp scouting or sheer luck, added on-ice talent that would form the nucleus of future championship teams, players like Elmer Lach, Ken Reardon, Butch Bouchard . . . .and Maurice Richard.

Hailing from Montreal's working class Bordeaux neighborhood, where he developed his powerful skating stride in winters spent on the nearby Riviere-des-Prairies (or North River), Maurice Richard soon made a name for himself as a prolific scorer in Montreal youth and junior leagues, sometimes playing on as many as three teams at a time. Unfortunately, he also earned the reputation for being brittle and prone to injury.

Promoted to the Canadiens' Quebec Senior Hockey League affiliate in 1940 after a promising junior career, the nineteen-year-old Richard crashed into the boards and broke his left ankle in the first game of the season. After missing the rest of the year, Richard returned to the team in the fall of 1941 and was progressing nicely, scoring eight goals in 30 games, when he broke his left wrist against an unforgiving goalpost. Luckily, Richard's wrist healed in time for him to return for the playoffs, where his two-goal opening game performance was good enough to earn him an invitation to the Canadiens' 1942 training camp.

At camp, Richard turned heads with his speed. And his addition to a squad of "Flying Frenchmen" that was particularly short of French players was welcomed by French-speaking fans and reporters.

2nd Period

On November 8, in his third game, playing on a line with Elmer Lach and Tony Demers at home against the New York Rangers, Richard scored his first NHL goal on a spectacular end-to-end rush. Former Canadiens star Newsy Lalonde, who predicted a bright future for the dark-haired young winger, was present to witness the feat.

Then disaster struck. With five goals under his belt in 16 games and gaining in confidence with every passing day, Richard broke his leg, this time the right one, in a December 28 game against the Boston Bruins.

Recounting the story in his 1953 *The Hockey Book*, author Bill Roche remarked that, "It really looked as though the Flying Frenchmen had picked an easily-bruised-and busted lemon. Richard seemed destined to only be Number One on the Canadiens' injury list."

Many gave up on Richard at that point. In fact, he almost gave up on himself. For a time, Richard considered leaving hockey behind. If he had, numerous Quebec folks songs would never have been sung, scores of books would never have been written, and a 2005 feature film about his life would never have been made. Dick Irvin and Tommy Gorman were among the few who still believed in Maurice Richard. Fortunately, they were the only ones whose opinions mattered.

The Rocket blasts off

Exchanging his number 15 for the number 9 made available by the departure of forward Charlie Sands (the second-last to wear that number for the team) and physically and mentally healed, Richard reported to the Canadiens' 1943 training camp determined to show everyone that he was in the NHL to stay. At practice one day, after observing one of his high-flying charges up the ice, teammate Ray Getliffe remarked that Richard looked like a "rocket" heading to the net. *Montreal Gazette* hockey reporter Dink Carroll, credited by many for giving Richard his iconic nickname, overheard the comment. And the rest is history.

It didn't hurt the newly dubbed Rocket's cause that the team, which finished the previous season in fourth place with a record of 19–19–2, had turned a corner of its own. With Rookie Bill Durnan in goal and forward Buddy O'Connor leading the offensive charge, the Canadiens stormed out of the gates. At the Christmas break, they sat in first place with a record of 14–2–3

Richard, bothered by a sore shoulder that caused him to miss a few games, started slowly, with only two goals and two assists to his credit until Dick Irvin reunited him with early season linemates Elmer Lach and veteran winger and team captain Hector "Toe" Blake for a December 30 game against Detroit.

The Punch Line, as they were dubbed by the press, took off that night, and so did the Rocket. "Canadiens Stretch NHL Lead to Nine Points by Whipping Wings, 8–3: Maurice Richard Bags Three Goals" read a headline in the next day's *Montreal Gazette*. Richard had a pair of assists to go with his hat trick, while Lach, with two goals and four helpers, had a six-point night. Blake had two assists.

With the Punch Line leading the way, the Canadiens dropped only three more games that season, finishing with an NHL leading 38–5–7 record. All five losses were suffered on the road.

In the final 30 games of that 1943–44 season, Richard scored 30 goals and added 20 assists, giving him a total of 54 points in 46 games, third behind Lach's 72 and Blake's 59.

While Montreal hockey fans enjoyed the wildly successful season, and fell in love with Richard along the way, they'd had their hearts broken before. Regular season success was nice, but after a thirteen-year drought, Montreal hockey fans had their sights set higher—on the Stanley Cup.

The Canadiens faced the third-place Toronto Maple Leafs in a first-round (semifinals) best-of-seven series, and things quickly got off on the wrong foot. Aware of Richard's surge in production (23 goals in the season's final 18 games), the Leafs assigned expert checker Bob Davidson to shadow him throughout the game. The Leafs' 3–1 win stunned the 10,850 Forum faithful. Toronto's strategy had worked. Not only did Richard's name fail to make the scoresheet, it wasn't mentioned at all in Dink Carroll's report of the game in the following day's *Montreal Gazette*. The only thing a frustrated Richard managed to do was promise Toronto netminder Paul Bibeault, a friend who had defended the Montreal net the past two seasons, that things were going to be different in Game 2, to be played back at the Forum two days later.

Indeed, the legend of the man who would become one of the greatest playoff performers in hockey history started to truly grow on March 23. Seeing Richard blanketed in Game 1, coach Irvin responded in Game 2 by shortening his bench and using Richard on different lines in an effort to free him from the pesky Davidson.

Collars tightened on many of the more than 12,243 fans squeezed into the Forum as the first period ended in a scoreless tie. Then the Rocket went off. In a controversial sequence, where the Leafs claimed a fan had grabbed Davidson's stick, Richard, after a passing play with Mike McMahon and Blake, fired a hard shot past Bibeault 1:48 into the second period. Seventeen seconds later, Richard struck again, spinning hard off his check and blasting a shot into the top corner. Lach and Blake had the assists.

With Richard in the penalty box for tripping, Toronto got within one when a Reggie Hamilton shot deflected off a Canadiens defender, past Durnan, and into the

The Canadiens' legendary Punch Line (front row) consisting of Maurice Richard (left), Elmer Lach (middle), and Hector "Toe" Blake (right) was formed during the 1943–44 season (Imperial Oil – Turofsky/Hockey Hall of Fame).

Montreal net. But Richard completed the natural hat trick after a beautiful play by Lach, and the period ended with a 3–1 Montreal lead.

Richard, who actually had two minor penalties in the second frame, wasn't done writing his name all over the game's scoresheet . . . or hockey's record books. Exactly one minute into the third period, he scored his fourth goal of the night on another beautiful feed from Lach. The Forum crowd erupted, but not for the last time that night. Richard was saving his best for last, this time using finesse rather than raw power. After taking a pass from Blake, he maneuvered around Hamilton on one skate, circled in front of the Toronto goal, and slid the puck between Bibeault's pads.

When the final buzzer sounded, the scoreboard read Montreal 5, Toronto 1, but it might just as easily said, as newspaper headlines across the country the next day did, "Rocket Richard 5, Maple Leafs 1."

Andy Lytle, writing in the March 24, 1944 edition of the *Toronto Star*, in an article bearing the headline "Remarkable Scoring Feat by Slim Young Habitant," described the scene this way:

"The sounds were deafening when Richard scored his third and fourth goals but when he gained the fifth by another burst that began over the red line, the tumult was so great that for several minutes time seemed to stand still as well as the pace of the game. Richard was surrounded and held an impromptu reception. Five goals by one player is an extraordinary feat at any time. To score that many in a playoff game is an achievement never duplicated by an individual since hockey was taken off the ponds of the country."

Lytle wasn't altogether right. Richard's five-goal performance only tied the record set by Canadiens star Newsy Lalonde in 1919. Toe Blake's five assists were indeed a record, though. Richard would go on to set a number of playoff records of his own.

The cheering at game's end momentarily turned to boos when the Forum's house announcer began calling out the traditional Three Stars in ascending order. The crowd was stunned to hear "La troisieme etoile, the third star . . . Maurice Richard." How could someone score five goals in a single game and manage no better than third star? Then, "La deuxieme etoile, the second star . . . Maurice Richard." Now most caught on, and a roar began to build, reaching a crescendo with the announcement of the first star, again ". . . Maurice Richard."

It had never happened before and never has since. One man was named all three stars in an NHL game. And not a single soul disagreed.

After the euphoria passed and heads cleared, there was still the matter of the semifinal series, now tied at one, to settle. The Leafs nearly reversed the tide in Toronto two nights later, but the Canadiens prevailed, 2–1 on a Ray Getliffe goal. Montreal then took Game 4, 4–1, before finishing off a dispirited Leafs team back at the Forum March 30, 11–0. Richard, Blake, Getliffe, and Murph Chamberlain each scored a pair for the Canadiens, who were now off to the Stanley Cup Finals against the surprising Chicago Blackhawks.

After a 5–1 Canadiens win in Game 1, Richard was at it again, scoring all three Canadiens goals in a 3–1, Game 2 victory. The Canadiens won a hard fought Game 3, 3–2, and were poised to win their first Stanley Cup since 1931.

Game 4, in Montreal, was the best of all. The Canadiens trailed 4–1 midway through the third period when Lach scored to cut the Chicago lead to two. With under four minutes remaining, Richard, on a pass from Blake, scored to get the Canadiens within one. The roar of the crowd had barely dulled when Richard struck again one minute and

15 seconds later on a centering pass from Blake. The Forum erupted again and the game had to be stopped to clear the ice of celebratory debris. The Blackhawks somehow managed to compose themselves in the final minutes. The game was headed for overtime.

Nine minutes into the extra frame, Captain Toe Blake took care of business, collecting a Butch Bouchard pass and banging the puck into the back of the Chicago net for his first goal and fifth point of the night. After dropping the playoff opener three weeks earlier, Montreal won eight games in a row to claim their fifth Stanley Cup. Blake finished the playoffs with 18 points while Richard notched 12 goals, both new records. The two heroes would figure prominently in Canadiens' glories still to come.

Up Close: Howie Morenz: The Stratford Streak

Howard William Morenz, simply "Howie" to hockey fans, was one of the NHL's first superstars. Nicknamed the "Stratford Streak" for his blazing speed and the Ontario town he moved to at age fifteen, Morenz made an immediate impact when he joined the Canadiens for the 1923–24 season. After a 13-goal regular season, Morenz scored four goals in four Stanley Cup games and helped the Canadiens win the coveted trophy for the second time.

Morenz led Montreal to two more Cups, in 1930 and 1931. He led the NHL in scoring in 1927–28, his 51 points making him the first player to ever reach 50 in a season. Morenz scored a career-high 40 goals in 1929–30 and claimed a second scoring title in the Cup season of 1930–31, again with 51 points. He placed in the NHL's Top 10 for points 10 times and led the Canadiens in that statistic for seven straight seasons.

After stops in Chicago and New York (Rangers), the three-time NHL MVP returned to the Canadiens, at age thirty-four, for the 1936–37 season. On January 28, 1937, Morenz badly broke his leg during a game against the Chicago Blackhawks. Hospitalized and despondent over what he felt certain was the end of his career, Morenz suffered a nervous breakdown. He died in the hospital on March 8 from a heart attack believed to be caused by a blood clot. On March 11, a public funeral was held for Morenz at the Montreal Forum. Some 50,000 people are said to have paid their respects. The next public funeral held for a Canadiens player took place at the then Molson Centre in 2000, when 115,000 people paid tribute to the fallen Maurice Richard.

Howie Morenz was among the first group of inductees when the Hockey Hall of Fame opened in 1945. In 1950, the Canadian press named him hockey's best player in the first half of the twentieth century. In 1998, the *Hockey News* magazine placed him at number 15 on its list of the Top 100 NHL Players of All Time.

THE MONTREAL MAROONS

After the demise of the Montreal Wanderers in 1918, English-speaking Montrealers were left without a team of their own to cheer for. While some switched allegiances to the mainly French-supported Canadiens, many applauded the arrival of another Montreal NHL team, the Maroons, in 1924. Founded by the owners of the newly built Montreal Forum, the team actually arrived without a nickname as the Montreal Professional Hockey Club, but fans soon dubbed them the Maroons after the color of their jerseys.

The Maroons were an almost immediate success, winning the Stanley Cup in only their second season. Amidst growing financial concerns, the Maroons nevertheless captured a second Stanley Cup in 1935 by winning three best-of-five playoff series in three straight games. In the 1935–36 playoffs, the Maroons were on the wrong end of the 1–0 score in the longest NHL playoff game in history when Detroit's "Mud" Bruneteau ended the game with a goal 16:30 into the sixth overtime period at the Montreal Forum.

With their financial situation worsening as the Great Depression dragged on, the owners of the Maroons tried in vain to sell their club. When they failed to find a buyer, they chose to suspend operations for the 1938–39 season. Dormant for years while its backers attempted to sell it, the Maroons franchise was eventually cancelled by the NHL in 1946.

2nd Period

The Rocket's Greatest Goal

11

The Montreal Canadiens of 1951–52, a few years into a rebuilding program initiated by new general manager Frank Selke in the late 1940s, were a mix of the old and new. And so, in a way, was Maurice "Rocket" Richard.

Selke inherited a powerhouse team when he came to Montreal from the Toronto Maple Leafs organization in the summer of 1946. But he immediately recognized that, apart from a core of stars, the Canadiens cupboard was nearly bare. He set about creating a farm system that would develop players for the NHL team, a formula he had applied with great success with the Maple Leafs, who, ironically, were now reaping the benefits. But Selke knew there would be lean years until the newest crop of Canadiens came into their own. And he was right. After finishing first in 1946–47, the team wound up fifth the following year and missed the playoffs for the first time since 1939–40.

The roster changes actually began shortly after Montreal won its sixth Stanley Cup in 1946. Selke traded longtime Canadien Buddy O'Conner to New York in 1947. Hector "Toe" Blake, the star left winger who combined with Elmer Lach and Richard to form the legendary Punch Line, retired in 1948. Forward Leo Lamoureux departed that same year, followed by Murph Chamberlain in 1949. Goaltender Bill Durnan and defenseman Ken Reardon followed them out the door after the 1949–50 season.

To replace them, between 1947 and 1952, Selke added new blood to the Canadiens roster. Players like Doug Harvey, Tom Johnson, Dollard St. Laurent, Floyd "Busher" Curry, Bert Olmstead, Richard "Dickie" Moore, and Bernard "Boom-Boom" Geoffrion would contribute to varying degrees in the early 1950s, but would be the bedrock of a future dynasty. But that's another story *(see Five Consecutive Cups, page 84)*.

Then there was Maurice Richard. Since his 50 goals in 50 games season of 1944–45 *(see The Rocket Scores 50 in 50, page 10)*, Richard's career was more roller coaster than rocket. In the first postwar season of 1945–46, he scored only 27 goals, giving ammunition to those who would diminish his mid-forties dominance as having taken place in a watered-down league. But he bounced back with 45 goals in 1946–47 when virtually all of the players who had served overseas were back with their teams, and won the Hart Trophy as the NHL's most valuable player. He later followed seasons of 20 and 28 goals with 43- and 42-goal years in 1949–50 and 1950–51.

One statistic of Richard's that would continue to climb every year was his number of penalty minutes. Frustrated with the close checking and other, more underhanded means of preventing him from scoring, Richard had begun to retaliate with increasing frequency and fury. In 1949–50, he accumulated 114 minutes in penalties.

With a meager 65 points and a record of 25–30–15 in the now 70-game NHL season, the Canadiens finished third in 1950–51, behind second-place Toronto (95) and Detroit, who'd finished atop the standings for a third straight season after collecting 101 points. But Detroit would win only two more games that year . . . and lose four. The Canadiens upset them in the first round, and the series hero was Maurice Richard, whose quadruple and triple overtime goals in games 1 and 2 gave the Canadiens a surprising 2–0 series lead.

Richard had another OT marker in Game 2 of the Stanley Cup Finals against Toronto, where all five games were decided in overtime, the only time in NHL history that has ever occurred. Unfortunately for the Canadiens and their fans, Maple Leafs players scored the other four. Nevertheless, Richard led all playoff scorers with nine goals that year.

Instead of building on their upset of the powerful Red Wings the previous spring, the Canadiens got off to a poor start in 1951–52. After winning three of four to start the campaign, the team won only one of their next eight.

Playing with Bert Olmstead on left wing, and a revitalized Elmer Lach at center, Richard eventually began scoring again and the team found its stride, winning nine times in 11 games between December 15 and January 3. But a mysterious stomach ailment and a groin injury sidelined the thirty-year-old Rocket for much of the winter and he played in only 48 of the team's 70 games that year. His season total of 27 goals was still good enough for fifth overall in the NHL.

The Canadiens youngsters stepped up to fill the void left by the ailing Rocket. Eventual Rookie-of-the-Year Geoffrion scored 30 times in his first full NHL season while newcomer Moore had 18 goals in 33 games. Elmer Lach, who became the NHL's all-time leading scorer when he passed retired Bruin Bill Cowley on February 23, finished the season with 15 goals and a league-high 50 assists. In a 22-game span between January 23 and March 13, the Canadiens went 14–5–3.

After back-to-back losses to Boston on March 15 and 16, Richard returned to the Canadiens lineup for a pivotal March 19 game in Toronto, the third to last game of the

2nd Period

season. With second place on the line for Montreal, Geoffrion, Butch Bouchard, and Richard each scored in a 3–0 victory. The Rocket's goal, scored at top speed while fending off a checker, reassured those who were concerned about him being ready for the playoffs.

Montreal finished second with 78 points, well behind dominant Detroit and their 100. The Canadiens would face fourth-place Boston in the first round. Trouble was, the Bruins had beaten the Canadiens seven times and tied them twice during their 14 regular season meetings. Eliminating them would not be easy.

The Canadiens won the series' first two games at the Forum, with Richard notching a pair in a 5–1 Game 1 win and Geoffrion potting a hat trick in a 4–0 Game 2 victory. But with the series now headed to Boston, the Canadiens picked the wrong time to ease off the gas pedal, and the Bruins tied the series with 4–1 and 3–2 home ice wins. And they weren't done. On April 3, back in Montreal, the Bruins surprised the locals 1–0 to take the series lead.

In what would turn out to be one of the most dramatic playoff games in NHL history, the Canadiens faced elimination three days later at the Boston Garden.

Trailing 2–0 after the first period after goals by Bruins captain Milt Schmidt and center Dave Creighton, the Canadiens found some life when winger Eddie "Spider" Mazur, who had spent the entire regular season with Buffalo in the American Hockey League, pounced on a Bill Reay rebound and scored to cut the Bruins lead to one.

The Bruins clung to their one-goal advantage in the third while the Canadiens pressed desperately. Eight minutes into the frame, Boston goalie "Sugar" Jim Henry was struck in the face with a hard Doug Harvey shot. His nose broken, Henry retreated to the trainer's room for repairs. When he returned after a seventeen-minute delay, he struggled to see through the severe swelling around his eyes.

Three minutes later, after a rare miscue by the normally sure-handed Schmidt, Richard picked up a loose puck, spun quickly, and fired a 30-foot shot past Henry and into the top right corner of the Bruins' net.

Both teams traded chances for the remainder of the third, but Henry and Montreal goalie Gerry McNeil barred the door.

The game remained tied through the rest of the third and a full period of overtime. Then, seven minutes into the second overtime period, Harvey rushed up the ice and fired a shot into Henry's pads. Canadiens rookie center Paul Masnick, called up that very day from the Canadiens' Cincinnati farm team, was "Johnny-on-the-spot," collecting the rebound from six feet out and firing it into the Boston net. The Canadiens were alive and headed back to the Forum for Game 7. For sheer drama, Game 6 would be hard to top.

Both the Bruins and Canadiens hobbled back to Montreal. After six hard-fought games, players from both sides were bruised and battered. "Sugar" Jim Henry applied hot

Respect: Wounded warriors Jim Henry of the Bruins and Montreal's Maurice Richard shake hands at the conclusion of the epic seventh game of the 1952 semifinals (Roger St. Jean/Hockey Hall of Fame).

and cold compresses to his eyes in an effort to keep the swelling down, and Richard was hobbling after injuring a knee. Even coach Dick Irvin, who was struck in the forehead by a wayward Milt Schmidt shot in the third period of Game 6, was battle-scarred. And it was about to get worse.

Dazed and confused

Game 7 on April 8, 1952 was more than "the hottest ticket in town"; it was the only ticket worth having. The *Montreal Gazette* reported that one scalper (or "ticket-reseller" in current politically correct parlance) outside the Forum was asking for the outrageous sum of $12 for a standing-room ticket that usually sold for under $2.

Inside, the Forum faithful were on edge as the puck dropped on Game 7. They breathed a little more easily after another Eddie Mazur goal put the home team in front less than five minutes into the first, but their relief was short-lived. At the 12:25 mark, Boston's Ed Sandford connected from the side of the net to tie the game at one.

The second period was scoreless, but by no means uneventful. In the early going, Richard mustered one of his patented rushes, and with only one destination in mind, the Boston net, tried to barrel his way through the Bruins' defensive pair of Hal Laycoe and Bill Quackenbush. Unfortunately for the Rocket, he never saw Leo Labine. The Boston forward, once described by author Stan Fischler as having "scant acquaintance with the rulebook," back-checking to save his life, hit the now off-balance Richard, who some say had already fallen to his knees, with a thundering body check.

What happened next has been described over the years in many different ways, not all of them compatible with each other. Whether it was a stick or Bill Quackenbush's knee, something struck Richard in the head as he fell . . . and the ice finished him off, opening a cut above his left eye. The Rocket was, as one wag later put it, "knocked colder than a bailiff's heart."

Some fans reportedly thought Richard, sprawled out on the ice and not moving, was dead or that his neck was broken. But smelling salts eventually revived the bleeding Rocket, and he was helped off the ice into the Forum clinic, where he reportedly lost consciousness again on the trainer's table while doctors closed the gash in his head with six stitches.

It's hard to fathom now, in this age of concussion protocols and "quiet rooms," but Richard eventually made his way back to the Canadiens bench, where he told coach Irvin he was ready to play. Many have suggested that he was in a semiconscious state when he took his usual seat next to Elmer Lach.

While Richard was being brought back from the dead, much of the third period had gone by. Sitting on the bench, blood from the newly stitched wound over his eye dripping down his face, Richard glanced up at the scoreboard, trying to determine the score and the amount of time left, but his blurred eyesight betrayed him. Lach had to fill him in: "Four minutes left . . . still 1–1." The next goal would almost surely win the game, and by extension, the series.

Although he knew the Rocket was still groggy at best, Dick Irvin was no fool. He wasn't about to leave one of the greatest clutch scorers in hockey history on his bench, especially with the teams playing 4-on-4 following major penalties to Hal Laycoe and Montreal's Billy Reay at the 13:55 mark. Richard went over the boards around the same time Butch Bouchard was deftly breaking up a Boston attack. The Canadiens' veteran defenseman came away with the puck, spotted the open Richard, and passed it up ice to him. The Rocket flew past the two nearest Bruins and eluded a stick check from another. That left a backpedalling Bill Quackenbush, one of the NHL's best skating and highly regarded defenders, between Richard and the Boston goal. But Quackenbush reacted almost perfectly, angling the onrushing Rocket towards the corner of the rink. It looked like Richard had run out of room, when, still traveling at top speed, he cut sharply to his left, skating almost horizontally to the goal line, and headed for the front of the net. Richard faked a shot, which momentarily froze Henry, then whipped a low, hard shot inside the left post. The goal light flashed red and the Forum erupted.

"The crowd of 14,598, largest of the series, saluted the brilliant play with a roar that shook the building. Programs, coins, newspapers, overshoes and anything that was throwable rained down on the ice. A squad of seven attendants took five minutes or more to clean the ice," wrote Dink Carroll in the following day's *Montreal Gazette*.

With 3:41 still to play, there was time for the Bruins to rally, but, stunned by the turn of events and unsettled by the still roaring crowd, they failed to mount a serious attack on the Montreal goal. The Canadiens defended furiously and Boston coach Lynn Patrick pulled Henry for a sixth attacker. But Billy Reay, newly released from the penalty box, sealed the win for the Canadiens with an empty-net goal with 34 seconds left on the clock.

The fans cheered for another five minutes after the final buzzer sounded and the Bruins and Canadiens came together for the traditional post-series handshake. That's when Roger St. Jean, a photographer for the *La Presse* newspaper, snapped one of the most iconic photos in sports history. It shows a clearly dazed Richard, blood dripping down his face from a large bandage over his left eye, staring intensely and firmly shaking the hand of Jim Henry, who, sporting two black eyes, leans forward, almost bowing. If that photo could be captioned with one word, that word would be "Respect."

Rocket Richard had and would continue to score some incredible goals during his career, more than one coming while carrying opposing defensemen on his back. But for the sheer power and determination with which it was scored, and the circumstances it came under, nothing could match the Game 7 winner of 1952. More than 60 years after he scored it, it is unanimously remembered as Richard's greatest goal.

Unfortunately, the man who had just scored it could barely remember his most recent exploit. Amidst the chaotic locker room celebrations, Richard tried to recall and explain to reporters what had occurred only minutes before. But it was all a blur. And when his father, Onésime Richard, entered the room and draped a congratulatory arm around his son's shoulder, the overwhelmed, confused, and clearly hurting Rocket broke down and sobbed.

Richard and the rest of the battered and battle weary Canadiens would go on to lose the Stanley Cup Finals in a four-game sweep to a Detroit Red Wings team eager to avenge the previous season's playoff upset.

As for the Bruins, their pain would linger for a while longer, with much of their future torment coming at the hands of the Canadiens. The two teams met again the following playoff season, this time in the Finals, and Montreal prevailed in six games to win its seventh Stanley Cup. The Rocket had a hat trick in Montreal's 7–3, Game 4 win and set up Elmer Lach for the Cup-clinching 1–0 overtime winner in Game 5.

With the addition of two more key pieces in Jacques Plante and Jean Béliveau just around the corner, the Canadiens were on the verge of becoming the greatest team in hockey history. If not for a horrifically unfortunate bounce the following year, and an incident involving the great Maurice Richard the season after, that team might have won eight Stanley Cups in a row.

Up Close: Bernard "Boom-Boom" Geoffrion

Born Bernard Andre Joseph Geoffrion in Montreal in 1931, the affable Bernie Geoffrion scored 393 goals over 16 NHL seasons, the first 14 of which he played with his hometown Canadiens.

Geoffrion had already earned his nickname when he came to the Canadiens in 1951 after a successful junior career. A reporter dubbed him "Boom-Boom" after watching him practice his powerful slap shot, which he claimed to have invented as a boy.

Joining the team late in the season, Geoffrion notched eight goals in only 18 games. The following year, his 30 goals would lead the team, which included his boyhood hero Maurice Richard, and he won the Calder Trophy as the NHL's 1951–52 Rookie of the Year.

Skilled and tough, Geoffrion would go on to play in 11 NHL All-Star Games and win the Stanley Cup six times. He won a controversial Art Ross Trophy as the NHL's leading scorer in 1955 and again in 1961, the same year he took home the Hart Trophy as the league's MVP and became only the second player after Richard to score 50 goals in a single season.

Geoffrion nearly died after colliding with a teammate during a Canadiens practice in 1958. Revived on the ice by a team trainer, he was rushed to the hospital (and given his last rites), where emergency surgery was performed. Plagued throughout much of his career by stomach issues likely caused by nerves, Geoffrion also had his nose broken 16 times and received over 400 stitches in his face and head.

With his production declining, Geoffrion retired from hockey in 1964 and pursued his dream of coaching with the AHL's Quebec Aces. Still only thirty-five years old, Geoffrion returned to the NHL with the New York Rangers in 1966, and scored 22 goals over two seasons before taking over as the team's head coach in 1968.

In 1972, he was named head coach of the expansion Atlanta Flames, a position he held until his firing after 52 games in 1974–75. In 1979, he took over for Scotty Bowman as bench boss of the Canadiens, but quit after 30 games for health reasons.

That Canadiens team included Geoffrion's son Danny, the grandson of Canadiens' legend Howie Morenz (Howie's daughter, Marlene, married "the Boomer" in 1952). Danny Geoffrion's son, Blake, became the fourth member of the Morenz-Geoffrion clan to play for the Canadiens when he joined the team in 2012. He chose the number

57 in honor of his grandfather Bernie's number 5 and his great-grandfather Howie's number 7.

Bernie Geoffrion passed away from stomach cancer on March 11, 2006, the same day the Canadiens were to retire his jersey at the Bell Centre. The ceremony went ahead as planned, with Geoffrion's family members on hand to see his number 5 raised to the rafters alongside his father-in-law's number 7.

Geoffrion was inducted into the Hockey Hall of Fame in 1972. In 1998, the *Hockey News* magazine ranked him 42nd on its list of the Top 100 NHL Players of All Time.

2nd Period

Five Consecutive Cups

12

If Montreal general manager Frank Selke had a dynasty on his mind in the spring of 1955, it wasn't his own Canadiens, winners of only one of the last nine Stanley Cups. Selke was thinking about the powerhouse Detroit Red Wings, who had captured the last two Cups and won the NHL regular season every year between 1947–48 and 1954–55.

The Boston upset of the powerful Red Wings in the first round of the 1953 playoffs opened the door for Montreal, who would go on to beat the Bruins in the Finals to win their seventh Stanley Cup. But the team's luck wasn't so great the following season, when an accidentally deflected puck in overtime against Detroit essentially cost them Game 7 of the Finals, or in the 1955 playoffs, when they lost to the Wings without the suspended Maurice Richard, again in the Finals, and again in seven games. But time did what it eventually always does, and as one dynasty started to fade, another began to emerge. And this time luck would have nothing to do with it.

Little by little, the Canadiens had closed the gap between themselves and the great Red Wings. In 1951–52, Detroit finished 22 points ahead of the second-place Canadiens. In 1952–53, they had 15 points more. In 1953–54, the difference was down to seven, and in 1954–55, the year the Canadiens forfeited a game to Detroit, two measly points separated the teams. Indeed, the last two Stanley Cup Finals had proven to Selke that any distance between the two teams was due to reasons less tangible than mere talent. He, like many hockey observers, believed the high-flying Canadiens were actually the better of the two teams—on paper, at least. But something was missing, and it was Selke's job to find it . . . and fix it.

Adept public relations spinners even then, a little more than two weeks after their Game 7 loss to Detroit, the Canadiens announced that coach Dick Irvin was leaving the team to take over as head coach in Chicago, where he had played for three years and held his first coaching job for another two. The truth of the matter was that Irvin, after 15 years, had been dismissed.

The suspension of Maurice Richard (*see The Richard Riot, page 150*) still loomed large in the Montreal front office, where it was believed that the team would have defeated Detroit had their volatile scoring star been allowed to play. And Selke blamed Irvin, who he believed purposely stoked the hot-tempered Richard's competitive fires, for the Rocket's increasingly out-of-control behavior.

Selke and the team's directors were also frustrated by Irvin's seeming inability to win the big games. Yes, he had helped bring three Stanley Cups to Montreal, but he'd also lost four finals in the past five years. Over his 26-year coaching career in Chicago, Toronto, and Montreal, Irvin's teams had appeared in 16 Cup Finals, but won only four.

Montreal newspapers were soon buzzing with talk of Irvin's successor. In their May 3, 1955 article announcing his departure, the *Montreal Gazette* offered up three former Canadiens as frontrunners for the vacant coaching job, all of whom were coaching in the team's vast minor league system: former defenseman Roger Leger, player-coach of the Shawinigan Falls Cataracts of the Quebec Hockey League, centerman Billy Reay, who held the same position with Victoria of the Western Hockey League, and former Punch Line pivot Elmer Lach, the bench boss of the Junior Canadiens. Two others were put forth as "dark horse contenders": former Junior Canadiens coach (and future Montreal general manager) Sam Pollock and Lach's former Punch Line winger and longtime team captain, Hector "Toe" Blake.

On June 8, the Canadiens introduced Toe Blake as the team's new coach. Blake was by no means a unanimous choice for the job—he'd feuded with Selke while coaching minor pro and junior hockey in Quebec. But, unlike Irvin, he was bilingual. And he had the support of some of his old teammates, like current assistant manager Ken Reardon and his old linemate, Maurice Richard.

Blake addressed those gathered at the press conference to announce his hiring in both French and English:

"I am stepping into a big pair of shoes in taking over from Dick Irvin. I have always considered him the best in the league. With the help of Mr. Selke and Mr. Reardon and the players, we will continue to keep Canadiens hockey name on top. The team won't let the fans down."

A dynasty in the making

As many would point out in the future, Blake inherited a formidable team. It included the NHL's top three scorers from the previous season in Bernie "Boom-Boom" Geof-frion, who had 75 points to Maurice Richard's 74 (in three fewer games due to his suspension) and Jean Béliveau's 73. The team's experienced defensive corps featured thirty-one-year-old Doug Harvey, who had just captured the first of his seven career

Norris trophies as the NHL's top defenseman. Most importantly, perhaps, the Canadiens had finally found stability in goal in the person of Jacques Plante, on the cusp of winning five consecutive Vezina trophies as the NHL goaltender allowing the fewest goals.

And there were newcomers, too, the most notable being nineteen-year-old Henri Richard. The 5-foot-8, 155-pound dynamo would center a line featuring his thirty-four-year-old brother, Maurice, and twenty-four-year-old Dickie Moore, a left-winger with two Art Ross trophies for leading the league in scoring in his bright future.

The Canadiens and their new coach wasted no time showing the rest of the NHL *its* future. The team gave up only three goals in winning the first four games of the season. In a 22-game span between October 29 and December 17, the Canadiens lost only once. In one of those games, a 4–2 defeat of Boston, the talent-rich Canadiens showcased what was perhaps the deadliest power play in hockey history. Jean Béliveau scored all four Canadiens goals, with three coming in a 44-second span with the man-advantage. In those days, players served all two minutes of any minor penalty they received, regardless of whether or not their opponents scored during their time in the sin bin. But not for much longer. After watching the Canadiens' power play run roughshod over opponents that season, the rest of the NHL, to Selke's chagrin, voted to change the rule. From 1956–57 on, minor penalties ended after a goal was scored. (In March 2016, as part of talks on measures aimed at increasing scoring, the NHL's Board of Governors discussed changing the rule back.)

The Canadiens' 45–15–10 record gave them exactly 100 points for the 1955–56 regular season, an astonishing 24 more than second-place Detroit. With 47 goals and 41 assists, Jean Béliveau captured the NHL scoring title and the Art Ross Trophy that went with it. Bert Olmstead set an NHL record with 56 assists and Jacques Plante allowed a stingy 1.86 goals against per game. As for the aging Maurice Richard, he stayed healthy and out of trouble, and finished third in scoring with 38 goals and 33 assists and 71 points, eight fewer than Gordie Howe of the Red Wings.

The Canadiens easily defeated the New York Rangers in a five-game semifinal, bookended by 7–1 and 7–0 wins at the Forum. And after Detroit beat Toronto in the other semifinals, also 4–1, hockey fans would get what they most desired, a Stanley Cup Finals series between the greatest team of the past decade and one with an even greater destiny.

The teams met for Game 1 at the Forum on March 31, and the Canadiens, perhaps feeling the weight of their own and their fans' expectations, stumbled out of the blocks. They trailed 1–0 after the first period and 4–2 after the second. Frank Selke and the Forum faithful began to fear the worst. But whatever Toe Blake said to his charges during the second intermission, it worked. Scoring three goals in a two-minute span, the Canadiens took a lead they would not relinquish, and added some insurance via a Claude Provost marker midway through the period to win 6–4.

Trailing 2–0, the Red Wings got back in the series with a 3–1 win on home ice. But a Plante shutout and pair of Jean Béliveau goals helped Montreal to a 3–0 victory that put them one win away from their season-long goal. They achieved it back in Montreal two nights later, beating the Red Wings 3–1 in front of 14,152 ecstatic supporters. Fortunately for Canadiens fans, the stars came out to play that night, and Béliveau, Maurice Richard, and Geoffrion each tallied as the Canadiens won their eighth Stanley Cup. More importantly, perhaps, they had done so by slaying a personal demon, the Detroit Red Wings. Béliveau scored a record seven goals in the five-game final, and had 12 overall in 10 playoff games. Four days later, nearly half a million Montrealers turned out for a parade to honor the new champions.

Marked by their opponents after their incredible successes the previous season, the team struggled out of the gates in 1956–57, losing five of their first eight games. The team was also hampered by injuries throughout the season. Geoffrion missed 29 games, the Richard brothers missed seven each, and Bert Olmstead was sidelined for six. Goaltender Jacques Plante, a lifelong asthmatic, missed nine games in November due to bronchitis. The team finished second with 82 points, 18 fewer than the previous season and six fewer than first-place Detroit.

Once the playoffs started, however, the Canadiens kicked into high gear. Facing fourth-place New York, Montreal took Game 1 of the semifinals 4–1 after a pair of goals by a healthy Geoffrion and singles by Maurice Richard and Béliveau. New York took Game 2 in overtime but the Canadiens bounced back with wins of 8–3, 3–1, and 4–3, the latter on Maurice Richard's fifth career overtime goal 71 seconds into the extra frame.

While Montreal was dispatching the Rangers, the Bruins once again surprised Detroit. The Canadiens would play Boston, a team that finished only two points behind them in the standings, for the Cup.

Game 1 of the finals featured a scoreless first period, and the Bruins led midway through the second on a Fleming Mackell goal. Then Maurice Richard, who at age thirty-five was one of the oldest players in the NHL, took over. He tied the game at one with his fifth of the playoffs at the 10:39 mark, then put the Canadiens ahead less than three minutes later. Geoffrion scored his eighth of the postseason less than two minutes after that. Then, after quick rest on the bench, it was the Rocket again, at the 17:09 mark. Richard wasn't done, either, notching his fourth of the game, assisted by Henri, at 18:17 of the third. The Bruins outshot Montreal 42–26, but had not counted on the old Rocket's explosion. His four goals in a Stanley Cup Finals game tied a record held by Canadiens legend Newsy Lalonde and Detroit's "Terrible" Ted Lindsay.

The Canadiens prevailed 1–0 in Game 2 on a Jean Béliveau tally and took a 3–0 series lead after another two-goal performance by Geoffrion. Fighting for their lives, the

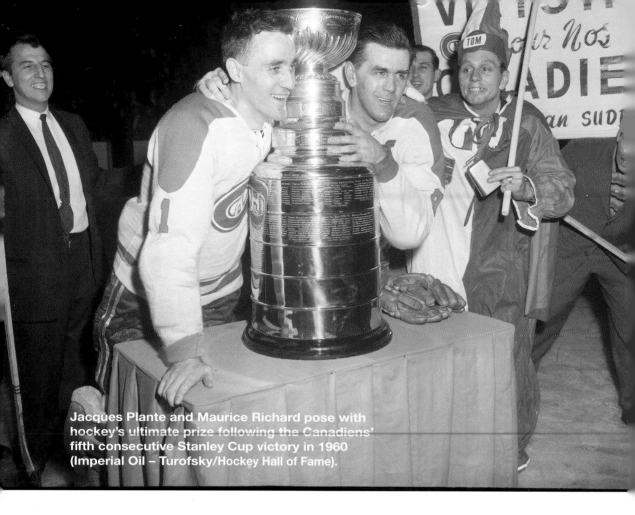

Jacques Plante and Maurice Richard pose with hockey's ultimate prize following the Canadiens' fifth consecutive Stanley Cup victory in 1960 (Imperial Oil – Turofsky/Hockey Hall of Fame).

Bruins won Game 4, 2–0, on a 29-save Don Simmons shutout, but the Canadiens were simply too strong, winning Game 5 by a score of 5–1 and taking home their ninth Cup. Geoffrion led all playoff goal scorers with 11.

Youth movement?

The Canadiens' 1957–58 season began and ended with a celebration of experience. But youth would rule in between. Maurice Richard began the season seven goals shy of the 500 mark. Already the NHL's all-time leading goal-scorer since surpassing Nels Stewart's 324 goals on November 8, 1952 (exactly 10 years after scoring his first), Richard had scored his 400th three years earlier, on December 18, 1954. The thirty-six-year-old Rocket didn't take long to hit the milestone once considered the be-all and end-all of scoring marks. On October 19, in the sixth game of the season and the 863rd of his career, Richard reached the 500-goal plateau, on a pass from Béliveau, in a 3–1 win over Chicago. Forum house announcer Jacques Belanger heralded the Rocket's 500th in special fashion: "Canadiens goal scored by Mr. Hockey himself . . . Maurice Richard."

The *Gazette's* Dink Carroll remarked that the Rocket, usually serious, "couldn't hide his happiness" and "was all smiles" after the game. But he wasn't smiling for long.

Eight games later, he suffered a badly lacerated Achilles tendon that sidelined him until mid-February. Richard played only 28 of his team's 70 games that season.

The Canadiens dropped the next two games after Richard's injury, then lost only one of their next twelve. They finished the season with 96 points, 19 more than second-place New York. Dickie Moore, who played the last month of this season with his left arm in a cast, won the scoring title with 84 points. Henri Richard, the twenty-two-year-old whose 52 assists led the league, finished second with 80 points.

After returning to the lineup on February 15, Richard was in fine form for the Canadiens' first-round matchup against the third-place Red Wings. He scored seven goals in what would be a four-game sweep, including his seventh (and final) playoff hat trick in the deciding game, a 4–3 Montreal victory. In contrast, thirty-year-old Gordie Howe (the real "Mr. Hockey"), a 33-goal scorer during the regular season and the NHL's MVP that year, scored only once in the series.

The only thing standing between the Canadiens and a third consecutive Stanley Cup, which would tie the modern era record set by the Toronto Maple Leafs from 1947–49, was the Boston Bruins. And they would give the Canadiens their sternest test to date.

The Bruins, who eliminated New York in six games on their way to the Finals, managed to keep Maurice Richard off the scoresheet for the first two games of the series, the second of which they won 5–2 to tie things at one. But the Richard brothers combined for three goals (Maurice with a pair), and alongside Jacques Plante teamed up to take the Bruins down by a 3–0 score in Game 3 back in Boston. The Bruins then won Game 4 to tie it at two going back to Montreal.

The Bruins jumped out to a 1–0 lead on a Fleming Mackell tally. Bernie Geoffrion then gave the Canadiens the lead with two goals 42 seconds apart in the second period, but Boston's Bronco Horvath tied the game in the middle of the third.

The overtime period that followed was the setting for the turning point in the series. If the Canadiens lost, they'd be facing elimination in Boston three days later, and their dream of three consecutive Stanley Cups would be in serious peril. Fortunately for them, they had the greatest clutch player and most prolific overtime goal scorer in history on their side.

With just over five minutes gone in the first overtime period, Toe Blake sent the line of Dickie Moore and the Richard brothers out for a crucial face-off in their own end. Off the face-off, the puck headed towards the boards where Moore narrowly beat a Boston defender to it. The Canadiens left-winger immediately threw the puck to the middle of the ice, where an onrushing Maurice Richard collected it on the Montreal side of the red line and sped towards the Bruins' zone. After crossing the Boston blue line, rather than taking the puck deep into the open corner, the Rocket swept sharply to his left and unleashed a wrist shot just as brother Henri was arriving in the Boston goalmouth. Bruins goalie Don Simmons never saw the puck that eluded his outstretched right pad and hit the back of the net to end the game. It was the 80th playoff goal of Richard's remarkable career, and his sixth overtime marker.

Back in Boston for Game 6, the Canadiens had no intention of letting the Bruins back in the series and attacked from the drop of the puck. Geoffrion scored 46 seconds into the game followed by Maurice Richard, with his 11th of the playoffs just over a minute later. Second period goals by Béliveau and Geoffrion gave Montreal a seemingly insurmountable 4–1 lead, but the Bruins answered with a pair of their own in the third to come within one with a little over six minutes to play. But Plante and the Canadiens held the fort, and with Simmons pulled for an extra attacker, Doug Harvey sealed the deal into an empty net with 51 seconds left on the clock. The Canadiens had won their 10th Stanley Cup.

Time for a tune-up

The champagne had yet to dry within the bowl atop the Stanley Cup before Frank Selke began plotting the Canadiens' course for a record fourth consecutive championship. Even in the midst of the record run, the Montreal GM had constantly tweaked his team's roster in order to ice the most competitive squad possible. In the summer of 1958, he was active again, selling veteran defenseman Dollard St. Laurent to Chicago and leaving Bert Olmstead unprotected in the NHL's annual intra-league draft. Their departures made room for rugged, 205-pound defenseman Albert "Junior" Langlois and twenty-one-year-old center Ralph Backstrom.

The injury bug nipped several Canadiens again in 1958–59, none more sharply than Maurice Richard, who was limited to 42 games after breaking his ankle in January. But the team was simply too deep to be affected. The Canadiens celebrated the 50th season in their history by scoring 53 goals more and allowing 43 fewer than any other team. They finished the season with 91 points, 18 more than second-place Boston. Dickie Moore, with an NHL record 96 points, was the NHL's top scorer, followed closely by Jean Béliveau and his league-leading 45 goals. The Canadiens captured their usual armful of trophies that year and added another to the team showcase when Backstrom won the Calder as the NHL's top rookie.

In the semifinals, they faced a determined Chicago Blackhawks squad, who tied the series at two after a pair of home ice wins. But the Canadiens took Game 5 back in Montreal on the strength of four first-period goals. Game 6 was a see-saw battle that featured a pair of Dickie Moore tallies. The game was tied at four when Montreal's Claude Provost notched the eventual game-winner with only 1:08 left in the third period to give Montreal the series win.

In their quest for a fourth straight title, the Canadiens would face the Maple Leafs, the only other team to win three straight Stanley Cups. But Toronto, which reached the Finals after an exhausting seven-game battle with Boston, was no match for the Montreal juggernaut further bolstered by the return of Maurice Richard. A Game 3 overtime win on a goal by Dick Duff was the high point for the Leafs, who fell in five games. The Canadiens won their fourth straight and 11th Stanley Cup in Montreal four nights later with a 5–3 series clincher. The game-winning goal, his 10th of the playoffs, belonged to the surprising Marcel Bonin, who had managed only 13 in 57 regular season games.

The Canadiens showed no signs of slowing down in the fall of 1960. If anything, they looked better than ever. After winning only two of the season's first five games, the team went undefeated in 18 contests between October 18 and November 29, winning the last eight of them. Another long winning stretch in January gave them a huge lead in the standings, and when all was said and done, the Canadiens finished first again with 92 points, 13 more than second-place Toronto. Half of the team's 18 losses that year occurred in the season's final 20 games, when they appeared to coast to the finish line.

Montreal's less than impressive stretch run, which featured five losses in the final eight games, gave a glimmer of hope to their semifinal opponents, the Chicago Black-hawks. Though their optimism seemed well founded, it did not produce results. Chicago dropped Game 1 of the series 4–3 despite outshooting the Canadiens 28–19. Game 2, in which they bombarded Jacques Plante with 40 shots, went to overtime, but Doug Harvey's goal 8:38 into the extra period, on Montreal's 25th shot of the game, put Montreal up 2–0.

The close call seemed to wake the slumbering Canadiens. Or maybe it was just Jacques Plante. The Canadiens netminder, who wore a mask (*see Jacques Plante Debuts the Goalie Mask, page 16*) for most of the 40 regular season wins he collected that year, posted two consecutive shutouts in Chicago to give Montreal a 4–0 series sweep. The Blackhawks' star winger, Bobby Hull, who won the NHL scoring title with 81 points and 39 goals that season, was limited to one goal in the series.

The Canadiens were bound for the Stanley Cup Finals for the 10th consecutive year, and their opponents were the young and improving Toronto Maple Leafs, who arrived by way of a 4–2 semifinal defeat of Detroit. Playing with great confidence in front of the spectacular Plante, the Canadiens took a three-goal lead in the first period of Game 1 on tallies by Moore, Harvey, and Béliveau. The Leafs got two back in the second, but Henri Richard scored an insurance marker early in the third and Plante stopped every one of the 11 shots he faced in the period. Game 2 was a similar story. Moore and Béliveau scored at 1:26 and 5:56 of the first and Larry Regan got Toronto within one with only 28 seconds left in the period. But that was it for the scoring. Plante stopped 18 shots in the second and eight more in the third.

2nd Period

Game 3 in Toronto was relatively uneventful except for what occurred 11:07 into the third period. With the Canadiens leading 4–1, Maurice Richard banged a Dickie Moore rebound past Toronto's Johnny Bower for career playoff goal number 82. In an unusual gesture, Richard reached into the Toronto goal and retrieved the puck.

Two days later, the Canadiens put an exclamation mark on their season and remarkable five-year run, becoming the first team since the 1952 Red Wings to sweep a playoff season. Jean Béliveau scored twice and Harvey and Henri Richard once each, and Plante picked up his third shutout of the playoffs as the Canadiens took the game and the series 4–0 to win their fifth consecutive Stanley Cup, a feat that remains unmatched.

The team that Frank Selke began assembling more than a decade earlier is widely recognized today as the NHL's greatest dynasty. Other teams may have had better individual seasons, but no team ever dominated so completely, and for so long.

Of the 26 players who played a playoff game with the Canadiens from 1956 to 1960, twelve of them, including Maurice Richard, were part of all five Cup-winning teams. On the same page as an article on the team's fifth Cup win, *The Gazette's* Dink Carroll, in his column "Playing the Field," addressed the elephant in the locker room—the future of the fading star, under the headline "The Rocket and Retirement."

When asked if his retrieving of the puck in Game 3 meant that he was hanging his skates up, Richard was evasive. The truth was, he still hadn't made up his mind. But when training camp started in the fall of 1960, the thirty-nine-year-old Rocket was on the ice with his Canadiens teammates. So it came as a surprise to many when, on September 15 at the Queen Elizabeth Hotel, the Canadiens assembled the media for the announcement of Richard's retirement. The unasked question on many lips was "did he go on his own, or was he shown the way out?"

The Canadiens enjoyed another fine season in 1960–61, their first without Maurice Richard in nearly 20 years. The team took first place for the fourth straight season with a record of 41-19-10, but when the playoffs came around, it was a case of "third time's the charm" for their first-round opponents, the Chicago Blackhawks. Chicago goalie Glenn Hall shut out the Canadiens in Games 5 and 6, and in one of the biggest upsets in hockey history, the Blackhawks eliminated the Canadiens 4–2. The most successful run by any team in NHL history was over.

Up Close: Hector "Toe" Blake

Hector "Toe" Blake was born in Victoria Mines, Ontario in 1912. His nickname came from a younger sibling's struggle to pronounce his first name, which came out as "Hec-toe" instead.

After playing minor league hockey in Northern Ontario and Hamilton for six years, Blake broke into the NHL with the Montreal Maroons in 1934–35, but played only eight games with the team. He caught on with the Montreal Canadiens organization the following season and became an NHL regular with them in 1936–37. In 13 seasons with the Canadiens, Blake won two Stanley Cups (1944 and 1946) and was the NHL's scoring leader and MVP in 1939. In 1943–44, he joined Elmer Lach and Maurice Richard to form the prolific Punch Line. A three-time first team All-Star, Blake retired as an NHL player in 1948 after badly fracturing his ankle in a game.

After coaching in Montreal's minor-league system for parts of eight seasons, Blake became the big team's head coach in 1955, and proceeded to lead the team to five consecutive Stanley Cups. The Blake-led Canadiens won three more championships in the 1960s, and Blake retired after the 1967–68 season with a total of eight Stanley Cups in 13 years, a record surpassed by Scotty Bowman in 2002. After his retirement, Blake and his family remained in Montreal, where he tended to Toe Blake's Tavern, the legendary watering hole he opened near the Forum in 1952.

Toe Blake was inducted into the Hockey Hall of Fame in the player's category in 1966. In 1998, *The Hockey News* magazine ranked him at number 66 on its list of the Top 100 NHL Players of All Time. He passed away from complications of Alzheimer's disease at the age of eighty-two in 1995.

Up Close: Doug Harvey

Douglas Norman Harvey was born in Montreal in 1924. A veteran of World War II and an outstanding baseball and football player, Harvey played on Montreal Junior, Navy, and amateur hockey teams before turning professional with the Montreal Canadiens in 1947.

Now widely considered to be one of the greatest defensemen in hockey history, Harvey was criticized for his risky style of play early in his career. A skilled skater and passer who liked to join and even lead the rush, he helped redefine the defense position, making it acceptable for blueliners to become part of a hockey team's attack.

Harvey played 14 seasons in Montreal, where he won six Stanley Cups and six Norris Trophies as the NHL's top defenseman. A free spirit who often rankled hockey's establishment, Harvey was part of a group that attempted to put together a player's association in the late 1950s, a fact that irked his bosses in Montreal. He also had a reputation for being too fond of alcohol, and the Canadiens used this and other excuses to trade him to New York ahead of the 1961–62 season, an arrangement that also made Harvey the Rangers' new head coach. Despite the change in scenery and added responsibilities, he won the 1962 Norris Trophy, his seventh. Harvey left New York during the 1963–64 season and played in the minor leagues for four years before signing on with the expansion St. Louis Blues in time for the 1968 playoffs. A 10-time NHL first team All-Star, Harvey played 70 games in 1968–69, and at age forty-five, represented the Blues in the 1969 All-Star Game (his 13th).

In 1966, the Confederation Arena in the Montreal neighborhood of Notre-Dame de Grace, where he grew up, was renamed the Doug Harvey Arena in his honor. He was inducted into the Hockey Hall of Fame in 1973, but skipped the ceremony to go fishing. The Canadiens retired his number 2 in 1985. Harvey died on December 26, 1989, two days after his sixty-fifth birthday. In 1998, the *Hockey News* magazine placed him at number 6 on its list of the Top 100 NHL Players of All Time.

Dryden Debuts as
Canadiens Shock Bruins

13

Facing the powerful, defending Stanley Cup champion Boston Bruins in the first round of the 1971 playoffs, the mediocre Montreal Canadiens, with little to lose, turned to an untested young goaltender that they had acquired seven years earlier from the Bruins themselves. The trade was so inconsequential at the time that nobody in Boston, or Montreal for that matter, could even recall it. But they would remember his performance in the 1971 playoffs for a long time.

After winning back-to-back Stanley Cups in 1968 and 1969, the Canadiens missed the playoffs for the first time in 22 years in 1969–70. Their 97 points saw them finish tied for fourth place in the East with the New York Rangers but lose the "goals-for" tiebreaker by two. It was a long, unhappy summer for the team and its fans.

After sharing the Vezina Trophy with the inimitable Lorne "Gump" Worsley in 1968, Canadiens goaltender Rogatien "Rogie" Vachon was one of the heroes of the 1969 Cup victory, winning seven of the eight games he played and posting a stellar 1.42 goals against average. Despite a significantly increased workload the following season, after Worsley sat out most of the year (and was subsequently traded), Vachon continued to play well, posting a record of 31–18–12. But it was not enough to get the Canadiens into the playoffs.

His nerves frayed from the stress, Canadiens coach Claude Ruel, who had succeeded the legendary Hector "Toe" Blake after his retirement in 1968, resigned after a rocky patch in November and December of 1970. One-time Canadiens player Al MacNeil, the team's thirty-five-year-old assistant coach who had been player-coach of the Canadiens' American Hockey League affiliate, the Montreal Voyageurs, the previous season, replaced him. In mid-January 1973, with the Canadiens once again flirting with the middle of the standings, general manager Sam Pollock traded three players to the Detroit Red Wings in exchange for star winger Frank Mahovlich (who would be joining his younger but taller brother, 6-foot-5 center Pete). The nine-game unbeaten streak that followed in February improved the team's fortunes immensely.

Unfortunately, the second-place New York Rangers were too far ahead to catch, and with the playoff format of the time, the third-place Canadiens seemed destined for a first-round date with the first-place Bruins, who had pretty much manhandled them all year.

Not entirely at ease with his team's goaltending, particularly that of backup Phil Myre, Pollock called up twenty-three-year-old goalie Ken Dryden from the Voyageurs on March 7, the final day for roster moves.

Raised in Islington, Ontario, just outside of Toronto, Dryden was chosen 14th overall by the Bruins in the 1964 NHL Amateur Draft of players not already sponsored by an NHL team. But in what would later go down as one of the worst trades in sports history, Boston immediately shipped the sixteen-year-old to Montreal as part of a pre-arranged package deal. Rather than report to the Canadiens after his junior career, Dryden enrolled at Cornell University, where he helped lead the Big Red to an NCAA championship in 1967. After graduating in 1969, he was briefly part of the Canadian national team program. Dryden made his professional debut in 1970 with the Voyageurs, where he played in 33 games while taking law classes at Montreal's prestigious McGill University.

In a brief *Montreal Gazette* item headlined "Habs Bring Up Dryden" the day after his call-up, reporter Pat Curran wrote:

"The McGill law student joins Canadiens as goalie insurance for the rest of the season and playoffs. The move raises the question on the status of Phil Myre, who hasn't played since Feb. 6 when he was beaten four times in a 6–3 loss at Los Angeles."

Dryden made his debut on March 14 in a 5–1 defeat of Pittsburgh. He played five more games, including part of a March 20 matchup against Buffalo where the opposing goaltender was his older brother, Dave. With Dryden alternating with Vachon, the Canadiens put together an impressive six-game winning streak between March 18 and 28. On March 21, at New York's Madison Square Garden, Dryden made 47 saves in a 6–2 win over the second-place Rangers.

Dryden played in six games, winning them all and posting an impressive 1.65 goals against average in the process. But in the eyes of Canadiens management, the newcomer was doing nothing more than having a successful apprenticeship. He was not a serious part of the team's short-term plans.

Two of the Canadiens' last three games were against the mighty Bruins, and, still in search of a playoff starter, the team split them between Myre and Vachon. But the results were disastrous, 6–3 and 7–2 losses. Now what?

A year after missing the playoffs, with a first-round date with Boston looming, and the team's goaltenders both having an off season, the expectations for the Canadiens on April 6, 1971 were not exactly high.

As Dryden himself later explained in his seminal hockey book, *The Game,* the Canadiens' 1970–71 roster looked like a formidable one in hindsight, but the team, full of stars from the 1960s and mid-to-late 1970s, was ". . . a little too old and a little too young, both past its prime and before it. Indeed, of all its players, only Yvan Cournoyer was at his peak in 1971."

What's more, the team's captain, best player, and top scorer, Jean Béliveau, had announced that the season, his 19th complete one, would be his last. Everyone expected the team to go through the motions, lose, and try again next year, when they would have the first overall choice in the amateur draft thanks to Pollock's clever maneuverings.

Pollock and MacNeil, therefore, had nothing to lose then when they named their starting goaltender for the series—Ken Dryden.

The Bruins, led by defenseman Bobby Orr and goal-scoring machine Phil Esposito, were coming off one of the greatest seasons an NHL team had ever had. Along the way, they had shattered dozens of scoring records—most goals by a team (399), most goals in a season (76), and most points by an individual player (152 for Esposito). Bobby Orr scored 37 goals, set a new record for assists with 102, and won his second consecutive Hart Trophy as NHL MVP. The Bruins had the NHL's four leading scorers, for the first time in history, and seven of the top eleven. And when Johnny Bucyk hit the 50-goal mark, he and Esposito became the first ever teammates to score that many in a season. What chance did the Canadiens have?

As expected, the Bruins took Game 1 in Boston, 3–1, on solid goaltending by Gerry Cheevers and goals by Orr, Wayne Cashman, and Fred Stanfield. The Canadiens' standout was Dryden, who made 39 saves and earned himself at least another start.

The same can't be said for Boston goalie Gerry Cheevers, who some said saved the day for the Bruins. In an unusual move by Bruins coach Tom Johnson, he replaced his Game 1–winning goalie to honor a promise he'd made to his other goaltender, Eddie Johnston. It took a little while, about 43 minutes to be precise, but the unnecessary change ended up backfiring . . . badly. Meanwhile, MacNeil's faith in Dryden paid off in spades.

The Canadiens jumped out to an early Game 2 lead when Yvan Cournoyer put one past Johnston only 3:32 into the first period, but Bobby Orr, a minute later, and Ted Green scored a little more than a minute apart to give the Bruins a 2–1 lead.

Smelling blood, the Bruins jumped all over Dryden and the Canadiens in the second. Johnny McKenize, Cashman, and Derek Sanderson scored six minutes apart to give the Bruins a 5–1 lead midway through the second. That was the bad news for the Canadiens. But it was also good news, because there was more than half a game still to play. And with 4:27 left in the second, Henri Richard stripped the puck from an over confident Orr, broke in alone on goal, and beat Johnston with a nifty deke to make it 5–2. But the Bruins were unshaken. They were a period away from a 2–0 series lead and they had a three-goal lead.

Had Richard not scored, it's possible that MacNeil may have turned to Rogie Vachon for the third. But we'll never know.

Tough guy John Ferguson, who had come out of his brief retirement in mid-November to help the struggling team, explained the mood in the dressing room between periods to the authors of the 2002 book *The Game I'll Never Forget*:

"I think it's at that point that we tapped into the Montreal Canadiens tradition. We were a team that did not panic. We were confident . . . you were expected to win when you were a Canadien. We took the ice for the third period with that in mind."

No one on the Canadiens understood the traditions and expectations more than thirty-nine-year-old Jean Béliveau, who first played with the team in 1950 and had been part of nine championship teams. The captain took charge of the game by scoring twice in the first 4:22 of the third period to get the Canadiens within one. Then, midway through the period, Jacques Lemaire intercepted a Ken Hodge pass intended for Bobby Orr at the Canadiens blue line, dashed the length of the ice, and calmly lifted a hard shot high into the corner over the flopping Eddie Johnston to tie the game. Bobby Orr, arriving too late on the scene, slammed his stick in frustration. The Bruins, supremely confident minutes earlier, were suddenly in disarray.

A little more than five minutes later, Béliveau out-fought two Bruins for a puck behind the Boston net and slid it to Ferguson, left unguarded at the side of the goal by Bobby Orr. "Fergy" slammed the pass into the net for a 6–5 Montreal lead. With the Bruins pressing for the equalizer, Frank Mahovlich took a long lead pass from teammate Phil Roberto and mercilessly ripped a hard slap shot past a reeling Johnston for the fifth Canadiens goal of the period (on 14 shots). Dryden, meanwhile, stopped all 10 of the shots he faced in the final frame, further frustrating the flustered Bruins stars. The emotional Phil Esposito, who Dryden denied time after time in both games, was the most perturbed of them all. In interviews, he took to calling the lanky 6-foot-4 goaltender a "giraffe" or an "octopus."

Final score: Montreal 7, Boston 5.

The Canadiens had stunned the Bruins, but the series was far from over. And Dryden, allowing five goals, had been rescued by his veteran teammates. But would he hold up? That was the question on everyone's mind when the series headed to Montreal.

With Cheevers back in goal for the Bruins, Esposito finally scored his first of the series 29 seconds into the game, on the power play (after Pete Mahovlich took a penalty at the 0:01 mark!), and the Bruins breathed a collective sigh of relief. Espo was back on track. All was right in the Bruins' world. But things didn't turn out that way. Dryden stopped the next 13 shots he faced in the period, all 14 he saw in the second, and nine more in the third, many coming from the stick of Esposito. Frank Mahovlich and Jacques Laperrière scored for Montreal in the second and Montreal hung on for the 3–1 win.

Esposito was beyond frustrated; he was apoplectic. *Sports Illustrated* magazine, in a post-series report, described it this way:

"Midway through the third period of last Sunday's showdown between Montreal and Boston, the old seigneurs and brash young lords of hockey, Ken Dryden stretched all 42 inches of his left arm across the mouth of the Canadien net and speared a couldn't-miss shot by Phil Esposito. Esposito, Public Enemy No. 1 to goaltenders, having scored the criminal total of 76 goals during the season, stared at Dryden, cursed him—'You thieving giraffe!'—and then slammed his curved stick against the glass behind the goal."

The Bruins, most notably Bobby Orr, solved the "thieving giraffe" in a 5–2 Bruins win the next day to knot the series at two. Orr scored his third of the night into an empty net.

"Now it's down to the best two out of three and there's no way the Canadiens are going to beat us in Boston," Esposito told reporters after the game. "No way. Believe me." And this time he was right. In a case of near déjà vu, the Bruins took a 5–1 lead into their dressing room, and the Canadiens scored two goals to get within two of the lead midway through the third. But the first goals of the series by Bucyk and Hodge gave Boston a 7–3 victory. The Bruins put 56 pucks on Dryden during the game, a remarkable 23 in the first period alone. As the teams left the ice the Garden crowd yelled at Dryden, who had turned down an offer from Harvard University to play pro hockey in Montreal—"The Bruins ain't Hahvud, kid." Red Fisher of the *Montreal Star* wrote, "The strut returned to the Bruins' stride."

The Bruins returned to Montreal for Game 6 needing only one win to eliminate Dryden and the Canadiens. But the Canadiens refused to go away. After Boston's Fred Stanfield tied the game at 2 early in the second, the Canadiens roared back with four unanswered goals, outshooting Boston 43–32 in an eventual 8–3 victory.

The series headed back to the hot, loud pressure cooker the Bruins called home, the Boston Garden, for Game 7. All eyes were on Ken Dryden. Hodge scored at the 6:50 mark, but Frank Mahovlich and rookie Rejean Houle gave the Canadiens the lead on two of the 18 shots they fired at Cheevers in the first period. Boston responded with 16 shots on Dryden in the second, but the period's only goal came off the stick of Canadiens defenseman J. C. Tremblay at 15:35. Mahovlich, with his seventh goal of the playoffs, scored only 14 seconds into the third to put Montreal up 4–1, but Johnny Bucyk replied 48 seconds later for Boston. For the final eighteen and a half minutes of the third period, the desperate Bruins pressed the Canadiens. Attacking in wave after wave, the highest scoring team in NHL history fired everything they had at Dryden. They thoroughly dominated play, outshooting the Canadiens 18–7 in the final period,

2nd Period

Ken Dryden, striking his famous relax-mode pose in this 1972 photo, was the NHL's Rookie of the Year for 1971–72, almost a full season after helping the Canadiens upset the powerful Boston Bruins in the spring of 1971 (Frank Prazak/ Hockey Hall of Fame).

but to no avail. The Canadiens and the goaltender nobody had ever heard of six weeks before had pulled off one of the greatest upsets in NHL history.

After the game, Esposito looked across the ice at the mob of reporters surrounding Dryden and said, "The better team won, but Dryden deserves about 75 percent of the credit."

"Dryden was better than we had ever dreamed," said Bobby Orr.

The Canadiens moved on to the semifinals, where they defeated the Minnesota North Stars in six games. The North Stars started former Canadien Gump Worsley in the series, but switched to Cesare Maniago after Montreal's 7–2, Game 1 win.

In the Stanley Cup Finals, Dryden and the Canadiens were the underdogs once again when they faced the West Division–winning Chicago Blackhawks.

Chicago directed an incredible 56 shots on Dryden over three periods but still need overtime to take the series opener at home, 2–1, on a Jim Pappin goal early in the extra period. The Canadiens returned to Montreal down 2–0 in the series, but won Game 3, 4–2, on a pair of third-period goals by Cournoyer and Frank Mahovlich, then tied the series with a 5–2 Game 4 win in which Dryden made 30 saves.

The teams traded home wins in games 5 and 6, with the Mahovlich brothers delivering third period heroics in the latter, which ended 4–3, and the series returned to Chicago for a seventh and deciding game.

The Canadiens trailed the game 2–0 midway through the second period, but tied it on goals by Lemaire and Henri Richard. Then Richard, who had feuded bitterly with Al MacNeil throughout the Finals, scored what would prove to be the Cup winner on a beautiful individual effort early in the third. Late in the game, Dryden made three great stops, including a desperate lunging leg save on Jim Pappin in the dying minutes. The Blackhawks pulled goaltender Tony Esposito for a sixth attacker, but failed to score. The Canadiens won their 17th Stanley Cup and Ken Dryden took home the most unexpected Conn Smythe Trophy ever as playoff MVP, almost a full year before he would win the Calder Trophy as the NHL's Rookie of the Year.

TOE BLAKE'S SHOES TOO BIG FOR AL MACNEIL

Canadiens coach Al MacNeil coached the Montreal Canadiens to a most unlikely Stanley Cup in 1971, but his road to hockey glory that spring was fraught with potholes. The unilingual Anglophone was first criticized in the press and by fans over his decision to start Ken Dryden over the popular and more experienced francophone Rogie Vachon. Then, during Game 2 of the semifinal series against the Minnesota North Stars, he infuriated veteran John Ferguson by replacing him with rookie Bobby Sheehan in the third period.

2nd Period

Ferguson, a player who gave his heart and soul to the team between 1963 and 1970 and who had come out of retirement in November to help the struggling Canadiens, exploded in rage on the bench and left for the dressing room.

Things got worse for MacNeil during the Stanley Cup Finals when he benched thirty-five-year-old Henri Richard for what he considered a penalty. After the game, Richard, who would soon succeed Jean Béliveau as team captain, ripped MacNeil before the assembled reporters. "He's incompetent. The worst coach I've ever played for," said Richard, who in truth had only had two other coaches in his 16-year NHL career. That was MacNeil's biggest problem. Like Claude Ruel, before him, he wasn't Toe Blake.

Richard's rant caused a media firestorm back in Montreal, with columnists and radio show callers asking for MacNeil's head. Some callers to the Forum literally called for his head, and the Canadiens took these death threats so seriously they hired security specialists to keep watch over their coach during Game 6 of the Finals.

After the season, MacNeil offered to go back and coach the American Hockey League's Voyageurs, who coincidentally were moving to Halifax, in his home province of Nova Scotia, and Sam Pollock took him up on it. MacNeil coached the Voyageurs to three championships in his six seasons there before taking the head coaching position of the Atlanta and then Calgary Flames for three seasons. From there, he became the team's director of player personnel and pro scouting in 1982. He was the Flames' assistant general manager in 1989 when they beat the Montreal Canadiens in the Stanley Cup Final.

Good vs. Evil: The Series That Saved Hockey

14

The 1976 Stanley Cup Finals pitted the Montreal Canadiens, the NHL's most-skilled team, against its toughest, the two-time defending champion Philadelphia Flyers, who had relied heavily on brawn and intimidation on their way to becoming the first expansion team to win a Stanley Cup three years earlier. Some saw no less than the future of pro hockey itself at stake when the two contrasting styles met head-on for the championship.

By the spring of 1976, the barbarians were no longer at the gates. They were living inside the city walls, gobbling the food and guzzling the wine with their feet up on the furniture. And they'd been there for two years. The place was a mess.

In the early 1970s, with its talent pool diluted by expansion and the departure of established players for the upstart World Hockey Association, the NHL had moved towards a more physical, often outright violent style of play. Teams like the St. Louis Blues and "Big, Bad" Boston Bruins regularly played physical and often dirty hockey, but the Flyers, who soon came to be known as the Broad Street Bullies, were goon hockey's chief proponents . . . and proud of it. Their lineup was peppered with the league's fiercest fighters, players like Dave "The Hammer" Schultz, Bob "Hound Dog" Kelly, and Jack McIlhargey. Several others, although not purely goons, like Don Saleski and defenseman Andre "Moose" Dupont, were not shy to drop the gloves.

The Flyers were led by their somewhat eccentric coach, Fred Shero, nicknamed "The Fog" because he was often lost in thought. Although he came to be known as a brilliant strategist, his recipe for winning was a simple one, which dismayed those longing for the skill-based beautiful game of days gone by.

"There are four corners in a rink and there are two pits, one in front of each net," Shero once said. "To win a game, you've got to win the corners and the pits. You give punishment there and you take it, which is why we have more fights than most teams."

The team's on-ice leader, meanwhile, summed up the Flyers' play this way:

"You don't have to be a genius to figure out what we do on the ice," said team captain, Bobby Clarke. "We take the shortest route to the puck and arrive in ill humor."

Indeed, Clarke had already shown that he would do whatever was necessary to win. In Moscow, during the legendary 1972 Canada-Russia Summit Series, he accepted a mission to "take care" of the talented Valeri Kharlamov, delivering a deliberate, two-handed whack that broke the Soviet star's ankle.

Some NHL players were even known to come down with a mysterious illness known as The Philly Flu when faced with the prospect of playing the Flyers in the boisterous and hostile Philadelphia Spectrum. But with the Flyers using their bruising style to win, many other NHL teams felt compelled to play along. Soon, almost every team lined up goon-type players, better suited to scrapping than skating and scoring. Bench-clearing brawls became routine in the NHL's version of the Wild West. And the Flyers wore their black hats with pride.

That's the most common version of the tale of the Broad Street Bullies. But it overlooks one key aspect of the Flyers and the success they enjoyed—they could play hockey, and play it well. Many of them could, anyway.

In 1972–73, Rick MacLeish became the first player on an expansion team to score 50 goals, a feat he came within one of repeating in 1976–77. Winger Bill Barber of the Flyers had 50 in 1975–76 and scored 40 or more on four other occasions. Reggie Leach would follow a 45-goal campaign in 1974–75 with a 61-goal season the following year, and scored 50 in 1979–80. Pure goons aside, the Flyers' depth forwards were strong, seasoned veterans who could play a two-way game. The defensive corps was not nearly as skilled, but tough and experienced, and was backed up by future Hall of Famer Bernie Parent, who won the Vezina Trophy as the NHL's best goaltender and the Conn Smythe Trophy as the playoff MVP in the Flyers' Cup years of 1974 and 1975.

Then there was Bobby Clarke. In 1973, 1975, and 1976, he won the Hart Trophy as the NHL's Most Valuable Player. He was among the NHL's top 10 scoring leaders every year between 1971–72 and 1977–78, finishing second twice, in 1972–73 and 1975–76, when he had six fewer points (and 100 more penalty minutes) than Montreal star Guy Lafleur.

All roads lead to Philly

The last team to beat the Flyers in a playoff series prior to 1976 was the Montreal Canadiens, on their way to their 18th Stanley Cup in 1973. And in the fall of 1975, the Canadiens knew the road back to the top would, one way or another, take them through Philadelphia. There would be no detours.

The Flying Frenchmen of the early to mid-1970s were the NHL's fastest and most creative team, but they were no angels either, and could defend themselves when they had to. The Canadiens had memorable, fight-filled games against the Flyers in 1973 and 1974, when Montreal defenseman Larry Robinson sought out and punched the notorious Schultz to the ice during a bench-clearing brawl.

The two teams faced each other in back-to-back games during the 1975–76 preseason. The first game, a 5–4 Flyers win at the Montreal Forum, featured fearsome hitting, 24 penalties, and a winning goal by none other than Dave Schultz, who infuriated the Canadiens by roughing up their new captain, 5-foot-7 Yvan Cournoyer. The next night, a Sunday at the Spectrum in Philadelphia, the Canadiens hit back. With Montreal ahead by a wide margin, twenty-one-year-old Doug Risebrough, who had tangled with Schultz the night before, went after Clarke. Both benches emptied and fighting broke out all over the ice. The referees handed out 10 fighting majors during the game, which was called off with 1:35 to play. But even though the Flyers went on to win two of the four regular season contests between the two teams, which included a tie, the Canadiens had made a statement. They were not going to be pushed around.

By Christmas, the Flyers and Canadiens had established that they were the two best teams in the NHL. But it was in non-league action that their contrasting styles were most dramatically revealed. On New Year's Eve, as part of a series of games against two barnstorming Soviet club teams, the Canadiens faced off against the powerful Central Red Army squad at the Montreal Forum. The game, which has been recognized by many as the finest of all time (*see The Greatest Game, page 164*), was dominated by Montreal but ended in a 3–3 tie.

Eleven days later, the Flyers hosted the same Red Army team, which had beaten the New York Rangers and Boston Bruins during their tour. From the drop of the puck, the Flyers pounded the skilled visitors. The Soviets, after a brutal attack from behind on Valeri Kharlamov by Flyers defenseman Ed Van Impe, even left the ice in the first period, unprepared and unwilling to absorb the punishment dished out with impunity by the Flyers. After some heated off-ice negotiations, they returned 15 minutes later to continue the game. But their hearts were no longer in it. The Flyers won 4–1. Only the brilliance of Red Army netminder Vladislav Tretiak kept the score close, as Philadelphia outshot them 49–13. After the game, Red Army coach Konstantin Loktev told reporters, "We have never played [against] such animal hockey."

Showdown at the NHL Corral

The Canadiens finished the 1975–76 season atop the Prince of Wales Conference with a record of 58–11–11 for 127 points, scoring 337 goals while allowing only 174. The Flyers won the Campbell Conference with a 51–13–16 record and 118 points, scoring 11 more goals than the Canadiens but giving up 35 more.

In the quarterfinals, the Canadiens swept the Chicago Blackhawks while the Flyers had their hands full with the Toronto Maple Leafs. Philadelphia took a 2–0 lead, but Toronto took Game 3, 5–4. The Flyers fell behind 5–2 in the second period then did the expected: they stopped playing hockey and started setting the table for the next game with thuggery. The penalty-filled game took 3½ hours to play, and after the smoke had cleared, three Philadelphia players found themselves facing criminal charges—Don Saleski and veteran Joe Watson after swinging their sticks at fans and a Toronto police officer from the penalty box, and Mel Bridgman for his on-ice assault of Toronto's Borje Salming. Bob "Hound Dog" Kelly was also charged after Game 6 for throwing his glove into the stands and striking a female usher. Philadelphia won the series with a 7–3 home ice win in Game 7.

In the semifinals, Montreal beat the New York Islanders and the Flyers dispatched Boston, each series ending in five games. Hockey fans would get their wish—the two best teams in hockey would face each other for the game's ultimate prize. And to some, there was more than a big silver trophy at stake. Author D'Arcy Jenish, in his book *The Montreal Canadiens: 100 Years of Glory*, summed it up this way:

"Many said the future of the game hung in the balance. If the Flyers won, mayhem would prevail. If the Canadiens triumphed, speed and finesse would rule."

Unfortunately for the Flyers, they would be without two key players for the series, making their quest for a third straight title even more difficult. After suffering a neck injury in the preseason, star goaltender Bernie Parent played only 11 games all year. And although he suited up for the series as a backup for starter Wayne Stephenson, he did not play. Nor did injured sniper Rick MacLeish, who had the Cup-winning goal in the 1974 Finals, and 22 and 20 points respectively in the two Cup-winning playoff seasons of 1974 and '75.

For the most part, well aware that the lethal Montreal power play would destroy them if they took too many penalties, the Flyers stayed away from the style of play for which they were feared. That's not to say the series wasn't a physical one. It was, with both teams throwing heavy body checks whenever the opportunity presented itself. Each game was played at a furious pace.

Game 1, played at the Forum on May 9, was, as the old timers like to say, a "doozy." Reggie Leach stunned the excited Forum faithful into silence 21 seconds into the game, blasting a shot from the left face-off circle past Montreal goalie Ken Dryden for his 16th of the playoffs and a new NHL postseason record. At the 13:22 mark, Flyers winger Ross Lonsberry fired in a pass from Bridgman to give the defending champs a 2–0 lead they took into the dressing room after 20 minutes of play.

Urged on by the home crowd, the Canadiens came out for the second with more life and tied the game on goals by Jim Roberts and Larry Robinson. Larry Goodenough restored the Flyers' lead on the power play at 5:17 of the third, but Jacques Lemaire followed up with a weak backhand past Stephenson. Then, with only 1:22 to play, defenseman Guy Lapointe gave the Canadiens their first lead of the night with a hard shot from a sharp angle. A diving save by Dryden on what seemed like a sure Jimmy Watson goal with five seconds left preserved the victory for Montreal.

Game 2 was another hard-fought and tightly played affair. The turning point in the then scoreless game came fifteen minutes into the second period when Lemaire stripped Goodenough of the puck during a Flyers power play, raced in alone, and picked a corner on Stephenson. Guy Lafleur, on the power play, gave the Canadiens a 2–0 lead early in the third. Then, midway through the period, the 6-foot-3, 225-pound Robinson threw a body check they are still talking about in both cities. Gary Dornhoefer tried rushing the puck up along the wall and into the Montreal zone, but Robinson sliced over with speed and cut off the opening, slamming into the Flyers' winger with such force that it opened a space in the boards several inches wide. A Forum worker had to come onto the ice and bang them back into place with a hammer, but the impression made by the collision remained. (Dornhoefer stayed in the game, but later said that he spat blood for three days after the hit.) Dave Schultz scored his second goal of the playoffs late in the period, but the Canadiens held off the Flyers the rest of the way. Dryden made 24 saves for the win. Montreal had played just well enough to win each game, but headed to Philadelphia leading the series 2–0.

The Flyers trailed the series but felt confident they could right their ship on home ice. The Canadiens, for their part, had not won a game in the Spectrum in three years. For good luck, the Flyers replaced the national anthem with a recording of Kate Smith singing "God Bless America." Over a five-year period, the team would post a record of 36–3–1 after playing the radio star's rendition of the Irving Berlin song. The Flyers and the crowd were pumped up, maybe too pumped up. Bill Barber took an elbowing penalty at 1:52 and Montreal's Steve Shutt made them pay, putting a self-described 65-foot "knuckleball" past Stephenson. But if the Flyers were fazed, they weren't for long. Reggie Leach blasted two sharp angle shots past Dryden for his 17th and 18th of the postseason and the Flyers took a 2–1 lead into the second. But Dornhoefer took an elbowing penalty of his own with only one second to play in the period, and the Canadiens started the second with the man-advantage. Shutt tied the game just over a minute into the period. Midway through the third, Montreal defenseman Pierre Bouchard, who had scored one goal in 66 regular season games, directed a long shot towards the Philadelphia goal that found its way past a screened Stephenson for a 3–2 lead. The Flyers managed only a handful of shots on Dryden, and suddenly the Canadiens, without dominating any of the three games, had a stranglehold on the series. The Spectrum jinx was broken. But the Canadiens were not celebrating, despite their 3–0 lead. Among themselves, they'd decided that they would do everything in their power to prevent the series from returning to Montreal. They wanted to sweep the Flyers in front of their own fans.

For Game 4, the Flyers pulled out all the stops, bringing Kate Smith herself in to rally the troops. This time it worked, with Leach blasting an incredible 19th goal of the playoffs past Dryden only 41 seconds in. But the period ended 2–2 after power play goals by Shutt, the suddenly offensively gifted Bouchard, and Bill Barber. The teams exchanged more power play goals in the second, Dupont with his second and Cournoyer with his third of the playoffs.

The third period was played at a frenetic pace, with both goaltenders tested several times. The Flyers went on the power play after a Bob Gainey holding penalty at 11:26, and the Flyers narrowly missed taking the lead after Gary Dornhoefer collected a Lonsberry rebound and looked to have beaten Dryden high to the glove side. Dornhoefer even raised his stick in celebration, but the Canadiens netminder got a piece of the shot with his glove and then pounced on the loose puck laying dangerously in the goalmouth to snuff the threat.

The game remained tied until the 14:18 mark, when Guy Lafleur, the NHL's leading scorer, who had been uncharacteristically quiet in the series, whacked a centering pass from Pete Mahovlich over Stephenson's blocker to give the Canadiens a 4–3 lead. The Flyers dug down deep for a response, but it was the Canadiens who had the final answer.

Led by Guy Lafleur (left) and Doug Jarvis (right), Canadiens players pour from the bench after defeating the Philadelphia Flyers in the 1976 Stanley Cup Finals (AP Photo).

Less than a minute later, Lafleur collected a loose puck near the left corner and found an open Mahovlich, who fired a backhand past Stephenson's for a two-goal lead. The Flyers pressed desperately, pulled their goaltender for an extra attacker, and had a few good scoring chances, but the Canadiens were content to ice or dump the puck and kill the last few minutes of the game. When the game clock hit 0:00, the Canadiens joyfully spilled over the boards to celebrate their 19th Stanley Cup.

The best team had won the series, but did good really win out over evil? In Philadelphia, fans would point out the absence of the missing goal scorer and the All-Star goaltender, which might have made a difference in the three one-goal games. In Montreal, they would point to the four-game sweep, and to the future. The Flyers remained competitive, became more skilled, and returned to the Stanley Cup Finals in 1980, but the high-flying Canadiens would dominate, and by extension change, hockey for the rest of the 1970s and beyond.

The Conn Smythe Trophy: When losers win

Since it was first handed out in 1965, members of the Stanley Cup-winning team have been awarded the Conn Smythe Trophy as the playoffs' Most Valuable Player all but five times. In the 1976 playoffs, nobody on the Cup-winning Canadiens had shone particularly brightly. Playing behind an extraordinary defense corps, goaltender Ken Dryden won 12 of 13 games and posted a strong goals against average of 1.92. And the team's defensive forwards, like Bob Gainey and rookie Doug Jarvis, had succeeded in keeping most of their opponents' top scorers in check, but not all of them. So ultimately the Professional Hockey Writers' Association decided to give the 1976 trophy to Flyers' right winger Reggie Leach.

With five goals in the team's 6–3 semifinal-clinching win over Boston on May 6, Philadelphia's Reggie Leach tied the single-game playoff record set by Montreal's Maurice Richard in 1944 and the playoff season record of 15 by Yvan Cournoyer.

Nicknamed the Riverton Rifle for his Manitoba birthplace and his hard shot, Leach would score four more goals in four games in the finals for an astonishing total of 19 in 16 games and, after goaltenders Roger Crozier in 1966 and Glenn Hall in 1968, became only the third member of the losing team to be awarded the Conn Smythe Trophy. Two more players, goaltenders Ron Hextall (1987) and Jean-Sebastien Giguere (2003), have won as members of the losing team since, making Leach the only non-goalie in the category.

In 1985, Edmonton's Jari Kurri tied Leach's playoff goals record, his 19 tallies coming in 18 games.

Too Many Men

15

With apologies to the gentlemen who penned the lyrics for "Three Little Words," the three little words that still stab at the hearts of Boston Bruins fans some 37 years later are "too," "many," and "men," short for hockey's dreaded minor penalty for having too many men on the ice. In Montreal, on May 10, 1979, the words were music to the ears of scores of Canadiens fans.

As if Boston sports fans hadn't suffered enough after the "Bucky F*cking Dent" episode seven months earlier, when the hated Yankees defeated their beloved Red Sox in a one-game, winner-take-all division tiebreaker, with the coup-de-grace delivered by the light-hitting New York shortstop . . . all after blowing what was once a 10-game American League East lead. Now this.

In 1978–79, the Montreal Canadiens were seeking a fourth consecutive Stanley Cup title. The class of the NHL since 1975–76, they finally faced some serious competition, most notably from the New York Islanders, who were but a brick shy of building a dynasty of their own. When Montreal, undefeated in their previous eight games, lost the season's final one, 1–0 to the Red Wings in Detroit, the Islanders passed them for first place in the overall standings, their 116 points one better than the Canadiens' final total.

The Boston Bruins, whom the Canadiens had defeated in the 1977 and 1978 Stanley Cup Finals, were no pushovers either. After the departures of Bobby Orr and Phil Esposito a few years earlier, the offensive juggernaut of the early part of the 1970s had transformed itself into a self-described "Lunch Pail Athletic Club" of blue-collar heroes, in the image of their bombastic head coach, Don Cherry.

After winning the Norris and Adams divisions respectively, the Canadiens and Bruins each earned a first-round bye in the playoffs, and both teams cruised to easy, four-game sweeps in the quarterfinals, Montreal eliminating Toronto and Boston taking out Pittsburgh.

That last-game loss in the regular season would back come to haunt the Canadiens. In the semifinals, the first-place Islanders would face the weakest remaining team, the fifth-place New York Rangers, who had surprised fourth-place Philadelphia a round earlier. The Canadiens would have to face the third-place Bruins . . . again.

Today, the Canadiens-Bruins rivalry is considered one of the greatest in pro sports history, in North America, at least, right up there with Yankees-Red Sox and Lakers-Celtics. But by the spring of 1979, it was a decidedly one-sided one. The two teams had met in the playoffs 17 times in their shared history, with the Canadiens winning all but two of the series (1929 and 1943), and the last 13. But the Bruins were closing the gap, and after losing the last two Cup Finals, hungry for revenge. The teams had met four times during the regular season, with mixed results. The Canadiens took two of the contests by 6–1 and 3–1 scores, with the two others ending in ties, the last a 3–3 draw in Boston on April 1.

The series kicked off on Thursday, April 26 at the Forum in Montreal. The Bruins, on second-period goals by Jean Ratelle and Don Marcotte, took a 2–1 lead into the third period, but the Canadiens regained it after tallies by Guy Lafleur and Pierre Larouche. Doug Jarvis added an empty-netter with 27 seconds to play to seal the 4–2 win. The Bruins jumped out to an early 2–0 lead two nights later, in Game 2, on goals by Rick Middleton and Peter McNab. But Montreal answered back, scoring three times in a span of 1:24 to take a 3–2 lead. They added two more in the third for a 5–2 win.

Desperate, Don Cherry took a gamble. Veteran goaltender Gerry Cheevers had been decidedly unimpressive in the third-period of Game 1, and gave up five goals on only 20 shots in Game 2, so Cherry replaced him with thirty-year-old Quebec native Gilles Gilbert, who had not started a playoff game in three years, for Game 3. The move paid off for Cherry and the Bruins, who won Game 4, 2–1, on a late goal by defenseman Brad Park, and took Game 4 in overtime on Jean Ratelle's seventh goal of the postseason. The series was tied 2–2.

Outshooting the Bruins 30–22, the Canadiens easily took Game 5, 5–1. But Cherry stuck with Gilbert and the Bruins won Game 6, 5–2, on the strength of a surprising hat trick by winger Stan Jonathan. With the score 4–2, Montreal coach Scotty Bowman, in anticipation of Game 7, began resting star players like Guy Lafleur, a 52-goal scorer during the regular season. Despite being closely shadowed throughout the series by defensive specialist Marcotte, whom Cherry had ordered to follow his man wherever he went, including the men's room (according to the cliché from that time), Lafleur had still managed to score five goals in the series and seven in the first nine playoff games. It was crucial that he be well rested for Game 7.

Game 6 was a chippy one, with a number of Canadiens players complaining about slashes and high-sticks. Earlier in the series, Cherry had grumbled about what he considered to be one-sided officiating in Montreal. It was the one thing he and his boss, Bruins general manger Harry Sinden, could agree upon. Sinden, who had been known to blame his team's woes in the city on ghosts inhabiting the Forum, also liked to crack

2nd Period

wise on what he considered three certainties in life: "Death, taxes, and the first penalty in the Forum." In his postgame meeting with reporters, Cherry couldn't resist a last bit of gamesmanship. "Look, the penalties were even in the games here. Is there any reason they can't be in Montreal?"

After the game, both teams had learned who the winner of Game 7 would meet in the Cup finals when the New York Rangers, led by former Bruins star Phil Esposito, completed a six-game upset of the Islanders. Suddenly, the door to Cup glory seemed wide open.

On May 10, 1979, the puck dropped on what would become one of the most memorable games in hockey history. Both teams stuck to clean hockey, and the first penalty in the Forum that night was a pair of offsetting minors to Boston's Bob Miller and Canadiens winger Mario Tremblay. The Canadiens fired a whopping 15 shots on the Boston goal in the first frame, while the Bruins responded with 10, and the period ended with the score tied 1–1.

Boston veteran Wayne Cashman, a cantankerous old foe who seemed to harbor a special dislike for the Canadiens, almost did them in by himself in the second period, scoring first at the 0:27 mark and giving the Bruins a two-goal lead with another with 3:48 to play.

The Canadiens headed to their locker room dejected, down by two, their quest for a fourth straight Cup in serious jeopardy. But a pep talk by injured captain Yvan Cournoyer and words of encouragement from several other veterans buoyed their spirits.

The third period became a coaching chess match, with lines juggled and players constantly matched to different situations. Bowman, in an effort to free him from the checking of Marcotte, double- and triple-shifted Lafleur, and after an injury to Guy Lapointe midway through the period, relied almost entirely on the duo of Larry Robinson and acting team captain Serge Savard on defense. Cherry, as he had done all game long, used only nine forwards.

The Canadiens and their fans came to life when forward Mark Napier cut the lead to one at the 6:10 mark. Two minutes later, with Montreal on the power play after a questionable hooking call against Boston's Dick Redmond, the second soft call by referee Bob Myers against the Bruins in the game, Guy Lapointe blasted a shot through heavy traffic and past Gilbert to tie the game. Guy Lafleur assisted on both goals.

With fatigue setting in and the fans on the edge of their seats, Rick Middleton suddenly and cruelly silenced the Forum, bouncing a puck off Dryden's arm and into the net from behind the goal line. With just under four minutes remaining, the Bruins had re-taken the lead, 4–3.

"Savard was closest to the play," Dryden later wrote in his hockey classic, *The Game*. "He let out a groan of curdling sadness, as if it was over."

Then it happened. With time and hope running out for the Canadiens, the Bruins became confused at their own bench after Lafleur stopped in for only a brief moment at his. Marcotte left the ice, then quickly returned after seeing the Canadiens' star jump back into the fray. But so had another Bruins player . . . or two. The play carried on for several seconds, with veteran linesman John D'Amico trying repeatedly to warn the Bruins about their bad math. The next to notice were the Forum fans, who began shouting, some standing and pointing, as if to count the players on the ice, 1,2,3,4,5,6 . . . "Too many men!"

D'Amico, after waiting for the Bruins to correct their mistake, could wait no longer, and blew the play dead. No official wants to impact a crucial game with a borderline call at a crucial time, but D'Amico had no choice; the Bruins' self-declared power play had gone on too long. Myers skated to the penalty box to assess the penalty, and play-by-play man Danny Gallivan, calling the game on the *Hockey Night in Canada* telecast, summed things up for the viewers at home with one of the greatest understatements of all time:

"Well, this is a terribly inopportune time for the Boston Bruins to pick up a penalty of that nature and of that magnitude . . . with two minutes and 34 seconds remaining, and they're that far away from winning this series with a goal lead," he said. "But there's going to be an application of tremendous pressure by the Canadiens now as they go all out to get that tying goal."

Bowman called a time-out to rest his exhausted players. He then sent Lafleur, Jacques Lemaire, Bob Gainey, Robinson, and Savard, all future Hall of Famers, out for the power play. Savard lined up on right wing, with Lafleur behind and far to the right hoping for a pass that would spring him free. The play worked and Lafleur was able to put a high backhand on net that Gilbert juggled. The crowd roared with excitement. Seconds later, Robinson missed the net with a hard blast from the left point, and then Savard, parked in front, narrowly missed jamming in a pass out from Lemaire. Cue more screaming from the fans.

The play was finally whistled dead when two players fell on the puck near the left boards. The Bruins then called a time-out of their own to rest Gilbert, Marcotte, and the other Boston penalty killers.

With 1:06 left in the penalty and a face-off to Gilbert's right, Bowman replaced Gainey with Steve Shutt. The Bruins eventually took control of the puck and fired it down the ice to Dryden, who relayed it to Lafleur with 55 seconds left in the penalty. Lafleur took the puck to the right of the Montreal net, then spun in a circle in an effort to ditch the persistent Marcotte and headed up ice.

Now back to you, Danny:

"Lafleur coming out rather gingerly on the right side, he gives it up to Lemaire, back to Lafleur . . . he scores!"

2nd Period

It was a play they had made countless times before, in practices and games. Lafleur would skate up the ice and hit Lemaire, waiting at the blue line, with a long pass, then follow quickly up behind him and accept a drop pass. This time he stepped into it with full force, ripping a quick slap shot from three feet outside the top of the right face-off circle, just as Marcotte reached out to stick check him. Gilbert kicked out his right pad, but the puck flew by and into the net, just inside the right post. The game was tied. The Canadiens had new life and their fans in the Forum and at home exploded with joy.

Curiously, although they raised their sticks, smiled, and patted each other on the back, the Canadiens didn't celebrate their season-saving goal with the vigor it might have merited, not by today's over-the-top standards, anyway.

Gilbert, for his part, sat on the ice, stunned. And Danny Gallivan uttered another epic understatement:

"This has got to be heartbreaking for the Boston Bruins."

The final 1:14 of the period passed and the teams headed for their locker rooms. The Bruins told themselves that it wasn't over, but in their hearts they knew that they had failed to take advantage of a momentous opportunity. The drained Canadiens, who had

Physically and emotionally drained members of the Bruins and Canadiens take part in the traditional handshake line at the conclusion of Game 7 of the 1979 semifinals (Mecca/Hockey Hall of Fame).

bombed Gilbert with 17 shots in the third period, consoled themselves with the thought that if they were tired, the Bruins might be too, perhaps even more so.

In the overtime period, the Canadiens, urged on by 17,453 screaming fans, outshot the Bruins 8–3, the eighth one coming at the 9:33 mark when third-line winger Yvon Lambert, after a key play by Savard in the Canadiens' end, steered a Mario Tremblay crossing pass beyond Gilbert to send Montreal to the Stanley Cup Finals. This time, the team celebrated with the panache the moment deserved, spilling over the boards and piling onto Lambert and Savard in the corner to Gilbert's right.

The Bruins were crushed. But they remained loyal to each other. Although many knew the identity of the man-too-many, they never revealed it. Don Cherry, who won the Jack Adams Trophy as the NHL's Coach of the Year in 1976, was fired, or, rather, not rehired, by the Bruins when his contract ran out after the season.

Eleven days after eliminating Boston, the Canadiens won their fourth consecutive and 22 Stanley Cup, beating the New York Rangers in five games, the final one on home ice, no less (*see Unlucky Bunny, below*).

It was the end of an era, with big changes ahead for the team and many of the key contributors to its success. But that was all still in the future. For the fourth year in a row, the Canadiens had another parade to take part in, which Montreal mayor Jean Drapeau and the City announced would take place on its "usual route."

2nd Period

UNLUCKY BUNNY

After eliminating the Bruins, and with the surging New York Islanders out of the way, the Canadiens may have thought they could waltz their way to a fourth consecutive Cup. Instead, they got a big surprise in Game 1 of the Stanley Cup Finals.

Playing a rare Sunday matinee, the heavily favored Canadiens looked like they were still in bed when the puck dropped. The Rangers scored twice on seven shots in the first and twice more, once on the power play and once shorthanded, on six second-period shots.

With his team trailing 4–1 after two, partially to shake his slumbering team, Montreal coach Scotty Bowman replaced goaltender Ken Dryden, who had played every minute of every playoff the Canadiens played since 1971. Michel "Bunny" Larocque, who stopped all nine of the shots he faced, provided solid relief. But the Canadiens failed to score either. The three-word headline in the following day's *Montreal Gazette* was: "Rangers Stun Canadiens."

Bowman announced that Larocque would start Game 2, played two days later. But as fate would have it, after waiting years for his crack at the Canadiens starting goaltender's job, Larocque was struck flush in the mask by a hard shot from teammate Doug Risebrough during the pregame warm-up and had to abdicate his newly acquired throne.

Admittedly unprepared after only five minutes' notice, Dryden gave up two goals on three shots in a little over six minutes, and the boo birds who had blamed him for the Game 1 loss descended once again. But the Canadiens picked up their sagging star with three quick goals to take the lead and won the game, 6–2.

The turning point in the series came at New York's Madison Square Garden in Game 4, with the Canadiens leading the series 2–1. The teams headed to overtime after the third period ended with the game tied 3–3. A Canadiens victory would give them a chance to end things at home in Game 5. Larry Robinson appeared to give Montreal the win with a long slap shot at 6:07 of the first overtime, but the red light failed to come on as the puck quickly exited the net and play continued. The Canadiens' bench was in an uproar. The blown call could have proven disastrous for the Canadiens, but Bowman calmed his troops and Robinson's defense partner, Serge Savard, on a rare foray into the offensive zone, scored on a pass from Guy Lafleur 1:15 later.

The Canadiens won Game 5, and their 22nd Stanley Cup, with a 4–1 win at home on May 21, the first championship captured on Forum ice since Cup number 15 in 1968.

The Good Friday Massacre 16

On April 20, 1984, a Good Friday, in the considerably Catholic province of Quebec, the Montreal Canadiens and Quebec Nordiques took their still blossoming rivalry to another level, and gave hockey, not to mention each other, a black eye in the process.

The Canadiens of 1983–84 were but a shadow of the 1970s dynasty that won its fourth consecutive Cup in 1979. After that season, the team lost head coach Scotty Bowman to the Buffalo Sabres, team captain Yvan Cournoyer and goaltender Ken Dryden to retirement (very early, in the case of the latter), and first-line center Jacques Lemaire, who went to Switzerland to begin a coaching apprenticeship that would ultimately bring him much success. A fifth straight Cup, it seemed, was best left to the Canadiens of the late 1950s, the only ones ever to accomplish that achievement.

Other stars left in the years that ensued, and those who stayed were aging, some more gracefully than others. The Canadiens were succeeded as Cup champions by another dynasty, the New York Islanders, who were now taking their Drive For Five more seriously than the previous champions had.

New powerhouses were also emerging, like the young Edmonton Oilers, who had joined the NHL in the fall of 1979 along other former World Hockey Association teams; the Winnipeg Jets; the Hartford Whalers; and the Quebec Nordiques. Suddenly, the Canadiens had competition within their own province, too. And what a competition it was.

The Battle of Quebec

Since the folding of the Montreal Maroons in 1938, the Canadiens had had a monopoly on the hearts of Quebec hockey fans. But with the arrival of the Nordiques, strange new dividing lines were drawn. The big-city Canadiens were known to have voted against the merger with the WHA in the first place. And with their wealthy English owners, they found themselves cast as the establishment team, supported for the most part by English and French Montrealers. The upstart, provincial Nordiques, meanwhile, decked out in uniforms inspired by the Quebec flag, won the hearts of young francophones across the rest of the province. In the heyday of Quebec nationalism, some even tried to position the teams on either side of the province's political Great Divide, separatism vs. federalism. As with most stereotypes, this was often but not always true. What is true is that personal relationships, between friends and within families, suffered because of the rivalry. Some homes had to institute a "no hockey" rule at the dinner table to keep the relative peace. Violence is known to have broken out at some gatherings, particularly when alcohol was involved.

Members of the media in each city, although supposedly impartial, were not immune to the madness. Normally sane television reporters would engage in nasty exchanges, which sometimes included fisticuffs in press centers . . . and in bars after games. And when they weren't fighting each other, they would stoke the rivalry's fires on the airwaves and in the pages of newspapers.

Then there was the beer war aspect. The Canadiens were owned by rich and powerful Molson Breweries, while the Nordiques were run by O'Keefe Breweries. And one simply did not drink the beer of their hated rival. Beer sales, carefully monitored in Canada, were said to be affected by the outcome of games and playoff series.

The Nordiques missed the playoffs in their first NHL season, and the two teams played lively but relatively clean hockey in their first dozen or so encounters, which they split almost evenly, with each team winning at home more often than not. The rivalry seemed to pick up steam with the arrival of Quebec's firebrand young coach, Michel Bergeron, and took off for good when the teams faced each other in the first round of the 1982 playoffs.

Each game was marked by numerous post-whistle scrums and cheap shots; Game 1 in particular featured a number of misconduct penalties as well as a fight late in the third period. Things exploded midway through the first period of Game 4 at Quebec City's Le Colisée. With the Canadiens just having taken a 1–0 lead, a fight broke out between Montreal's Jeff Brubaker, called up especially to add some muscle to the Canadiens lineup, and Quebec tough guy Wally Weir. Soon everyone but the goalies had dropped their gloves and was going at it. It took several minutes before order was restored, and once it was, 159 minutes in penalties were handed out. More fighting ensued in the third after the Canadiens had taken a 4–1 lead, and more again in the dying seconds, with Montreal ahead 6–2. In a pattern that would repeat itself, feisty Quebec forward Dale Hunter, who would go on to become one of the greatest agitators the game has ever seen, seemed to be in the middle of everything all night long. No saints, either, were the Canadiens' scrappy Mario Tremblay, tough-as-nails forward Chris Nilan, and Dale Hunter's little brother, Mark. Remember those names.

The teams met at the Forum in Montreal for the deciding game two days later. With the season on the line, both squads stuck to hockey this time. The Canadiens dominated the game outrageously, outshooting the Nordiques 35–18 on the night and 15–5 in the third period. But Quebec Bouchard was outstanding, and the game headed to overtime, tied 2–2.

All it would take to end Round 1 of what would come to be known as the Battle of Quebec was one shot. Unfortunately for the Canadiens and their fans, that's exactly what happened when Dale Hunter collected a loose puck beside the Montreal net after a broken play and tucked it past goaltender Rick Wamsley only 22 seconds into OT. One shot, and the Canadiens' season was over.

The rivalry intensified over the next two seasons, and by the time the teams met again in the 1984 playoffs, it was a full-out feud. Nothing, it seemed, was off-limits. During one regular season game, the hell-raising Mario Tremblay, after a Canadiens goal, is rumored to have sidled up to Daniel Bouchard, the Nordiques' overtly religious netminder, and quipped, "Where was your Baby Jesus on that one?"

It was an unlikely meeting. The Canadiens, the weakest of the eight playoff qualifiers in their conference, eliminated the heavily favored Boston Bruins in the division

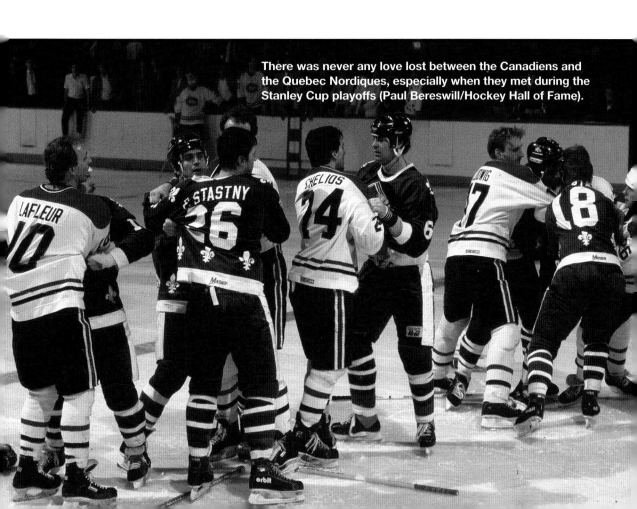

There was never any love lost between the Canadiens and the Quebec Nordiques, especially when they met during the Stanley Cup playoffs (Paul Bereswill/Hockey Hall of Fame).

semifinals thanks to the goaltending of rookie Steve Penney. Thrust into the starting goaltender's job after only four regular season appearances, he allowed just two goals in the three-game series. Quebec, meanwhile, surprised the higher ranked Buffalo Sabres in a three-game series marked by several fights.

The teams split the first two games of the series, during which a number of fighting majors and misconduct penalties were handed out, in Quebec City. The Canadiens took Game 3 in Montreal and the Nordiques won Game 4, 4–3, on an overtime goal by Bo Berglund. The Canadiens scored three times in under three minutes in the third period of Game 5 on their way to a 4–0 win and 3–2 series lead. The game, like the two before, was fight-free. It was all was quiet on the Quebec front. Maybe too quiet.

The Canadiens returned to the Forum, where tickets were going for $500 a pop on the sidewalk outside, intent on ending Quebec's season. But the Nordiques had apparently decided that they would not go down without a fight, and 23 seconds into the game, Wilf Paiement and Canadiens rookie, Mike McPhee, dropped the gloves and engaged in a spirited tilt. Center Peter Stastny, the Nordiques' best player and the NHL's fourth-leading scorer with 119 regular season points, opened the scoring at the 5:12 mark. Several minor penalties were handed out, including offsetting minors to Chris Nilan and rugged Nordiques defenseman Pat Price at 17:23, and Quebec team captain, Mario Marois, was assessed a penalty at the 20:00 mark, a portent, perhaps, of things to come.

"A brawl to end all brawls"

When he wasn't sitting in the penalty box after mixing it up with a Canadiens player, Dale Hunter spent the second period stirring the pot, bumping Steve Penney and jawing between whistles. With only 12 seconds left in the period, following a penalty to Montreal's Bobby Smith, Canadiens center Guy Carbonneau bumped into Bouchard, and was immediately fallen on by Hunter, who had lost his stick on the play. As the siren sounded to end the period, Hunter pushed Carbonneau's head into the ice and held him there. While the two combatants started rolling around, the other players on the ice milled over and took sides. Then both benches emptied and players began seeking each other out to correct past injustices, or perhaps, for reasons more sinister, if you believe Michel Bergeron.

"This . . . is . . . bad," said *Hockey Night in Canada*'s Bob Cole.

Chris Nilan jumped in and began pummeling Quebec's Randy Moller, badly bloodying his face. Other players began leaping into piles of bodies, punching furiously. Peter Stastny, a non-fighter who should have taken a tip from Canadiens' Guy Lafleur and stayed out of things, became involved with Tremblay, who proceeded to pummel his bigger dance partner, breaking his nose.

The two backup goaltenders, Montreal's Richard Sevigny and Quebec's Clint Malarchuk, became entangled. Dale Hunter, curiously, had made his way over to the Quebec bench.

At one point, 14 pairs of players were engaged with each other, exchanging various degrees of unpleasantries.

The final and most serious hookup made its way to the corner to the left of the Quebec net. With a linesman in between, trying to separate them, Quebec's Louis Sleigher and Montreal defenseman Jean Hamel seemed to have reached the end of their bout when Mario Tremblay skated over to pull Hamel away. Sleigher, who clearly decided the fight was not yet over, threw a vicious left-hand punch that caught the distracted Hamel in the eye, knocking him out cold and dropping him to the ice like a sack of potatoes. While teammates and the Canadiens' medical staff tended to the fallen Hamel, Sleigher was led away and both teams finally headed for their dressing rooms.

"A great hockey series has been spoiled with this eruption at the siren of the second period," Bob Cole said.

In their dressing room, the Canadiens grew furious when they saw Hamel and learned the extent of his injuries—an injured shoulder from the fall and severe damage to his eye from the punch. But chaos reigned as overwhelmed referee Bruce Hood and linesmen John D'Amico and Bob Hodges tried to sort out what would eventually add up to 222 minutes in penalties.

Unbeknownst to the officials, who were still trying to deal with the brawl's aftermath, both teams returned to the ice for the third period, skating in circles to warm up. And in an oversight that would have calamitous consequences, nobody told the players who were to be ejected for their parts in the punch-up about their fates, so they were all out there skating around and eyeing each other: Nilan, Tremblay, and Sevigny on one side and Stastny, Malarchuk and . . . Louis Sleigher on the other.

"I still remember going out and seeing the guys who shouldn't have been there still on the ice," Carbonneau would recall later. "That was a shock. Once those guys were back on the ice, they had nothing to lose."

The Forum's house announcer was reading the long list of penalties he'd just been handed when all hell broke loose. Near the red line, Montreal's Mark Hunter threw his gloves down and took off in pursuit of Sleigher, who was immediately surrounded by teammates. A large pack of players came together in the middle of the ice, and Mike McPhee and Quebec's Wally Weir started throwing punches.

"Ah . . . here she goes again," said Bob Cole, his Newfoundland accent suddenly more pronounced.

Quebec coach Bergeron would later complain bitterly that the Canadiens had purposely targeted his better players, and he appeared to have a strong case. Richard Sevigny

2nd Period

went after Dale Hunter before he was restrained again by Malarchuk, who warned him that Hunter would "kill him" in a fight. "That's not the point," Sevigny replied.

At one point, a few Canadiens cornered Sleigher, with Mark Hunter in particular swinging a stick at the Nordiques' marked man.

Bob Cole: "Hunter is swinging his stick at Sleigher. Sevigny is punching Dale Hunter."

On and on it went; a large pack of players roamed all over the Forum ice, pushing and grabbing and jumping into piles to get at one another. And through it all, almost comically, the Forum announcer kept reading the litany of penalties from the period before.

Mark Hunter continued to go berserk, chasing after Sleigher, and at one point was intercepted by his own brother, who was then savagely tackled by Mario Tremblay. Tremblay himself was set upon by a pack of Nordiques, including Peter Stastny, who began raining blows on his tormentor's back.

"This is a brawl to end all brawls," Cole said.

Twelve players were eventually ejected from the game, with Quebec clearly coming out on the short end of things in the talent department. But they still led the game 1–0, and two minutes after it finally resumed, Michel Goulet put them up 2–0. The Forum, which minutes before sounded like the Colosseum in Rome, was suddenly quieted.

Unfortunately for the Nordiques, goaltender Dan Bouchard, one of the only players not involved in the brawl, seemed to crack from the pressure of the situation.

Steve Shutt, years removed from his prime, found his old scoring touch, and tied the game with goals at 6:23 and 9:11 (a number somebody probably should have dialed long before). Then Rick Green, John Chabot, and Carbonneau each scored in a little over two minutes to give the Canadiens a 5–2 lead. The game ended 5–3. In the most crucial period of the season, Dan Bouchard allowed five goals on seven shots.

The game came to be known as the "Good Friday Massacre." And though many fans, Canadiens supporters certainly, reveled in the excitement and, especially, the outcome, some of the next day's newspapers crucified its participants.

The *Montreal Gazette*'s Michael Farber, under a headline reading "Forum Brawl Disgraced Game," wrote: "Shame on you, Montreal Canadiens. You were a disgrace to the uniform. Shame on you Quebec Nordiques. After spending two years trying to polish your image, you helped turn a playoff game into what would be mere burlesque if the fights weren't premeditated."

Riding the goaltending of Steve Penney, the Canadiens went on to win the first two games of the Conference Final against the New York Islanders, then lost the next four as the four-time defending champions pursued their Drive for Five.

The Islanders' quest, however, was interrupted by Wayne Gretzky and the Edmonton Oilers, who might have won four straight Cups of their own if not for some strange happenings in the spring of 1986. But that's another story (*see A Saint Is Born: Rookie Roy Channels Dryden, page 124*).

PENALTY-FREE-FOR-ALL

Three years after the Good Friday Massacre, another long and unusual brawl took place at the Montreal Forum during a playoff game . . . or, rather, before a playoff game.

Two days after the Canadiens defeated the Philadelphia Flyers 5–2 to stay alive in the 1987 Wales Conference Final, the two teams met back at the Montreal Forum for Game 6. The date was May 14, 1987.

All series long, at the end of each pregame warm up, Montreal agitator Claude Lemieux had been engaging in the ritual of firing a puck into the Flyers net after they left the ice. By Game 6, especially after losing Game 5 at home, the Flyers were fed up with Lemieux's little game. In fact, they expressly told him to cut it out. But Claude Lemieux, being Claude Lemieux, wouldn't listen.

Lemieux left the ice, but hung around until everyone else did, then, accompanied by teammate Shayne Corson, grabbed a puck and headed back out. Flyers tough guy Ed Hospodar and backup goalie Glenn "Chico" Resch followed the Montreal pranksters, and after Corson shot the puck into the empty Flyers goal, Hospodar, who hadn't played in the last four games of the series and was not expected to take part in Game 6, dropped his gloves and began punching Lemieux, who did not fight back. As Corson came to his teammate's rescue, Resch intercepted him.

Alerted to what was happening, players from both teams left their dressings and headed back out onto the ice, some fully dressed, some only partially, and some without skates. With the Forum fans roaring with excitement, the situation quickly escalated into a full-scale brawl. The main event featured the teams' two principal enforcers, Montreal's Chris Nilan and the only partially clad Dave Brown. The problem was, there were no referees on the ice to break things up, and the fighting went on for nearly 10 minutes. Finally, the officials appeared and order was restored.

The referees conferred with off-ice officials before coming to the conclusion that, as the NHL rulebook did not cover pregame situations, no penalties would be handed out.

The game was finally played, ending in a 4–3 Flyers victory. A few days later, the NHL fined members of both teams almost $25,000 for their parts in the fight.

During the summer, the league added a new rule to cover situations occurring before and after games.

2nd Period

A Saint Is Born: Rookie Roy Channels Dryden

17

When the Montreal Canadiens started the 1985–86 NHL season with an inexperienced coach and no number-one goalie, the chances of ending the team's longest Stanley Cup drought in more than 40 years seemed slim at best.

There were a number of reasons to be optimistic about the Canadiens immediately following the 1984–85 season. The team had ridden the hot goaltending of rookie Steve Penney to the 1984 conference final then won their division in 1984–85. Their defensive corps was one of the best in the league, their American Hockey League team had just won a championship, and several young prospects were coming down the pike. They also had experience and leadership, namely in the form of captain Bob Gainey and Larry Robinson, key figures in the team's 1970s dynasty. But, without warning, coach Jacques Lemaire, the man who most believed was largely responsible for the turnaround in the team's fortunes, resigned during the summer. Lemaire's replacement was thirty-eight-year-old Jean Perron, a former Canadian university coach who had served as a Canadiens assistant the previous season. Optimism turned to pessimism almost overnight.

Three's a crowd

The most intriguing plot line that emerged during the subsequent training camp was the competition for the position of backup goaltender. Under normal circumstances, the job would have automatically gone to twenty-nine-year-old Doug Soetaert, who posted a 14–9–4 record as Penney's backup in 1984–85. But the Canadiens organization wanted a closer look at nineteen-year-old Patrick Roy, one of the team's third-round picks from the 1984 NHL Entry Draft. Roy, who had faced a barrage of shots nightly for three years with the sad-sack Granby Bisons of the Quebec Major Junior Hockey League, had led the AHL's Sherbrooke Canadiens to the Calder Cup the spring before after playing only one regular season game.

To light a fire under Steve Penney, who had failed to impress during the early weeks of camp, Perron soon announced that the number-one goalie job was up for grabs, too. But Penney did not respond to the challenge, and as the regular season neared, the goaltending situation was more muddled than ever.

As the end of camp loomed, Perron was in a difficult situation. Roy had been the best of the three goalies in camp, but the young coach risked alienating the team's veterans, not to mention the goalie sent to the minors, if he kept Roy with the big team. So he and general manager Serge Savard made the unusual decision to start the season with three goaltenders. That didn't sit well with everyone, particularly Penney and Soetaert, who wondered why the young upstart couldn't head to the minors for some seasoning just like everybody else. They were even less pleased when Perron named his goaltender for the team's season-opening game in Pittsburgh—Patrick Roy.

It was a risky move by Perron, who would take the blame from fans and the media if Roy proved unready for the NHL. He was putting his neck, and his new job, on the line. But Perron saw something in Roy. Unlike Lemaire, a traditionalist who tried to get Roy to play a more stand-up style in training camp the year before, Perron always encouraged him to play his way, and arranged for the organization's dynamic young goaltending coach, Francois Allaire, to work almost exclusively with him.

Roy won that first game, and the next, but dropped a 7–2 decision in Boston that hurt his confidence. More losses followed. With nobody grabbing the number-one goalie job by the horns, the Canadiens won just four of their first 11 contests, allowing an average of more than five goals per game. The fans and media blamed the unusual three-man goaltending system, and Savard agreed. It was time to send Roy to the minors, he told Perron. But the coach held his ground, saying he needed more time to evaluate the rookie goalie.

With all of the goaltenders suddenly upping their games, the Canadiens finally got on a roll. A five-game win streak at the end of January gave them a record of 30–17–5. By the beginning of March the Canadiens led their division, but a horrible month, capped by a six-game losing streak, put their playoff chances in jeopardy. Some veterans began airing their grievances, privately and publicly. Among others, thirty-five-year-old Larry Robinson, in his 14th season and fed up with mediocrity after having won five Stanley Cups in his first seven seasons, complained about Perron's methods and criticized Roy's maddening habit of letting in weak goals.

A strong finish saw the Canadiens sandwiched between their two biggest rivals in the final standings, with one point more than third-place Boston and five points fewer than division-leading Quebec.

With both of the other goaltenders suffering injuries over the course of the season, Roy had ended up starting 47 of the team's 80 games, twice as many as Soetaert. Penney won only six of the 18 games he appeared in. Roy had the most wins, but Soetaert had the better numbers.

With a first-round, best-of-five series against Boston on the horizon, a guessing game emerged over the identity of the Canadiens' starting goaltender. But Jean Perron had no doubts. Patrick Roy was his man.

In hockey, as in most sports, reputations are made (or ruined) during the playoffs, and Patrick Roy started building his from the get-go. In Game 1 at the Forum, Roy was sensational. While his teammates appeared to be skating in their sleep, Roy made save after save to keep the Canadiens in the game. At one point, the Bruins were outshooting Montreal 11–1. But the period ended in a scoreless tie.

Louis Sleigher, one of the main villains in a notorious brawl between the Canadiens and Quebec Nordiques that had taken place at the Forum two years earlier (see *The Good Friday Massacre, page 117*), had apparently never heard the oft-repeated warning about waking a sleeping giant. Almost six minutes into the second period, the Bruins forward took a run at Robinson, who'd been having a bad game, aiming an elbow at the 6-foot-4 defenseman's head. After the two fought and Sleigher was given an additional minor penalty for elbowing, the Canadiens found themselves on the power play. Montreal's Bobby Smith scored with the man-advantage to give the Canadiens the lead, and then added another less than five minutes later. A Mike McPhee goal at 16:30 gave the Canadiens a 3–0 lead.

The third period was a fight-filled one, most notable for Round 2 of Sleigher-Robinson after the Bruin flattened Roy with a cheap shot behind the Montreal net. The Canadiens, looking more like a team than they had all season long, took the game, 3–1. Roy stopped 27 of the 28 shots he faced.

The Canadiens took Game 2, 3–2, on a late third-period goal, his second of the game, by Claude Lemieux, the Canadiens rookie who had scored only once in the 10 regular-season games he played (see *Up Close: "Pepe" Lemieux, page 129*). In Boston, two nights later, the Canadiens closed out the series on the strength of two third-period goals by Gainey, the second, and game-winner, coming while the Canadiens were shorthanded.

For journalists and fans of a certain age, the Canadiens' defeat of Boston brought back memories of 1971, when rookie netminder Ken Dryden led Montreal to an upset playoff series win over the defending champion Bruins (see *Dryden Debuts as Canadiens Shock Bruins, page 95*). But the Canadiens had gone on to win the Cup that year. Surely that was too much to ask for from this younger and less talented team 15 years later.

The Canadiens' opponents in the Adams Division final were the Hartford Whalers, who were coming off an upset of the division-leading Nordiques, who had beaten Montreal six out of the eight times the two teams had met in the regular season. But if the Canadiens and their fans thought they were catching a break by not facing the

Nords, they were soon in for a surprise. The Whalers took Game 1 in the Forum, 4–1. Montreal won the next two but Hartford responded with a 2–1 overtime win in Game 4. After a 5–3 Canadiens win in Game 5, Whalers goaltender Mike Liut stopped all 32 shots faced in Game 6 to lead Hartford to a 1–0 win.

The series headed back to Montreal for Game 7, and Liut was outstanding again. With 13 seconds left in the first period, and the Canadiens outshooting Hartford 9–6, Mike McPhee scored while killing a penalty to Lemieux and the Canadiens took a 1–0 lead to the dressing room. The score stayed that way until 17:12 of the third period when Dave Babych deflected a shot past Roy to send the game to overtime. Somebody's season was going to end on the next goal. At 5:55 of the overtime period, Claude Lemieux took matters into his own hands, picking up a loose puck behind the Whalers' net, driving to the top of the crease and whipping a short backhand past Liut. Lemieux took off in celebration, arms raised and almost running on his skates, and then fell to his knees, sliding to the ice as his teammates piled on top of him.

The Canadiens were headed to the conference final. Waiting for them were the unpredictable New York Rangers and their twenty-two-year-old goalie, John Vanbiesbrouck, whose 31 wins helped him earn that season's Vezina Trophy as the NHL's top netminder. After barely scraping into the playoffs, the Rangers had knocked off the first-place Philadelphia Flyers and second-place Washington Capitals to win the Patrick Division.

Roy made 26 saves in a 2–1, Game 1 win and the Canadiens easily took Game 2, 6–2. The teams headed to New York for Game 3, where the Rangers, desperate to get back in the series, fired 16 shots on Roy in the first period, which ended 1–1. Vanbiesbrouck stopped all 15 shots he faced in the second and the Rangers were leading 3–2 with 2:04 left to play in the third when Smith's fourth of the playoffs knotted the game at three. Then Patrick Roy pulled off one of the greatest overtime performances in NHL history.

To Canadiens fans, it seemed like the entire overtime period was being played in front of Roy's goal. The Canadiens took two shots on Vanbiesbrouck in the early going, but after that it was all Rangers. Just under five minutes into the extra frame, Roy made three consecutive saves from close in as the Rangers hammered away. Two minutes later, he had to reach behind him as a deflected shot from the blue line trickled inches from the goal line. Just shy of the nine-minute mark, on the Rangers' 13th shot of the overtime and 47th of the game, Roy stopped Tomas Sandstrom's close-range shot. The Rangers and their frantic fans were left shaking their heads.

The Canadiens, exhausted from chasing their opponents all night, spent the next minute repelling Rangers rushes and simply clearing their zone. They seemed to have no energy for attacks of their own.

Following a face-off to Roy's left, Montreal winger Mike McPhee blocked a Willie Huber shot at his own blue line and stumbled to his feet in pursuit of the loose puck. At the same time, on the other side of the ice, the Rangers' left defenseman and one of the linesmen working the game collided. McPhee, back on his feet, suddenly found himself on a 2-on-1 break with none other than Claude Lemieux, who took McPhee's pass and fired the puck into the top corner, beyond the outstretched glove of John Vanbiesbrouck, for the game winner, his eighth of the playoffs. This time, the Canadiens were almost too tired to celebrate.

"Except for a couple games in juniors, this is the best game of my career," Roy told reporters after the game. "I was feeling pretty good in the overtime." No kidding, kid.

The Rangers, on a 29-save shutout by Vanbiesbrouk, won Game 4 to extend the series, but the Canadiens closed things out with a 3–1 win back at home in Game 5.

On to the finals

In the first all-Canadian Stanley Cup Final since 1967, they Canadiens faced the Calgary Flames, who had caused the biggest upset of the 1986 playoffs by eliminating their provincial rivals and two-time defending Stanley Cup–champion Edmonton Oilers in seven games in the division finals before beating the Blues in the conference finals.

The Flames took Game 1, 5–2, and were close to taking a stranglehold on the series when Game 2 headed for overtime, tied 2–2. But the Canadiens acted like they had a plane to catch. Several of the fans in the sellout crowd in Calgary's Olympic Saddledome had yet to return to their seats when rookie Brian Skrudland, on passes from McPhee and Lemieux, scored only nine seconds into the extra frame. It remains the fastest over-time goal every scored.

The Canadiens took Game 3 back in Montreal, 5–3, and Roy earned his first career playoff shutout in Game 4, a 1–0 win, on Claude Lemieux's unassisted third-period goal, his 10th of the postseason. After the siren wailed to end the game, a long, ugly bench-clearing brawl broke out. Afterwards, the Flames accused Lemieux, in the middle of things as usual, of having bitten a Flames player's finger.

Biting and brawling aside, the Canadiens were one victory away from winning the Stanley Cup, but they would have to travel all the way back to Calgary first. The Canadiens took a 2–1 lead into the third period of Game 5 after goals by Gaston Gingras and Skrud-land. Midway through the third, Montreal defenseman Rick Green scored on a rare, and beautiful, offensive foray, and Bobby Smith made it 4–1 Canadiens 19 seconds later. With about four minutes to play, some Canadiens players had started to celebrate on the bench. They were soon brought back to earth when Steve Bozek notched his second of the night with 3:14 to play. Then, with Flames goalie Mike Vernon pulled for an extra attacker, Joe Mullen scored his playoff-leading 12th goal to close the Canadiens' lead to one. With new

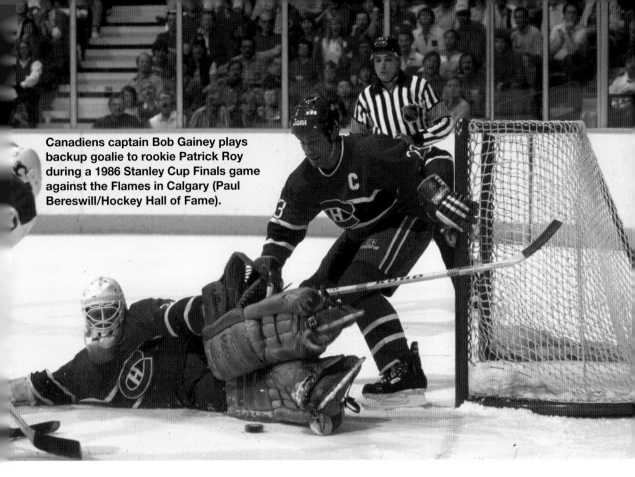

Canadiens captain Bob Gainey plays backup goalie to rookie Patrick Roy during a 1986 Stanley Cup Finals game against the Flames in Calgary (Paul Bereswill/Hockey Hall of Fame).

life, Calgary blitzed the Montreal goalmouth, but in the dying seconds Roy made a save on Mullen from close in and another on defenseman Jamie Macoun on the rebound.

"Patrick Roy," Canadiens defenseman Chris Chelios would say later, "made the biggest play of his life."

The final 14 seconds ticked off the clock and the Canadiens had their 23rd Stanley Cup. With a 15–5 record and 1.92 goals-against-average, twenty-year-old Patrick Roy became the youngest ever winner of the Conn Smythe Trophy as the playoffs' Most Valuable Player. Back in Montreal, his miraculous efforts earned him a new nickname as well—St. Patrick.

During the postgame celebrations, Brian Skrudland excitedly summed his fellow rookie's heroics, and his future.

"He was there right to the end, saving us. Look at that unbelievable save he made on Jamie Macoun in the last 14 seconds. He's going to be better than Dryden, better than Plante, better than any goaltender who has ever lived."

Up Close: "Pepe" Lemieux

Claude Lemieux won his second Stanley Cup with the New Jersey Devils in 1995, when his postseason-leading 13 goals helped him win the Conn Smythe trophy as play-off MVP. But it could easily have been Lemieux's second Conn Smythe win. Had it not been for the performance of fellow Canadiens rookie Patrick Roy, Lemieux might have been the MVP of the playoffs back in 1986.

Claude Lemieux actually made his Canadiens debut in 1983–84, playing eight games as an eighteen-year-old. He played one game the following season, against the rival Quebec Nordiques on January 24, 1985. And it was a typical Claude Lemieux game, with an assist, a minor penalty, and a fight against Nordiques leader Dale Hunter.

A 58-goal scorer in his last year of junior, Lemieux broke in for good late in 1985–86, recording a goal, two assists, and 22 penalty minutes in 10 games. But it was in the 1986 playoffs that he truly made himself noticed, scoring 10 goals and collecting six assists in 20 games. And the goals were important ones. Four were game-winners, with two coming in overtime and another late in a 1–0 game.

Lemieux was at his best when getting under his opponents' skin. His personality helped earn him the nickname "Pepe," as in the cartoon skunk, Pepe LePew. Unfortunately, like a skunk's noxious spray, his antics would also irritate his teammates and coaches, and he was traded to New Jersey in 1990.

Lemieux won his third Stanley Cup playing with the Colorado Avalanche and his friend Patrick Roy in 1996, and a fourth back in New Jersey in 2000. A consummate playoff performer, Lemieux retired (for a second time) in 2009 with 158 points in 234 playoff games. His 80 postseason goals earned him ninth place among NHL's all-time playoff goals leaders.

Cup Full of Overtime

18

On the 100th anniversary of the Stanley Cup, the team that had won it the most made a run for it again, and in the most unlikely of ways. Rather than dominating their opponents in the 1993 playoffs, the Montreal Canadiens often just got by, and game after game headed for sudden-death overtime, where the line between glory and devastating loss is the finest of all.

Former police officer Pat Burns brought a much-needed dose of iron-fist discipline to the young and talented Canadiens when he was hired prior to the 1988–89 season. The team, thanks in large part to the goaltending of eventual Vezina Trophy winner and first team All-Star Patrick Roy, racked up 115 points, the second-most in the NHL, and allowed the fewest goals. And both the team and Roy carried that success all the way to the Stanley Cup Finals. There were other good Burns years, too, like 1991–92, when the team won its division and allowed 29 fewer goals than any other team in the league. But in Montreal, what really matters is how you make out in the playoffs, and after three consecutive losses to the Boston Bruins in the Division Finals, the fans and even Burns's own players were grumbling. After all, the team had gone six years without winning the Stanley Cup.

Burns's relationship with the media, which was never great in the first place, also seemed to worsen with every passing year. Three weeks after suffering a humiliating four-game sweep to Boston in May of 1992, Burns was at his breaking point. On May 31, he resigned from what was once his dream job to take the same position with the Toronto Maple Leafs. Two weeks later the Canadiens held a press conference to introduce Jacques Demers as Pat Burns's successor.

Demers's approach to coaching was about as far removed from Burns's as it could be. A motivator and players' coach through and through, he soon earned the sarcastic nickname Mr. Positive from some of the more jaded members of the city's sports media. During training camp that year, he gathered his new players and told them, "We're going

2nd Period

131

to shock the hockey world and win the Stanley Cup." Some snickered, but others caught his infectious optimism.

With the team's head coach position now filled, Canadiens general manager Serge Savard set about improving its roster. Believing, like many of the team's fans, that an improved offense was the solution to their postseason woes, he brought talented scorers Vincent Damphousse and Brian Bellows on board via trades.

The changes did what they were supposed to do. The Canadiens finished the 1992–93 regular season with 326 goals, 59 more than the previous season. Trouble was, they gave up 280, 73 more than they had in Pat Burns's final year.

Canadiens goalie Patrick Roy had his best years playing behind Pat Burns's defense-first teams, winning three Vezina trophies as the NHL's top netminder. But with the team's new accent on scoring, his performance suffered in 1992–93. He wasn't awful, but he wasn't vintage St. Patrick either.

The perennial All-Star and avid hockey card collector took part that year in a campaign for Upper Deck trading cards in which giant billboards across the city were emblazoned with two words "Trade Roy." Ha Ha. Get it? Well, by January a newspaper poll showed that 57 percent of the team's famously fickle fans wanted to do just that.

After a difficult month of December, the Canadiens got on a roll in January and February, losing only five times in a 25-game stretch. But the team stumbled at the worst possible time, winning only seven of its last 18 games. Patrick Roy lost his last five regular season appearances.

Roy finished the season with a goals against average of 3.20, his worst, by far, since his rookie season of 1985–86. And though his regular season stats had been excellent over the past three seasons, his playoff performances had not. He was the team's best and most highly paid player, and as goaltender was an obvious target for frustrated fans and media members looking for a scapegoat. If the team failed again, much of the blame would fall on Patrick Roy's shoulders, and he knew it.

The Canadiens finished the season third in the Adams Division standings with 102 points, seven less than first-place Boston and two fewer than second-place Quebec, their two biggest rivals. Their late season swoon had cost them home-ice advantage in the first round of the playoffs. The Canadiens would face the Nordiques for Round 5 of the always-contentious Battle of Quebec.

The Quebec Nordiques had been one of the NHL's worst teams over the past few seasons, and had used their high positions in the draft to stock their team with excellent young players like Joe Sakic, the number 15 pick in 1987, and Mats Sundin and Owen Nolan, the number-one overall picks from 1989 and 1990. In 1991, they had the number-one pick again, and used it to select Eric Lindros, who refused to play for them and returned to Junior hockey for another season. On June 20, 1992, the Nordiques traded Lindros to

Philadelphia for young Peter Forsberg (the number 6 pick in the 1991 draft), All-Star goaltender Ron Hextall, Kerry Huffman, Mike Ricci, Steve Duchesne, Chris Simon, two draft picks, and $15 million. The Nordiques went from perennial cellar-dwellers to contenders overnight, doubling their number of points in one season from 52 to 104.

OT: Sunday April 18, 1993

The Nordiques were considered slight favorites when the puck dropped for Game 1, but with less than three minutes to play, the Canadiens had a 2–0 lead. And only the brilliance of Ron Hextall had kept the game that close. Patrick Roy, meanwhile, had blocked all of the 21 shots he had faced in the first two periods and half a dozen more in the third. Then, after a penalty to Montreal's Gilbert Dionne with 2:43 to play, disaster struck. Quebec's Martin Rucinsky, from close in, scored on the power play at 18:31, then with 48 seconds left to play, Roy let a seemingly harmless Joe Sakic shot get past him and the game was tied. At 16:49 of overtime, with Hextall having stopped eight Canadiens shots, Quebec's Scott Young stuffed a wrap-around past a careless-looking Roy. It was the worst-case scenario for the Canadiens star. Not only was he outdueled by Hextall, but he had also blown an easy win for his team.

The calls for Roy's backup, Andre Racicot, to take over only intensified when Roy allowed three first-period goals by the Nordiques in a 4–1, Game 2 loss. But, radio call-in shows be damned, Jacques Demers called Roy in to his office to reassure him. "Don't worry," he said. "I'm going to live and die with you."

OT: Thursday April 22, 1993

Quebec's Mats Sundin scored 77 seconds into Game 3, a contest Montreal absolutely had to win if it wanted to keep its hopes alive. Kirk Muller tied the game 1:30 into the second, and then the goaltenders took over. Through three periods, Roy stopped 29 of the 30 shots he had faced while Hextall made 37 saves. The desperate Canadiens threw everything they had at the Quebec net in overtime, and finally caught a break when Vincent Damphousse scored on the power play, the puck redirecting off a skate and past a furious Hextall at the 10:30 mark. The play was reviewed but the goal was still awarded. Nobody knew it at the time, but the Canadiens had just started a sequence that would defy all logic by the time it would end more than six weeks later.

OT: Monday April 26, 1993

Montreal tied the series at two with a hard-fought, 3–2 Game 4 win and the teams headed back to Quebec City for Game 5. The game would prove to be a dramatic one on many fronts. Directly off the face-off that opened the second period, with the Canadiens nursing a 1–0 lead thanks to a first period Mike Keane goal, Quebec's Mike Hough unleashed a high slap shot that found a gap in Roy's equipment and struck him on the collarbone. He collapsed in pain but soon rose to his feet and continued the game. But when Quebec's Andrei Kovalenko scored about 90 seconds later, it was clear that there was something seriously wrong with Roy. Immediately after the goal, he skated off the ice. The Patrick Roy haters back in Montreal finally got what they wanted, Andre Racicot. The Montreal backup goalie allowed two goals on 10 shots in the second, but the Canadiens put two of their own past Hextall and the period ended in a 3–3 tie.

Roy, meanwhile, had been given an injection of analgesic to numb the pain in his collarbone, but it didn't work, and he had to beg a reluctant Canadiens' doctor to administer another. "I have to get back in the game," he said. "Stick it right here, in the bruise."

The third period began with Ron Hextall in one net and Patrick Roy in the other. The teams exchanged goals, and for the third time in five games, overtime would be needed. The Nordiques took five shots on Roy, while the Canadiens managed only one. But that was all they needed as Hextall let a long, low Kirk Muller shot get past him for the winner.

Two nights later, back in Montreal, Hextall and the Nordiques completed their collapse. Roy made 28 saves and Paul DiPietro had a hat trick in the Canadiens' series-clinching 6–2 win. And they already knew who they would face next, the Buffalo Sabres, who had completed their sweep of the favored Boston Bruins four days earlier.

The Canadiens were listless in the Division Finals opener, firing only 22 shots on goal to the rested Sabres' 35. But Buffalo goaltender Grant Fuhr allowed four goals and Roy stopped the 13 he faced in the third and the Canadiens hung on to win, 4–3. Remember that score.

OT: Tuesday, May 4, 1993

Game 2 unfolded in much the same way. Montreal led 3–2 when Buffalo's Doug Bodger tied the game 44 seconds into the third. And for the fourth time in eight games, the Canadiens would play overtime. After some great hustle by rookie Ed Ronan cancelled out an icing call against the Canadiens, Denis Savard passed to Guy Carbonneau from behind the Sabres net and the Canadiens captain fired home his first of the playoffs for the game-winner. Canadiens 4, Sabres 3.

OT: Thursday, May 6, 1993

Same story, same score, same ending, except this time Patrick Roy was the busier of the two goalies. Gilbert Dionne, on a play he'll be explaining for the rest of his life, appeared to redirect a Patrice Brisebois shot past Fuhr 8:28 into overtime to give the Canadiens another 4–3 win. When the puck hit the back of the net, Dionne tapped himself twice in the chest as if to indicate that he had touched the puck on the way in, a gesture that was considered egotistical by many. But the Canadiens didn't care. They had a 3–0 series lead.

OT: Saturday, May 8, 1993

The Canadiens took a 3–1 lead into the third period of Game 4, but the Sabres refused to go down without a fight. Buffalo's Dale Hawerchuk scored on the power play at 12:30 to cut the lead to one. The Sabres pulled Fuhr and then tied the game on a Yuri Khmylev goal with 10 seconds left on the scoreboard. But the Canadiens were unfazed. They were getting used to this overtime business, their seventh of the playoffs so far. The Sabres shot on Roy 12 times, but he stopped them all. And at the 11:37 mark, Kirk Muller fired a slap shot from the left circle past a surprised Fuhr to end the game and series. The Canadiens had swept the Sabres, but the series was a lot closer than it looked. All of the games ended 4–3, and the last three had required overtime. Goaltending had been the difference.

The Canadiens had to wait to learn the identity of their next opponent. Most assumed that the team would face the two-time defending Stanley Cup champion Pittsburgh Penguins, who were led by Montreal native Mario Lemieux. But the New York Islanders pulled off the biggest upset of the 1993 playoffs by winning games 6 and 7 of the series, the latter in overtime.

Against the Islanders, the Canadiens took Game 1 of the Prince of Wales Conference Finals at the Forum in Montreal 4–1 on the strength of John Leclair's first two goals of the playoffs. Then . . . more OT.

OT: Tuesday, May 18, 1993

Canadiens center Paul DiPietro scored with 5:10 remaining in the third period to tie the game at three, and Game 2 was headed to overtime. And when the first extra period decided nothing, a fifth period was needed. Finally, at 6:21 of the second overtime, Stephan Lebeau scored his second goal of the playoffs and the game to give Montreal the win.

OT: Thursday, May 20, 1993

With the Islanders leading 1–0 late in the third, Vincent Damphousse's ninth goal of the playoffs sent the Canadiens to overtime for the eighth time of the postseason. And when Guy Carbonneau scored at 12:34, the Canadiens won their seventh overtime game in a row, a new single-season record. The team's 11th consecutive playoff win tied a mark co-owned by Pittsburgh and Chicago, which the Islanders put an end to two days later with a 4–1 home ice win.

The Canadiens closed out the series at the Forum on May 24, winning Game 5, 5–2. Once again, they had to wait to see whom they would face in the Stanley Cup Finals, the Los Angeles Kings or the Pat Burns–coached Toronto Maple Leafs. Canadian hockey fans dreamed of a Canadiens-Leafs series, a rematch of the 1967 finals won by the Leafs, their last Cup victory to date. Toronto was a goal away from making that dream come true when Los Angeles, on an overtime marker by Wayne Gretzky, pushed the series to seven games. And when the Kings, after another two-goal performance by Gretzky, won Game 7, 5–4, the dream died. The consolation for hockey fans would be a Stanley Cup Final between the legendary Canadiens and the Great Gretzky.

Whether it was rest from their eight-day layoff or simply the brilliance of Wayne Gretzky, the Canadiens fell to earth in Game 1 of the Finals in the Forum. With the Kings up 1–0, Gretzky did something no Canadiens player was able to achieve all game when he tipped Ed Ronan's crossing pass behind Kings goalie Kelly Hrudey. But the Great One made up for his gaffe, setting up Luc Robitaille's second goal of the game and then setting up a goal by Jari Kurri early in the third before putting his 14th of the playoffs into an empty net to seal the win. He finished the game with 4 points.

OT: Thursday, June 3, 1993

Kelly Hrudey was sensational again in Game 2, which featured one of the most controversial incidents in NHL playoff history. The Canadiens had somehow picked up on the fact a few Kings players were using illegally curved sticks, a common practice at the time, and probably still today (*see Marty McSorley's Illegal Stick, page 139*). But they wanted to wait for the right moment to use that knowledge. That moment came with Montreal trailing the game by a goal with only 2:45 to play. Jacques Demers asked the game's officials for a stick measurement on L.A.'s Marty McSorley. It was a huge risk. If the curve on McSorley's stick fell within the legal limits, the Canadiens would play the next two minutes shorthanded. But McSorley had failed to follow another common player practice and switch to a legal stick as the game's end neared, and this oversight cost him and the Kings dearly. McSorley's stick was measured and the curve determined to be too big . . . much too big. The call would ultimately change the direction of the series.

The Canadiens power play had been struggling mightily, so, with the upcoming face-off in Kings' territory, Jacques Demers pulled Roy for a sixth attacker. Thirty-two seconds later, Montreal defenseman Eric Desjardins scored his second goal of the night and sent the game to overtime.

The Canadiens caught another break less than a minute into overtime, when Desjardins joined a Canadiens rush, took a drop pass from Benoit Brunet, and ripped a slap shot that sailed over the Kings net. Normally, the puck would have caromed off the glass to the left, but the shot struck one of the metal dividers between the panes of glass and dropped straight down at the feet of Brunet, who collected it and sent it back to an open Desjardins, who then lowered his head and shot as hard as he could.

It all happened so quickly that Bob Cole, calling the game for *Hockey Night in Canada*, could barely keep with the action below:

"Desjardins following the play . . . here he is again . . . scores! Des-jar-dins! And the Canadiens win in overtime . . . his third goal of the game and the series is a brand-new one."

OT: Saturday, June 5, 1993

The stars came out for Game 3 in L.A. Not the star players, although they did too, but the rich, beautiful, and famous celebrities who came to witness the first ever Stanley Cup Final game played in Tinseltown. The Canadiens looked like they were about to spoil the party when they took a 3–0 lead 3:02 into the second on defenseman Mathieu Schneider's first of the playoffs. But the Kings stormed back with three consecutive goals of their own. Both goalies played flawlessly in the third and the Canadiens were headed for their 10th overtime of the playoffs. This was getting ridiculous.

Again, it took less than a minute to settle matters. The Kings didn't even manage a shot before John Leclair grabbed his own rebound and scored on a wild scramble 34 seconds into overtime to give Montreal a 2–1 series lead. The Canadiens' ninth consecutive overtime win broke the record they briefly shared with the New York Islanders, who had won eight overtime contests in a row over two seasons.

OT: Monday, June 7, 1993

Game 4 was strikingly similar to Game 3 in several ways. The Canadiens took a 2–0 lead on Damphousse's 11th goal of the playoffs, but Kings winger Mike Donnelly cut the lead to one just over a minute later. Then, with Montreal's Brian Bellows in the penalty box, Gretzky and Robitaille set up McSorley, whose shot beat Roy to tie the game with only five seconds left in the second period.

Back in the dressing room, the Canadiens were furious with themselves for letting another lead get away. Roy let his teammates vent for a while, then he put a stop to the negativity. "That's enough," he told them. "I'm going to stop everything. You guys just go out there and put one in."

True to his word, Roy shut down the Kings. And after one save, when a clearly frustrated Tomas Sandstrom took an extra whack or two at the covered puck, Roy winked at his old rival from the 1986 semifinals. The gesture, caught by television cameras, soon became part of the Patrick Roy legend.

Roy finished the third period with 15 saves. And he faced 10 more in overtime before Leclair, him again, tucked a loose puck beyond Hrudey for the Canadiens' tenth-consecutive overtime victory. They were going back to Montreal with a 3–1 series lead.

Demers made a surprising roster move for Game 5, surprising if you don't know the kind of person Jacques Demers is. He replaced defenseman Kevin Haller with Donald Dufresne, who had played 32 regular season games but had been left aside for the entire playoffs. His one appearance, if the Canadiens would go on to win the series, would earn him the right to have his name engraved on the Stanley Cup.

Los Angeles tied the game early in the second period, but it soon became apparent that overtime would not be necessary in Game 5. The Kings were mentally and physically exhausted, and it showed. Trailing 3–1 at the start of the third period, they could muster only five shots on Roy, for a total of 19 over the whole game. After Paul DiPietro scored his second goal of the game at 12:06 of the third, the countdown was on.

Hockey Night in Canada's Bob Cole, almost shouting to be heard over the roar of the Forum crowd, began his call with about 10 seconds left in the game:

"And now a 24th Stanley Cup banner will hang from the rafters of the famous Forum in Montreal. The Canadiens have won the Stanley Cup."

Joy: The Canadiens pose for a team picture after winning the 24th Stanley Cup in team history (Doug MacLellan/Hockey Hall of Fame).

Patrick Roy was awarded his second Conn Smythe trophy as playoff MVP. And when Gary Bettman, in his first championship ceremony since becoming NHL commissioner, handed the Stanley Cup to Guy Carbonneau, the first person the Canadiens captain passed it to was veteran Denis Savard, who had never won the Cup, and who had spent the past four games of the series in civvies behind the bench after injuring his foot in Game 1. Jacques Demers took in the whole scene, grinning broadly, his eyes glistening with joy.

Nobody could have imagined it at the time, but as of this writing, it was the Canadiens' last Stanley Cup victory, and the last by a Canadian team.

MARTY McSORLEY'S ILLEGAL STICK

Twenty-three years after it happened, some Los Angeles Kings players and fans are still angry about it. So is Barry Melrose, the Kings' coach from 1992 to 1995 and a hockey commentator on ESPN since 1996.

Most of the Kings don't actually have a problem with the Canadiens' request for the measurement of McSorley's big blade, or with the call rendered on the ice by referee Kerry Fraser, but they do have a beef for the way the Canadiens found out who was using illegal lumber.

Numerous theories have been floated over the years, implicating everyone from spying trainers to bribed police officers and security guards who broke into locked rooms. McSorley, for his part, claims the Canadiens hauled the Kings' stick rack into their dressing room and checked all the blades, an etiquette faux-pas right up there with secretly filming opponents' practices or deflating footballs in key games. The Canadiens, meanwhile, have mostly stuck to their original story, that some Montreal players noticed McSorley's blade on the ice, or that trainers and players saw it in the stick rack that was kept between the opposing benches during games. The curve was just so big, they said, that it was obvious.

Melrose, meanwhile, still insists that he would never stoop as low as the Canadiens did on June 3, 1993.

"Games are meant to be decided between the players, the heart and soul of the players, the passion of the players, the toughness of the players. I would never do that as a coach. I said that after the game and I still believe that today. Jacques didn't cheat or anything, it's in the rulebook, but I just don't think games should be won or lost for that."

3RD PERIOD

OFF THE ICE

1909: The Creation of Habs Nation

19

While the city's French-speaking fans now cheer on the Canadiens with an unmatched fervor, it took quite a long time for hockey fever to spread to Montreal's predominantly French-Canadian East End.

By the turn of the nineteenth century, Montreal was firmly established as the center of the hockey world. Organized ice hockey was born there in 1875 and the well-to-do English-speaking community's sporting clubs helped refine and popularize the game. Teams from the city won 24 of the first 44 challenges for the Stanley Cup, awarded to the game's champion team since 1893. But these were teams owned by, comprised of, and supported by members of Montreal's English-speaking minority. The first Cup winners, the Winged Wheelers of the Montreal Amateur Athletic Association, were members of a distinctly British sporting club, while the Montreal Shamrocks and Victorias were traditionally Irish and Scottish.

Then there were the Montreal Wanderers, who won four Stanley Cups (and nine Cup challenges) between their founding in 1903 and March 1910. Together with the Ottawa Hockey Club (a.k.a. "The Silver Seven" and later the Senators) the Wanderers dominated top-level hockey in Eastern Canada between 1903 and 1911.

French Montreal did have its hockey teams before the Canadiens were born. Although the city's East End was better known for its social clubs than sporting associations, in 1896, leading members of the French-speaking community formed one of the latter. L'Association Athlétique d'Amateurs le National (Le National for short) fielded a championship amateur lacrosse squad and teams in several other sports, including hockey. Two years later L'Association Athlétique d'Amateurs Le Montagnard was also founded. Both clubs eventually entered teams in senior-level leagues and hockey's popularity grew on the French side of town, but with the game's best and most experienced players suiting up for the more established crosstown teams, the teams were thin

143

on talent and eventually returned to the amateur side of the sport without achieving significant professional success.

The Canadian hockey landscape was an ever-changing one in the first decades of the 1900s. The rise of professionalism was changing the game and leagues and teams came and went. One of the stronger circuits, the Eastern Canada Amateur Hockey Association (ECAHA), was formed in 1905 through the merger of two other top-level associations. The ECAHA was an amateur league in name only, with several of its six founding franchises (The Montreal Hockey Club, Shamrocks, Victorias, Wanderers, Ottawa Hockey Club, and Quebec Bulldogs) employing pros. At the end of the 1908 season, the purely amateur Montreal Hockey Club and Montreal Victorias left the league, which dropped the first "A" in its name and soldiered on as a four-team professional league.

The powerhouse Montreal Wanderers and Ottawa Hockey Club were bitter rivals both on and off the ice, and animosities between them led to the breakup of the Eastern Canada Hockey Association in 1909. (In March 1909, Ottawa finally wrestled back the Stanley Cup, held by the Wanderers, except for two months in 1907, since March 1906.) A rink dispute was at the heart of the problems, which began in the fall of 1909 when the teams began organizing the 1910 ECHA season. The Wanderers had decided to move away from their West End fan base into the new Jubilee Arena on Ste-Catherine Street East, which their new owner, Patrick J. Doran, built and owned. It was a strange move by the Wanderers, who would be abandoning the renovated and much larger Westmount Arena for the 3,500-seat Jubilee, and their opponents, notably Ottawa, objected to the idea of sharing the resulting smaller revenues. The Wanderers were becoming a problem, and their rivals would employ a method to be rid of them that would be used against another troublesome franchise eight years later. The three other ECHA franchises simply dissolved the league to form a new one, leaving the uninvited Wanderers out in the cold. The new league was called the Canadian Hockey Association (CHA).

Ottawa, the Shamrocks, and the Bulldogs announced their CHA intentions at a league meeting at Montreal's Windsor Hotel on November 25, 1909. Also present that evening were representatives of other teams wishing to join them, including a contingent hoping to launch a team for the growing number of French-speaking fans. Then there was twenty-four-year-old John Ambrose O'Brien, the son of Michael John O'Brien, wealthy industrialist, future Canadian senator (1918–25), and owner of hockey teams, most notably Renfrew, Ontario's powerful Creamery Kings (named after the local dairy).

If they won't play you, join 'em

Having funded teams for years in mining and other minor-pro leagues, the wealthy O'Briens wanted in on big-time pro hockey.

They had unsuccessfully tried to challenge for the Stanley Cup, and the previous season, they had nearly lured Ottawa star Cyclone Taylor to their Federal League team with the promises of big money, earning them the scorn of their powerful Eastern Ontario neighbors in the process.

Shunned by the league's bigwigs that evening, particularly those from Ottawa, and thereby unable to make his pitch to join their league, the younger O'Brien instead found himself face to face with Wanderers representative and player Jimmy Gardner, who'd stormed out of the meeting upstairs and was fuming in the Windsor Hotel lobby. It wasn't a new idea in the Fall of 1909, but legend has it that the idea to officially launch a franchise for Montreal's French-speaking fans was Gardner's . . . once he'd calmed down. But the money behind it would be the O'Briens'.

The story, first told in a biography of Michael O'Brien, is recounted in author D'Arcy Jenish's superb centennial history, *The Montreal Canadiens: 100 Years of Glory*.

"Ambrose, why don't you and I start a league," Gardner said. "You've got Haileybury, Cobalt and Renfrew, and we've got the Wanderers. And I think if a team of Frenchmen was formed in Montreal it would be a real draw. We could give it a French-Canadian name. We'll call this team Les Canadiens."

While Gardner and O'Brien made plans downstairs, upstairs, the new CHA had awarded franchises to Le National and a new club, the All-Montreal HC, headed up by player-coach Art Ross.

On December 2, the new National Hockey Association (NHA) was founded. It would be comprised of the Wanderers and four mostly O'Brien-funded teams: Les Canadiens, Renfrew (soon to be nicknamed "The Millionaires" thanks to the huge salaries earned by their many new players), and entries in the small mining towns of Cobalt and Haileybury, Ontario. Now there were two senior level professional hockey leagues operating on more or less the same territory. The Canadiens franchise was officially admitted to the NHA on December 4 with the understanding that the O'Briens' involvement would be a temporary one. The team, whose official name was Le Club de Hockey Le Canadien, was to be turned over to French-Canadian owners as soon as possible.

Both leagues quickly drew up schedules that would begin in early January, still the custom at a time when ice rinks needed winter's help. With their first game scheduled to take place on January 5, the Canadiens had only a month to sign players and prepare for the season.

The first order of business for Les Canadiens was to hire someone to run the team. Their choice was Jean-Baptiste "Jack" Laviolette, a Belleville, Ontario–born veteran of the pro hockey circuit who had spent his formative years in Valleyfield, Quebec. The thirty-year-old Laviolette would serve as manager, coach, and captain, patrolling the point (or second line of defense), and it was his job to find and sign French-Canadian players to the team. The other NHA teams made his task somewhat easier by waiting until the Canadiens' roster was filled before signing any French players themselves.

Laviolette's first signing, that of his old friend and teammate Didier Pitre, actually ended up before the courts after the beloved "Cannonball" (he was known for his stocky build and exceptional speed) was tricked into signing for that other new French-Canadian team in town, Le National. A judge eventually settled things in the Canadiens' favor. Laviolette's next prize was Edouard "Newsy" Lalonde, a goal-scoring machine in both hockey and lacrosse who earned his moniker working in the print shop of the *Free Press* newspaper in his hometown of Cornwall, Ontario.

Drop the puck, already

On January 5, 1910, in the first game in their history, wearing blue and white jerseys adorned with a large "C," white pants, and red socks, the Montreal Canadiens took the ice to face the visiting Cobalt Silver Kings. Considering that there were now five teams vying for the disposable income of Montreal hockey fans, the estimated crowd of more than 3,000, mostly French-Canadians, at the Jubilee Arena was a pleasant surprise indeed for Canadiens' management.

In goal for Montreal was newcomer Joe Cattarinich, better known for his considerable lacrosse skills. Lining up ahead of him, at point, was Laviolette; at cover-point, Pitre; and at rover, Lalonde. Wingers Arthur Bernier and George "Skinner" Poulin lined up to the right and left of centerman Edmond Decarie. Lalonde opened the scoring with a spectacular play from his knees, and soon added another before the bell sounded to end the first half of the game (three-period games were not introduced until the following season) with the home team up, 3–1. But some shaky goaltending by Cattarinich saw the Canadiens trailing by two goals late in the second half. But, as they would so many times over the more than one hundred seasons that followed, the Canadiens refused to lose, and rallied to tie the game, 6–6, on late goals by Bernier and Laviolette. After some confusion, during which some fans even left the Jubilee thinking the game had ended, the teams and officials decided to end the deadlock with overtime. Cattarinich resisted an early Cobalt onslaught with a series of spectacular saves before Poulin sent the remaining fans home happy with the winning goal at the 5:25 mark. Final score: Les Canadiens 7, Cobalt 6. The *Montreal Gazette* edition of January 6, 1910 described the game as a "wild hurrah from start to finish."

What a shame, then, that such an exciting and memorable game would soon be erased from the record books. But pro hockey had not yet developed to the point where it could sustain so many teams in one area. There were not enough talented players to go around, and the competition for them sent salaries skyward.

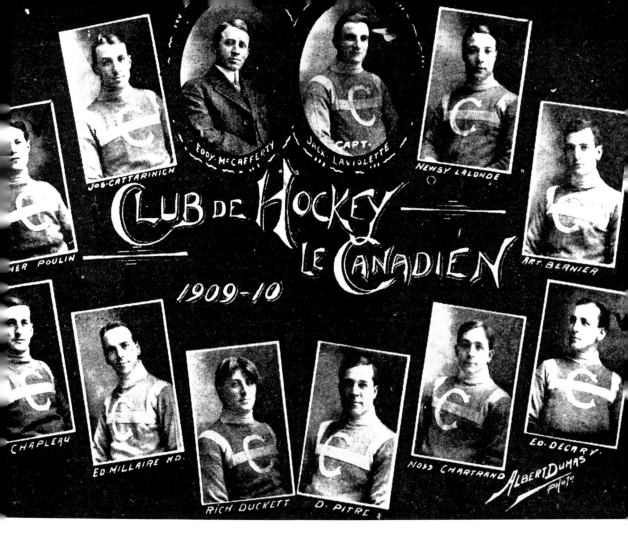

The first team: The 1909–10 edition of the Montreal Canadiens (Hockey Hall of Fame).

Something had to give and the CHA was the first to crack. Before the Canadiens could play again, the rival league folded after a series of poorly played and sparsely attended games. The Shamrocks and Ottawa joined the NHA, where they would be joined the following season by the Quebec Bulldogs. The All-Montreal HC simply disbanded.

Les Canadiens might have played only that one unofficial game had the owners of Le National accepted the O'Briens' offer to sell them the team and its players, but the asking price was too high and Le National temporarily closed shop before returning to the amateur ranks in 1911.

To the surprise of few, in French Montreal anyhow, the O'Briens had started to show their true colors—and they weren't those of Les Canadiens (blue and white or red, white, and blue). They were the white and red of the Renfrew Creamery Kings. The O'Briens had finally achieved their goal of being admitted to hockey's best league and had moved on to their next pursuit—winning the Stanley Cup. The Canadiens were an afterthought.

The season resumed January 19, with all games played before January 15 excluded from the standings. The Canadiens visited Renfrew, losing 9–4. They would go on to finish last in that inaugural NHA season with a record of 2–10. To make matters worse, home game attendance dwindled as the season progressed.

The O'Briens' talent-rich Creamery Kings, on the other hand, enjoyed much success before a series of losses in February threatened to knock them from contention. Before a crucial February 25 game against the visiting powerhouse Wanderers, Newsy Lalonde, the Canadiens' best player, was released from the team and then picked up by Renfrew. The Creamery Kings nevertheless lost that game to the Wanderers, who, as NHA champions, were later awarded the Stanley Cup.

The writing was on the wall in Montreal. The O'Briens clearly had no interest in supporting hockey in the city, and they proved that at season's end, essentially dropping Les Canadiens on the NHA's doorstep. After one final, and vain, attempt at winning a Stanley Cup, the O'Briens got out of the pro hockey game altogether after the 1911 season.

With the Canadiens in limbo at the end of the 1910 season, their players and a new franchise were awarded by the NHA to Montreal wrestling promoter George Kennedy, also the founder of the Club Athlétique Canadien, which became the official name of the new team. The bilingual Kennedy, who had objected to the O'Briens' use of the "Canadiens" name, paid $7,500 for the franchise and had new jerseys designed for his team. Gone was the blue jersey with the white "C," replaced by red uniforms with white and green bands and a green maple leaf crest. Kennedy also brought Newsy Lalonde back into the Canadiens' fold and hired Adolphe Lecours as coach, to take over for Laviolette (who stayed on as a player). He also moved the team from the Jubilee Arena to the Westmount Arena, and was the only NHA owner to make a profit in the 1910–11 season, in which the team would finish in second place with an 8–8 record. More significantly, Kennedy found a new goaltender in Georges Vezina, who would literally stick with the team for the rest of his life, and help lead them to the glory their growing legion of supporters so craved.

Up Close: The first Hab: Jack Laviolette

The Montreal Canadiens' first manager, coach, captain, and player were all the same man: Jean-Baptiste "Jack" Laviolette. Born July 17, 1879 in Belleville, Ontario, Laviolette honed his hockey skills on the rinks of Valleyfield, Quebec. A defender who loved to rush up the ice and score goals, Laviolette joined the Montreal Le National of the Federal Amateur Hockey League in 1903–04. The following season, he joined the Michigan Soo Indians of the professional International Hockey League, scoring 15 goals in each of his first two seasons. He returned to Montreal to suit up for the Shamrocks of the Eastern Canada Amateur Hockey Association for the 1907–08 and 1908–09 seasons.

Like all good hockey players, he was in the right place at the right time when the Montreal Canadiens were founded in 1909. The Canadiens needed someone with a French-Canadian name who could play and who knew the professional game, and Laviolette fit the bill in every way. Although he stopped acting as coach after the team's first NHA season, he would remain with them for a total of nine seasons. He retired in 1918 after a car accident cost him the use of his right foot. Jack Laviolette died at the age of eighty in 1960, and was posthumously inducted into the Hockey Hall of Fame in 1962.

THE END OF THE "FLYING FRENCHMEN"?

On February 17, 2016, following an injury to center David Desharnais, the Montreal Canadiens for the first time in their 107-year history played a game without a single player whose mother tongue was French. The team that debuted in 1909 with a roster featuring players named Laviolette, Lalonde, Pitre, and Bernier, and who over the years featured stars named Richard, Béliveau, Lafleur, Savard, Roy, Richer, and Carbonneau, had seen the number of French-Canadian players in its lineup dwindle as NHL hockey became a big business, and an international one at that. But there always seemed to be a French name or two on the back of a Canadiens jersey . . . until the winter of 2016. The team did, in fact, have four French-Canadians on their roster in 2014–15, second only to the Pittsburgh Penguins, who had six.

The utter lack of French-Canadian players on the Habs in early 2016 was bemoaned in a February 20 *Le Devoir* newspaper article by hockey writer Marc Tremblay, entitled "La fin des 'Flying Frenchmen'" ("The End of the 'Flying Frenchmen'"). Indeed, that this sad milestone would coincide with one of the worst losing sequences in team history was not lost on many of the Canadiens' most vocal critics.

The Richard Riot

20

There are some who would tell you the seeds of the Richard Riot in Montreal were sown September 13, 1759, when British soldiers under the command of General James Wolfe caught French forces, led by General Louis-Joseph, Marquis de Montcalm, by surprise near Quebec City and won a quick, strategic victory. Such a victory paved the way for the transfer of New France to British control within a year.

That France was much more interested in Caribbean colonies that produced valuable sugar products than in maintaining its grip on a frozen, sparsely populated, barren outcrop that delivered little more than fur by way of trade, has been lost on many of the generations that followed.

But the subsequent centuries of British colonial oppression, of cultural antagonism, and of feeling like second-class citizens in their own homeland finally erupted on a St. Patrick's Day evening in March 1955, the argument goes, after the hero of the French-Canadian population and Montreal Canadiens star forward, Maurice "Rocket" Richard, had been suspended for the remaining three games of the National Hockey League season and the entire playoffs.

It has been described as no less than the beginning of Quebec's "Quiet Revolution" against the stifling power of the Catholic Church, against English-speaking bosses, and against a conservative and autocratic Premier Maurice Duplessis, who ruled Quebec during what was referred to as "La Grande Noirceur," the Great Darkness.

Others, however, argue that the Richard Riot has taken on the trappings of a legend well after the event, a convenient story to fit the political and social context—that the riot was really nothing more than the reaction of furious, passionate hockey fans, who felt their hero had been treated with a manifest lack of fairness at a crucial moment in the season. It might have been the first time hockey fans smashed up Ste-Catherine Street in downtown Montreal, but it certainly wouldn't be the last (*see Montreal: Hockey Riot Capital, page 155*).

What, one has to ask, would have been the reaction had Richard's suspension for a multiplicity of sins occurred in, say, November?

Was it the trigger of a social revolution or just an angry explosion of hockey fans? The truth is likely a fair bit of both.

There certainly were linguistic underpinnings to the fracas, because the National Hockey League's president at the time, Clarence Campbell, was an English-speaking Montrealer (born in Saskatchewan) and Maurice Richard was a francophone from working-class Montreal, who happened to have as fierce a competitive instinct as he did talent with blades and stick. Richard himself had complained bitterly about what he and others saw as Campbell's demonstrable anti-French bias in dishing out discipline (or not) in an era where hockey was far more brutal than it is today.

"Richard Goes Insane"

It was, indeed, a different era in professional hockey. There were only six teams in the NHL, so they played each other far more frequently than they do now. The event that led up to the fateful riot occurred on March 13, 1955, during a game between Montreal and the Boston Bruins, in Boston. It was the 14th and last meeting of the clubs in the regular season. These days, teams in the same conference might only meet each other on four occasions during regular-season play—hardly enough opportunity to get a really good hate going on. Unless there's a history.

So here's what happened to spark the discipline meted out to Richard and the subsequent riot that caused an estimated $100,000 in property damage (that would be nearly $1 million today), and resulted in 37 people being hurt and 100 people arrested.

In a game on March 13 at the Boston Garden, the Bruins' Hal Laycoe, who had once been a Canadiens' defenseman, high-sticked Richard and cut him for five stitches. Referee Frank Udvari signaled a penalty, but play continued because Montreal had the puck. When the whistle finally blew, Richard went crazy. He confronted Laycoe, who had already dropped his gloves in anticipation of a fight. Instead of punching him, Richard whacked Laycoe with his stick, hitting him in the face and shoulders. Richard, pulled away by linesmen, continued to pursue Laycoe, eventually smashing his stick in two over the latter's body. One linesman, Cliff Thompson, got hold of Richard, but only briefly, and Richard spun and punched the linesman twice in the face.

On the spot, Richard was given a match penalty and an automatic fine of $100. For the record, Laycoe received a five-minute major for high-sticking (drawing blood), and a 10-minute misconduct for later throwing a bloody towel at the referee in protest over his own penalty.

Richard then left the ice, aided by the Canadiens' trainer. *Montreal Herald* sportswriter Vince Lunny wrote that Richard's face resembled a "smashed tomato."

3rd Period

Boston police later tried to arrest Richard, but were blocked from entering the Montreal dressing room and were persuaded by the Bruins management that the league would handle things.

How the league would deal with Richard sparked a riot four nights later.

Richard brought considerable baggage into a hearing Campbell ordered for March 16, 1955, at his Montreal office. By that time, Richard was one of the league's most penalized players. His seemingly uncontrollable temper and the violence that flowed from it were already legendary, and not just because he hit opponents with his stick or his fists. He had physically assaulted officials (a taboo in professional sport) and had already slapped a linesman earlier in the 1954–55 season, during a December game against the Toronto Maple Leafs. That weighed heavily. Campbell was doubtless under significant pressure from other team owners to "do something" about Richard, who was widely seen outside Montreal as being out of control. (The day after the fateful game, the *Boston Herald* ran the banner headline: "RICHARD GOES INSANE.")

The hearing in Montreal's massive Sun Life Building (a symbol of the English dominance of Montreal's business world) was attended by Richard; a bandaged-up Laycoe; Thompson, sporting a black eye; and representatives of both teams. The hearing lasted about three and a half hours. It seemed all of Montreal was holding its breath, waiting for the result that would finally come in the early evening.

Richard had pleaded that he was dazed and confused and had struck the linesman by mistake, thinking he was Laycoe. Campbell was having none of it: "I am also satisfied that Richard did not strike linesman Thompson as a result of a mistake or accident as suggested." Campbell also cited Richard's rap sheet as a repeat offender against officials.

"Whether this type of conduct is the product of temperamental instability or willful defiance doesn't matter," Campbell wrote in a statement. "It's a type of conduct that cannot be tolerated by any player—star or otherwise. Richard will be suspended from all games both league and playoff for the balance of the current season."

It was the longest suspension Campbell would issue during the 31 years he served as NHL president.

There were many, including Detroit Red Wings star Gordie Howe (himself no angel), who thought Richard was lucky to get away with that. A lifetime suspension might be more appropriate, a number of hockey observers suggested.

Most Montrealers didn't see it that way. They flooded the airwaves and newspaper telephone lines to vent against the unfairness of it all, observing that once again the Anglo establishment had trampled on a French-Canadian hero and that prejudice and bigotry were behind this patently unfair decision that would mortally wound their beloved team.

Their feelings would be made even more clear the next night, the first game Richard would miss because of his suspension, although he would likely have been in no condition to play, given the continuing symptoms of concussion, for which he sought medical attention. (In those days, however, such symptoms were not likely to have stopped someone like Richard from hitting the ice—and opposing players).

The Canadiens were playing host to the Detroit Red Wings at the iconic Montreal Forum, at the corner of Ste-Catherine Street and Atwater Avenue. There was a lot on the line. The Canadiens and Wings were locked in a virtual tie for the league lead and the home-ice advantage that first place would provide in the playoffs.

Things got ugly quickly, both on the ice and off. The Wings got off to a 4–1 lead by the end of the first period, but what had really stirred the crowd was Campbell's arrival (with one of his secretaries) midway through the period. He was pelted with eggs, vegetables, peanuts, galoshes, and boos. Outside, across Ste-Catherine Street, a crowd of about 6,000 young men had gathered. And they were angry.

Red Storey, who refereed that game, later said Campbell should never have been there, that had the NHL president stayed away from the game, "we woulda had no riot. But he dared the public."

While police were successful in keeping that crowd from storming the Forum, they were having less luck inside. During the first intermission, one man, pretending to be a friend of the NHL president, stepped up to Campbell and extended his hand, as if to shake. Campbell did likewise, and the man slapped him in the face and punched him, before being dragged away. Then a tear gas bomb went off, not far from Campbell's seat. The chaotic rush for the exits caused the Montreal Fire Chief to halt the game. It was declared a forfeit, and the Wings were awarded the victory, the first time such a thing had happened. (The Red Wings ended the season in first place with 95 points. The Canadiens, playing without Richard, dropped the March 20 season finale to Detroit, 6–0, and finished second with 93.)

To make matters worse, the suspension cost Richard what would have been his first (and only) NHL scoring title. Canadiens winger Bernie "Boom Boom" Geoffrion, with a three-point night in Montreal's 4–2 defeat of the New York Rangers on March 19, passed his teammate to claim the title, his 75 points in 70 games one better than Richard's 74 in 67. For his accomplishment, Canadiens fans booed Geoffrion.

With the forfeit, there was more for the crowd outside to be furious about. Fifteen thousand Forum spectators suddenly joined the thousands already in the street. In short order, people began taking out their frustrations on store windows. They overturned cars, set newsstands on fire, and began a riot that extended several blocks down Montreal's main commercial street.

Records of the day indicate that, within several blocks of the Forum, more than fifty stores were looted and/or vandalized. A dozen police officers and more than twenty

NHL President Clarence Campbell is attacked by an irate fan in the Montreal Forum on the night of the infamous Richard Riot (Le Studio du Hockey/Hockey Hall of Fame).

others were hurt. The riot lasted into the early hours of the next morning and Ste-Catherine Street was left a shambles.

While such shenanigans are not uncommon following major sports victories or defeats in this era, the Richard Riot was the first. Nothing of this scale had happened before, and Montreal (in fact, all of Canada) was reeling.

Richard went on the radio the next day to plead for calm. It seemed to work.

But questions remained. Where did all that anger come from? Why could something so inconsequential as a hockey event provoke people to commit such—until then—unheard of acts of violence and vandalism?

This is where we return to the debate about whether the Richard Riot was the trigger of Quebec's rising up over the next decade against the English establishment or just the manifestation of the world's most passionate hockey fans reacting to what they perceived as an unjust penalty against their team and against the hero they adored.

In the end, it is impossible to separate the two. There is no question that there was a strong anti-Anglo streak to the response to Campbell's decision, and his foolish decision to attend the game against Detroit. But remember Storey's view that, without

Campbell's presence, the riot wouldn't have occurred. And don't dismiss the proposition that, had this taken place in November, the consequences would have been dramatically different.

Without Richard in the lineup, the Canadiens failed in their bid to repeat as Stanley Cup champions. They reached the Finals, but were defeated in seven games by the Detroit Red Wings.

MONTREAL: HOCKEY RIOT CAPITAL

The participants in the Richard Riot of March 17, 1955 were angry about the suspension handed down to their hero by NHL President Clarence Campbell. But in 1986, 1993, 2008, and 2010 riots that caused millions of dollars worth of damage to downtown Montreal, stemmed from joyful occurrences. In the first two cases, thousands of happy Montrealers descended on the downtown core to celebrate the Stanley Cup championships won by the Canadiens. That's how it all started, anyway.

On May 25, 1986, moments after the Canadiens won their 23rd Stanley Cup in Calgary, between 5,000 and 10,000 people converged on Ste-Catherine, where stores were looted and cars were overturned and set ablaze. The riot caused approximately $1 million in damages. In an article headlined "Rioting, Looting, Mar Habs' Cup Win," the *Montreal Gazette* reported that the Montreal police had only forty officers on duty and took hours to make their presence felt. A Quebec court later ruled in favor of merchants who sued the city, finding the police criminally negligent.

On June 9, 1993, after the Canadiens won Cup number 24 at the Montreal Forum, it was the same story, but even worse. Despite the presence of nearly a thousand police officers, rioters destroyed fifteen city buses and forty-seven police cars, with damage estimates ranging between $2.5 and $10 million. More than 150 people, including forty-nine police officers, were injured and 115 people were arrested. Eyewitness accounts suggested that some of the looting that took place was organized.

In 2008, a simple first-round win over Boston was all it took to send some hockey celebrants over the edge again. A number of downtown businesses were looted and sixteen police cars were burnt or smashed. Damages were estimated at approximately $500,000. Two years later, after a second-round elimination of Pittsburgh, twenty-five people were arrested and a number of stores were looted.

Passing the Torch in June 1971

21

Three weeks after the Montreal Canadiens won their 17th, and possibly most unexpected Stanly Cup to date, a series of events transpired that would help the team win five more in the next eight years.

One would think that the general manager of a team who had just won the Stanley Cup (*see Dryden Debuts as Canadiens Shock Bruins, page 95*), and just one year after missing the playoffs, would have a little time to enjoy the spoils of victory and relax. But heading into the annual NHL meetings in Montreal in early June of 1971, Sam Pollock had a lot on his plate, and a good deal of it was unpleasant.

On June 1, Pollock fielded questions on the status of the team's head coach and best player, and he had no answer in either case.

Sticky situation number 1 involved Jean Béliveau, the team's captain and top scorer in the 1970–71 season. At age thirty-nine, and after 18 full seasons with the team, "Le Gros Bill" as he was affectionately known, had been openly contemplating retirement for some time. Popular logic had it that Béliveau, who had just won his 10th Stanley Cup as a player, would choose to go out on top and hang up his skates before his upcoming fortieth birthday. That said, losing the team's leader and top scorer wasn't a prospect Pollock relished. And although Béliveau was slowing down, having him around for one more year to help mentor some young players, with one in particular coming to mind, would be helpful indeed.

"I don't know what Jean plans to do," Pollock told the *Montreal Gazette*'s Ted Blackman for a June 1 column entitled "How to Please Everyone: Pollock's Giant Problem." "I wouldn't be honest if I did say that it would be strange not to see Jean Béliveau playing for the Montreal Canadiens, even if you know it'll happen one year. I don't want to say more, I don't want to put any pressure on him. It's his decision."

Then there was the even pricklier case of head coach Al MacNeil, who took over behind the bench after his predecessor, Claude Ruel, resigned before Christmas, and then guided the team to the Stanley Cup. Along the way, he'd been sharply criticized by some veteran players, namely Henri Richard, who would be named captain after Béliveau's eventual departure. The situation, which had French-English political overtones, got so bad that the unilingual MacNeil received death threats during the Stanley Cup Finals. Pollock had already wavered from his original stance in support of his coach, and was now answering noncommittally. Meanwhile, the members of the press busied themselves by bandying about the names of possible successors, like retired player Dickie Moore, former junior coach Roger Bédard, Jean Béliveau, and longtime Pollock protégé Scotty Bowman, dismissed mid-season from his job as coach and general manager of the St. Louis Blues.

One other piece of business was resolved on June 4, when John Ferguson, who came out of retirement on November 17, 1970 to help the stumbling Canadiens, announced that he was hanging up his skates for good after eight rough and tumble seasons. But Pollock placed his name on the team's protected list anyway.

Taking care of business

When the NHL meetings got under way on Monday, June 7 and with the Amateur Draft slated for June 11, Al MacNeil was still the coach of the Canadiens, and Béliveau was still team captain . . . but not for long. On June 9, the Canadiens formally announced that Béliveau was retiring as a player to take on the position of vice president of Corporate Relations with the team.

On Friday, June 11, the Canadiens added two key pieces to the puzzle that would soon be the team's 1970s dynasty, simultaneously announcing MacNeil's voluntary departure to take over the American Hockey League affiliate Voyageurs and the identity of his successor. MacNeil's choice was made easier by the fact the farm team, which had played the previous two seasons out of the Forum in Montreal, would be moving to Halifax in his home province of Nova Scotia.

In a *Montreal Gazette* article with the headline "MacNeil—Class in a Touchy Situation," MacNeil told reporter Pat Curran what most had already figured out.

"I knew because of the controversy that there was no way I could stay on as coach."

His replacement was thirty-eight-year-old Scotty Bowman, who would go on to be the most successful coach in NHL history. But that was still decades away.

For most of his hockey life, the bilingual Bowman had been a loyal Canadiens company man. After Bowman's junior playing career ended in 1954, Pollock (his former coach and then the Canadiens' director of player personnel) asked him to supervise the youth teams the Canadiens sponsored in Verdun, his home town, just a few minutes southwest of the Montreal Forum. He moved through the ranks quickly over the next decade, serving as assistant to Pollock in a variety of functions, most of them related to coaching. He coached the Canadiens-affiliated Peterborough Petes of the Ontario Hockey Association for three seasons, and then, after Pollock succeeded Frank Selke as Montreal general manager in 1964, Bowman guided the Junior Canadiens for two years.

Bowman himself would have made a young but capable successor to Toe Blake, who coached the Canadiens from 1955 to 1968, and Pollock tried to convince him to remain in the fold, but in 1967, when Blake's tenure continued, Bowman accepted the position of assistant coach with the expansion St. Louis Blues. Bowman took over as the team's head coach after 16 games in that first season and became coach-manager after the second. In his first three seasons, Bowman guided the Blues to two West Division titles and three consecutive Stanley Cup Finals. But he tangled with ownership early in 1970 and was fired. Other teams courted him, but his heart was in Montreal. During the 1971 Stanley Cup Finals in Chicago he spoke to Pollock, who told him, "You're hired. I just don't know yet what job I can give you."

The next order of business was the Amateur Draft, where the Canadiens owned six of the first twenty-five picks thanks to some shrewd maneuverings by the man some called "Trader Sam" a full year before.

French-Canadian superstars had led the Canadiens since Maurice Richard in the mid-1940s, and with Béliveau expected to retire shortly, Pollock knew that it would be important to replace him with another to continue the "Flying Frenchmen" tradition. The Canadiens had managed to wangle themselves the first pick on three previous occasions. In the very first draft, in 1963, they selected Garry Monahan first overall, followed by goaltender Michel Plasse in 1968 and Réjean Houle in 1969.

With the expansion Buffalo Sabres and Vancouver Canucks selecting first and second respectively, Pollock realized that the biggest prize of the 1970 draft, Junior Canadiens star center Gilbert Perreault, would be long gone before the Canadiens picked in the number 5, 6, and 10 spots (thanks to earlier trades), so he traded the tenth pick and prospect Ernie Hicke to the Oakland Seals, who had their hearts set on a player named Chris Oddleifson, who had scored 31 goals in 59 games with the Winnipeg Jets of the Western Canadian Hockey League. In return the Canadiens received an Oakland player named Francois Lacombe, cash, and the Seals' first pick in the prospect-rich 1971 draft.

A number of 1951-born, 1971 draft eligible French Quebecers had started to distinguish themselves as early as 1969, and by 1970, two began to emerge as the potential top prize, center Marcel Dionne of the Ontario Hockey Association's St. Catharines Black Hawks, and winger Guy Lafleur of the Quebec Major Junior Hockey Association's Quebec Remparts.

Guy Lafleur grew up in the pulp and paper town of Thurso, Quebec, located about thirty-three miles northeast of Ottawa, Ontario. When he outgrew the little backyard rink his father built, Lafleur, who would sometimes sleep in his hockey equipment to get a quick start on the following morning, would sneak into the local rink through a hole cut in its wall to practice before school. By the age of ten, he was already becoming famous in Quebec hockey circles after scoring 30 of his team's 48 goals as an underage player at the famous Quebec Pee-Wee tournament. After one hat trick, he was photographed alongside his hero, Jean Béliveau.

At the age of fifteen, Lafleur left home to play for the Junior B Quebec Aces. In 1968–69, his third season with the team, he scored 50 goals and 60 assists in 49 games. In 1969, Lafleur joined the fledging major junior Quebec Remparts, and his exploits began filling the 10,000-seat Colisée de Québec. He scored 103 goals and 67 assists in 56 games that season. Lafluer almost single-handedly revived hockey's fortunes in the provincial capital, which had sagged badly after Béliveau left the city in 1952 after starring with the Quebec Aces and Citadelles for five seasons. With the Remparts, Lafleur wore the same number 4 jersey as his idol.

"That man is my hero," he told *Sports Illustrated* in March 1971. "I may never be able to play hockey like him but I'd like to be the man he is."

That season Lafleur scored an incredible 130 goals and 79 assists for 209 points, and led the Remparts to a Memorial Cup, Canada's junior hockey championship.

Drummondville, Quebec-born Marcel Dionne for his part had 55 goals and 77 assists in 54 games in 1969–70, and 62 goals and 81 assists in only 46 games the following year, a new scoring record in the more defense-oriented Ontario league.

Pollock had his eye on both young stars, especially Lafleur, who was becoming a household name in Quebec. But in the fall of 1970, with the Seals' first pick already in hand, he had no way of knowing where the usually hapless team, who had just become the California Golden Seals, would finish in the standings. In 1969–70, they had tied the Philadelphia Flyers for the league's second worst record. If they improved, the pick would drop and he would probably lose out on both players.

After the Seals started the 1970–71 season by going winless in the first nine games, visions of Guy Lafleur in a Canadiens uniform danced in Pollock's head. But the Los Angeles Kings started to mess with Pollock's grand plans. After a strong start, the Kings went into a terrible tailspin. Winning only four of their next 29 games, including one over the Canadiens, the Kings had a record of 11–23–8 and 30 points on January 16, only one more than the Seals, who at 13–28–3 had two more wins but five more losses.

To make matters worse, the Kings had already traded their first pick in the draft to . . . the powerful and archrival Boston Bruins. Now Pollock was imagining Guy Lafleur in black and gold.

To bolster his chances, Trader Sam got on the phone with his L.A. counterpart, Larry Regan, and on January 26 sent veteran Ralph Backstrom, the 1958–59 Rookie of the Year, to the Kings for two players and a 1973 second-round draft pick. Pollock always maintained that he was doing a favor for the increasingly unhappy Backstrom, a center who had spent his entire career playing on the third line below Jean Béliveau and Henri Richard. Backstrom, who was going through a divorce, had repeatedly asked to be traded, specifically to the west coast.

Regardless of his intentions, things worked out very nicely indeed for Pollock and the Canadiens. Even though the Kings only won 11 games the rest of the season, including a 6–3 defeat of Montreal on February 6, they finished third-last in the West Division, with 18 more points than the last-place California Golden Seals. Sam Pollock would have the first overall pick in June.

What followed at the draft in Montreal on June 11 is described as follows in D'Arcy Jenish's book, *The Montreal Canadiens: 100 Years of Glory*:

"'California regretfully defers its number one choice to the Stanley Cup champion Montreal Canadiens,' replied general manager Gary Young.

'Canadiens' turn,' said Campbell.

'Time, please, Mr. Campbell,' Pollock shouted for effect. Then, smiling broadly, he said, 'Mr. Campbell, Montreal Canadiens choose Guy Lafleur of the Quebec Remparts.'"

The front page of the next day's *Montreal Gazette* showed a photograph of a smiling Lafleur and new Canadiens coach Scotty Bowman under the caption "Couple of newcomers."

The Canadiens' famous torch, which Béliveau had received from the failing hands of Maurice Richard in 1960, had now been passed to nineteen-year-old Guy Lafleur.

After choosing Lafleur, with the number seven pick the Canadiens chose winger Chuck Arnason, who would play in only 36 games with Montreal and 401 total during his NHL career, over 10 NHL seasons. They had more luck with their third first-round pick, at the 11 spot, speedy Ottawa '67s winger Murray Wilson, who would go on to win four Stanley Cups with the team between 1972–73 and 1977–78 before injuries derailed his career at the age of twenty-eight.

The Canadiens' first choice in the second round, the 20th overall pick, was explained in only eleven words in the following day's *Montreal Gazette*:

"The Canadiens also chose Larry Robinson, a tough defenceman from Kitchener."

Robinson would go on to play 20 NHL seasons, winning six Stanley Cups, two Norris trophies as the NHL's best defenseman, and one Conn Smythe Trophy as playoff MVP in the 17 years he spent in Montreal.

On teams coached by Scotty Bowman, and with Robinson as a teammate, Guy Lafleur won five Stanley Cups, three NHL scoring titles, two Hart trophies as the league's most valuable player, and one Conn Smythe Trophy.

A hero drops in: Canadiens legend Jean Béliveau pays a visit to a young Guy Lafleur in the Quebec Remparts locker room (Photo Moderne/Hockey Hall of Fame).

With Robinson, Sam Pollock and the Canadiens had gotten lucky. With Guy Lafleur, they made their own luck

Scotty Bowman would coach Lafleur and Robinson to one Stanley Cup in 1973 and four consecutive ones from 1976 to 1979. He won one Stanley Cup with the Pittsburgh Penguins in 1992, and his third Cup, his ninth overall, with the Detroit Red Wings in 2002, surpassing the previous mark of eight held by the man he almost succeeded, Toe Blake.

CANADIENS BUNGLE FIRST PICK IN 1980 DRAFT

Incredibly, in June of 1980, only one year after winning their fourth-consecutive Stanley Cup, the Canadiens once again found themselves with the top pick in the NHL Entry Draft.

"Trader Sam" Pollock was the man responsible again, once more dealing with a lowly team. On September 13, 1976, Pollock sent minor-leaguers Ron Andruff and Sean Shanahan to the Colorado Rockies for the option to swap first-round picks in the 1980 draft, almost four years down the line. And when the first-year Rockies finished dead last at the end of the 1979–80 season,

Montreal would happily exercise its option. Trouble was, Pollock, having resigned after the 1977–78 season, was not around to decide how to use the pick.

The debate over who to choose raged in newspapers and on radio call-in shows for weeks. The consensus choice was Doug Wickenheiser. The belief at the time was that the Canadiens needed a big center to work with Guy Lafleur, and the 6-foot-1, 186-pound center, who had scored an amazing 89 goals and 81 assists for 170 points with the Regina Pats in his last year of junior hockey, fit the bill.

The choice most popular among French-speaking fans was local boy Denis Savard, who had starred for three years with the Montreal Juniors. Only 5-foot-10 and 170 pounds, Savard was a magician with the puck who notched 63 goals and 118 assists in his final junior year. (For parts of three seasons on the Juniors, he centered "Les Trois Denis," a highly successful line completed by his boyhood teammates and friends, Denis Cyr and Denis Tremblay. Not only did they share the same first name, but they were all born on the same day, February 4, 1961. From 1977 to 1979, with the Juniors, they combined for 665 points.)

On draft day, June 11, 1980, at the Montreal Forum, Montreal general manager Irving Grundman and the Canadiens announced their proud selection of . . . Doug Wickenheiser. It was a choice they would come to regret. Wickenheiser would play only three and a half seasons in Montreal. He would go on to play 556 NHL games with five different teams, never topping the 25-goal season he enjoyed with the Canadiens in 1982–83.

Denis Savard, meanwhile, went third overall to the Chicago Blackhawks. A nine-time NHL All-Star, Savard scored over 100 points five times in Chicago, including 119 in his second season, 1981–82. He scored a career-high 47 goals in 1985–86, and 131 points in 1987–88.

The Canadiens, and Grundman's successor, Serge Savard, tried to redeem themselves by acquiring Denis Savard in a trade before the 1990–91 season. But after missing significant time with injuries in Chicago the two previous years, Savard wasn't the same player. He scored 28 goals in each of his first two seasons, but never managed more than 70 points. In the 1992–93 playoffs, Savard had no goals and 5 assists in 14 games as the Canadiens went on to win their 24th Stanley Cup, and he was traded to the Tampa Bay Lightning the following season. He finished his career back in Chicago in 1997 having played 1,196 games, and was inducted into the Hockey Hall of Fame in 2000.

In exchange for Savard, the Canadiens sent co-captain and 1989 Norris Trophy winner Chris Chelios to Chicago. Chelios would go on to win two more Norris trophies as the NHL's top defenseman and play in a total of 11 All-Star games. He retired in 2010 after playing in 1,651 NHL games.

Doug Wickenheiser died tragically in 1999, at the age of thirty-seven, from a rare form of cancer, just five years after retiring from professional hockey.

3rd Period

The Greatest Game

22

It wasn't a dramatic playoff game, or an epic regular season game; it was simply an exhibition game, albeit an unusual one, taking place mid-season. But many people, including an author who devoted an entire book to it, consider it to be the greatest hockey game ever played.

A common sportswriting cliché is to place the word "meaningless" before "exhibition game." But this was anything but. Given the context and its many storylines, the December 31, 1975 game between the Montreal Canadiens and the Central Red Army team of the Soviet Union was a meaningful one in every way.

The game was the third played in an event called Super Series '76, in which two club teams from the U.S.S.R., the Soviet Wings and the perennial powerhouse Central Red Army, each played four games against a total of eight different NHL teams. The Series came more than three years after the thrilling Summit Series of 1972, in which a team of top Canadian NHL players played eight games against the national team of the U.S.S.R., four taking place in cities across Canada, and four in Moscow. That series, narrowly won in an epic comeback by Team Canada, had served as a wake-up call to those who took international hockey superiority to be a Canadian birthright.

Game 1 of the series, on September 2, 1972 at the Montreal Forum, saw Team Canada take an early 2–0 lead but fall 7–3. The smug smile on the faces of the many who had predicted an easy, eight-game sweep for Canada was harshly wiped off as the Soviets displayed a level of skill and strategic brilliance few had thought them capable of. In the process, they made the Canadian game look slow, lumbering, and devoid of imagination. After the four games played in Canada, the Soviets held a 2–1–1 lead.

Some heroic and even underhanded play by Team Canada late in the series in Moscow helped avoid what would have been a complete and utter humiliation. And even after the dramatic win, there was surprise over the quality of the Soviet game, and considerable hand-wringing over the state of Canadian hockey. Had Team Canada lost, there would surely have been cries for a Royal Commission to look into the matter.

That said, North American hockey took a long time to heed the warning of 1972. Goon hockey continued to make gains in the NHL, culminating in consecutive Stanley Cup wins in 1974 and 1975 by its chief proponents, the Philadelphia Flyers.

Now the "Russians," as most in the hockey world continued to call them, were coming back, and even though seven of the eight games would take place in US cities, Canada's national pride would be at stake. It was the Cold War, fought on a second front. And those charged with defending Canada's hockey heritage would be the only Canadian-based team in the Series, the Montreal Canadiens.

The Canadiens of 1975–76 were a dynasty in the making, months away from what would be the first of four consecutive Stanley Cups (*see Good vs. Evil: The Series That Saved Hockey, page 103*). Fifth-year coach, Scotty Bowman, who guided the team to a championship in 1973, preached a new commitment to defensive hockey, with impressive results. They were still the Flying Frenchmen, with the likes of Guy Lafleur, who in 1974–75 finally had the season that was expected of him when the team drafted him first overall in 1971—53 goals and 119 points—and who would go on to win his first of three consecutive Art Ross trophies as the NHL's top scorer. But with a defensive corps led by the "Big Three" of Serge Savard, Guy Lapointe, and Larry Robinson, and excellent two-way players like Bob Gainey and Jacques Lemaire, the Canadiens had become the league's stingiest defensive team as well, one who could count on the stellar netminding of twenty-eight-year-old All-Star Ken Dryden. In the 37 games they played before facing the Red Army the team led the NHL with a record of 25–5–6. And Dryden, in 31 games played, could boast of a goals-against-average of 1.72.

The Red Army team, meanwhile, was a well-oiled and talent-packed machine, purposely stacked by the Soviet hockey establishment and perennial champions of the U.S.S.R's domestic league. The Super Series edition of the squad featured no fewer than 15 members of the country's celebrated and decorated national team, including 12 who had played in the Summit Series, a number of whom were known to North American fans for their performances back in 1972. This included dazzling forward Valeri Kharlamov, team captain Boris Mikhailov, and twenty-three-year-old goaltender Vladislav Tretiak. What's more, the team borrowed two of the top national team players from other Soviet clubs for their North American tour.

The Red Army wasted no time showing what they were made of, beating the New York Rangers 7–3 in Madison Square Garden on December 28. Towards the end of the first period, Kharlamov gave his team a 4–1 lead with a spectacular power play goal, barreling through a wall of Rangers players at the New York blue line before flicking a high shot over goalie John Davidson. The goal was the highlight of what would be

AN INTERNATIONAL HOCKEY EVENT

goal

U.S.S.R. vs. NHL

The official Super Series '76 program (Hockey Hall of Fame).

an almost total domination of the Rangers, and the other teams slated to play the Red Army swallowed hard in realization of what faced them.

Scotty Bowman, however, watching the game at home, had noticed a flaw in the Red Army's game, confirming an observation he'd previously made while watching game film of the Soviets, which he thought the Canadiens could exploit.

The Red Army arrived in Montreal on December 29 to a city a buzzing with excitement in anticipation of a meeting between two of the most successful hockey teams in the world. The Canadiens were excited, too. Fully comprehending what was expected of them, especially after the Soviet Wings beat the Pittsburgh Penguins 7–4 in the second game of the Series, they practiced and prepared for the contest with a rarely seen vigor and purpose. Many openly expressed their nervousness, especially the six Canadiens—Savard, Lapointe, Dryden, Yvan Cournoyer, Pete Mahovlich, and Don Awrey—who had been part of the 1972 Team.

"You're damn right I want to win," Mahovlich told the *Montreal Gazette.* "It's important to me."

The media, meanwhile, ratcheted up the hype, with Milt Dunnell of the *Toronto Star* going so far as to say that a win by the Russians would be the "real shocker" North American hockey needed.

"It might bring home the horrible truth to the elders of the NHL that they are no longer retailing the best brand of their product in the world."

Back in Montreal, the sportswriters at the *Montreal Gazette* were making their predictions. Columnist Tim Burke foresaw a 6–4 Canadians victory while Doug Gilbert anticipated an 8–4 Red Army win. Al Strachan, for his part, predicted a 3–2 Canadiens win, but in an another story under the headline, "Dryden Can't Hide Feelings about beating Russians," he noted, "No matter how well the Canadiens play tonight, they can't possibly hope to beat the Central Red Army team without a big effort in goal."

No pressure, Ken.

The decision to hold the game on New Year's Eve in Montreal added another dimension to what would be an especially electric atmosphere. While hockey fans across the country gathered in homes, arrived early at parties, or came together in crowded bars, many in the Forum crowd of 18,975 arrived dressed to the nines. There would be New Year's Eve parties and galas to attend after the game, and a Canadiens win would help fans ring in the New Year with joy and optimism. There was a true sense of occasion. The event had taken on a special magnitude. It was more than just a hockey game.

Meanwhile, in Moscow, where the game was being broadcast live, it was already 1976.

After player introductions, in which Kharlamov and Tretiak were singled out by the Forum crowd for loud cheers, an official face-off ceremony was held and the teams exchanged gifts (the only gift exchange to take place in the Super Series), and the great

Danny Gallivan, who would handle the play-by-play on the *Hockey Night in Canada* broadcast that night, remarked to his partner, Dick Irvin: "Well, Dick, there seems to be, and we are thankful for it, a great spirit of camaraderie here between these teams, starting the game, anyway."

First Period

Finally it was time for referee Wally Harris to drop the puck and let one of the most anticipated games in history get under way. With the unusual Canadiens forward line of speedsters Bob Gainey, Murray Wilson, and Guy Lafleur, a winger who lined up at center for the face-off, Scotty Bowman was about to show the Red Army the awesome pace at which this game would be played.

Barely 20 seconds into the game, Gainey sent Wilson in on a breakaway with a long pass, but Tretiak, in a scenario he would repeat throughout the night, held his ground and made the save.

Scotty Bowman's strategy immediately became clear as the Canadiens forechecked their opponents relentlessly, causing them to cough the puck up in their own end. On this night, the Soviets would get a taste of their own medicine as they watched the Canadiens control the puck for long stretches.

Just over three minutes into the first period, Canadiens left winger Steve Shutt collected a loose puck near the red line, skated into the Soviet zone, and from the top of the face-off circle, ripped an absolute rocket of a slap shot that went into the top corner to Tretiak's left. The Forum exploded with joy as Shutt and his linemates celebrated with an enthusiasm usually reserved for the biggest of occasions. In their hearts and minds, this was one such occasion.

The Canadiens never stepped off the gas and continued to pressure the Soviets in their own zone. They were soon rewarded for their efforts and awarded a power play after Red Army defenseman Valeri Vasiliev was caught hooking Doug Risebrough. Tretiak and the Soviet penalty killers stymied Shutt, Cournoyer, and Mahovlich, but less than a minute after the penalty expired, big left winger Yvon Lambert, after an inspired shift with his linemates, twenty-one-year-old Doug Risebrough and nineteen-year-old Mario Tremblay (the youngest player in the game) picked up a loose puck and beat Tretiak between the legs. It was 2–0 Canadiens and the Red Army had yet to register a shot on Ken Dryden. Before he finally had to make a save midway through the first period, Dryden had not been tested for nearly an hour—by his own teammates in the warm-up.

The period ended with the Canadiens outshooting the Soviets 11–4. If not for the brilliance of Tretiak, who made several difficult saves, the Canadiens might already have run away with the game.

Second Period

The second period was almost a carbon copy of the first—except for two little details.

The Canadiens came roaring out of the gates to start the second. They narrowly missed going up 3–0 when Mahovlich, on a beautiful individual effort, had what seemed like a sure goal taken away when Tretiak made an incredible, last-second pad save. Then Lambert had another great opportunity at the left post on a pass from Tremblay and Wilson's backhand struck the crossbar behind a beaten Tretiak. The crowd shrieked in disbelief.

The Soviets were hanging on for dear life when Vasiliev hit Boris Mikhailov with a long pass that caught the Canadiens off guard. The onrushing Red Army captain gained the Montreal zone with speed, cut to the middle, and unleashed a quick, hard wrist shot that Dryden appeared to initially save, but the puck nicked his glove before slowly crossing the goal line. It was the Red Army's first shot of the second period.

Midway through the period, Cournoyer restored the Canadiens' two-goal lead during a power play, and the rest of the second was played at a frantic pace as Montreal sought to put the game away, but Tretiak managed save upon miraculous save.

The Red Army seemed to gather itself near the end of the period, resulting in a number of dangerous forays into the Canadiens' zone, and Dryden was forced to make a good save, his first of the period on what was only the Soviet's second shot, on a dangerous wrister by Vladimir Petrov. Minutes later, Petrov stick-handled his way into the Canadiens' zone and found a speeding Kharlamov with a soft saucer pass at the same time he was splitting the Canadiens' defense. The quick and nimble Soviet star then slid a backhand along the ice and beyond a helpless Dryden to make the score 3–2. The Red Army had scored twice on three shots in the period. After two periods, the Canadiens were outshooting the Soviets 22–7. Tretiak was the story of the game.

Third Period

As they had all game long, the Canadiens came out firing to start the third, taking four dangerous shots during an early power play. But Tretiak stopped them all. About 90 seconds after the end of the man-advantage, Montreal defenseman Don Awrey challenged for a loose puck along the boards in the neutral zone, but the puck got past him and suddenly the Soviets were on a 2-on-1 break at top speed. The Red Army's Viktor Shluktov lifted a soft pass over the stick of a diving Larry Robinson to send Boris Aleksandrov into the clear. Again, Dryden got a piece of the young winger's wrist shot with his glove, but the puck somehow found its way through and trickled across the goal line. The game was tied and the Forum crowd was stunned silent.

The remaining 15:56 passed in a blur while the Canadiens tried to regain the lead over the tiring Soviets, but the scoring chances that materialized were snuffed out by Tretiak. One of the best scoring opportunities of the period occurred when Vladimir Popov batted a puck past a rattled Dryden only to strike the goalpost.

The Forum crowd found its voice again in the game's final minutes, urging the home team on. And their enthusiasm almost paid off. On a play that began on a Serge Savard rush with 1:20 to play, Canadiens center Jacques Lemaire had a golden opportunity after a deflected Bob Gainey pass found him alone in front of Tretiak. The Soviet goaltender kicked out his left pad to stop a quick shot and the rebound came right back to the spinning Lemaire, and he fired a backhand towards Tretiak, who fell to his knees and closed the space between his pads before the puck could find its way through. The game ended after one more close call when Dryden stopped but then lost sight of a Boris Mikhailov backhand from the slot. The Canadiens' big netminder desperately looked for the puck while Mikhailov briefly and mistakenly raised his hands in celebration, but the puck was collected and cleared by Guy Lafleur. The Canadiens had dominated the game from start to finish, outshooting their visitors 38 to 13, but all they had to show for it was a 3–3 tie.

Pete Mahovlich, who had wanted to win so badly, and played so wonderfully, was visibly distraught. Ken Dryden, who desperately wanted to make up for some shaky performances in 1972 with a strong one in this game, was crushed. And while his critics laid much of the blame at his feet, his coach and teammates were more understanding. It could not have been easy, they said, facing those sudden Soviet rushes after such long periods of inaction.

The feeling of disappointment, for Canadiens fans and players alike, was soon replaced by one of pride when the reality of what they had all been a part of began to dawn on them. The game had been an exciting one from the first drop of the puck to the final siren, played at top speed, with skill and passion, and heart and soul, but also respect. There was none of the dirty play that so often raised its ugly head in NHL games. Instead, it was hockey the way it should be played—hard, breathtakingly fast, and thoroughly entertaining, a beautiful thing to behold. The following day's newspapers would second that emotion.

In his *Montreal Gazette* column, under the headline "A Night of Nights for Canadiens," Tim Burke placed the game among the finest sporting events he had ever seen, calling it ". . . an event worthy of being framed in Churchillian grandeur, so that if Le Club de Hockey Canadien should last a thousand years, remember this one as their finest hour.

"In what was probably the most important and far-reaching sporting event ever held in this country, the Canadiens resurrected one of our proudest heritages and enshrined it with an unrivalled display of determination and sportsmanship."

Another headline over an Al Strachan game story summed things up perfectly. "Now That's How You Play Hockey, Comrade."

Back on the ice, at game's end, the night's Three Stars—Tretiak, Mahovlich, and Cournoyer—also seemed to suddenly seize the spirit of the moment, posing for photos, smiling broadly, with their arms draped over each other's shoulders as the crowd applauded loudly. It was far cry from the experience the Red Army team would have 11 days later in Philadelphia, when they would suffer their only loss of the Series. But that's another story.

VLADISLAV TRETIAK, HONORARY MONTREAL CANADIEN

The Super Series visits by club teams from the U.S.S.R. continued on and off until 1991, when the Soviet Union was in its final days and many of the best Soviet players were already playing in the NHL.

Helping to feed the hockey-watching public's appetite for more top-notch international competition in a time when professionals were not allowed to play in the Olympics, the Soviet National team visited Canada to play in the Canada Cup tournaments in 1976, 1981, 1984, 1987, and 1991. In February of 1979, the team came to New York to face a squad of NHL All-Stars in the three-game Challenge Cup at Madison Square Garden. The NHL team, which featured seven Montreal Canadiens, won Game 1, 4–2, and the Soviets took the second game, 5–4. In the third and final game, the Soviets humiliated the NHL stars 6–0.

For most of these games, Vladislav Tretiak, the star of the New Year's Eve game in Montreal, defended the Soviet goal. Over the years, he continued to be a revered figure in hockey circles, particularly in Montreal, and he dreamed of finishing his great career in a Canadiens uniform. His old rival Serge Savard, while serving as Canadiens' general manager, chose the thirty-year-old with the team's ninth pick, 138th overall, in the 1983 NHL Amateur Draft. But Soviet officials turned down Tretiak's request to leave and he retired from hockey in 1984 at age thirty-two.

In 1989, Tretiak, who won three Olympic Gold Medals and 10 International Ice Hockey Federation World Championships over his illustrious career, became the first Soviet to be inducted into the Hockey Hall of Fame. He finally made it to the NHL in 1990, when the Chicago Blackhawks hired him as a goaltending coach. He ran a popular goaltending school in Montreal in the 1990s that continues to operate in the Toronto area.

3rd Period

In 1996, Tretiak was a special guest at the ceremony for the closing of the Montreal Forum (*see Shutting Down a Shrine, page 45*), and in 2007 he was on hand to pay tribute to his goaltending rival Ken Dryden when the Canadiens retired his number 29 jersey.

In 2010, Tretiak was named the general manager of Russia's Olympic hockey team. The final torchbearer at the 2014 Olympics in Sochi, Russia, he now serves as the president of the Russian Ice Hockey Federation.

Captain Courageous
Conquers Cancer

23

Hockey stars are accustomed to applause, whether for scoring goals, winning games, or receiving awards. It's what players, and fans, live for. But the ovation Canadiens captain Saku Koivu received on April 9, 2002 was different: it was long, it was loud, and there were tears.

The applause started before Koivu emerged from the dressing room, intensified when he hit the ice, and lasted a full eight minutes. The crowd chanted "Saku! Saku! Saku!" and the national anthem was barely audible. Several times the referee attempted to start the game, but the fans, many of whom had brought homemade signs with them bearing Koivu's name, kept cheering. The visiting Ottawa Senators saluted Koivu by banging their sticks on the boards while the man himself stood at center ice, nodding and occasionally smiling, embarrassed by the sustained outpouring of love and support from the Montreal fans.

They were there to congratulate Koivu—a dazzling playmaker, stick-handler, and skater—not on his hockey exploits, but on his perseverance and courage in battling non-Hodgkin's lymphoma. It was the Canadiens' 80th game of the season, but Koivu's first. Diagnosed with Burkitt's lymphoma seven months earlier, Koivu's life had hung in the balance. While his teammates were at the rink, their captain was undergoing a grueling course of chemo and radiation therapy, including forty injections to the spine.

The story of Koivu's cancer went well beyond the sports pages. It was shocking that such a vigorous young athlete was stricken, and inspiring that by February his cancer was in remission. At that point, most expected Koivu to return to the NHL the following season, if at all. But Koivu has an exceptional work ethic, and once cleared to resume training, he made it his mission to return to the ice in time for the playoffs. Given how much weight and strength he had lost, this was a seemingly impossible task, but Koivu pulled it off with three games to spare.

Saku Koivu salutes the Bell Centre crowd on the night of his return to action after missing most of the 2001–2002 season following cancer treatment (Pierre Obendrauf/Montreal Gazette. Reprinted by permission).

Koivu played over eight minutes in that first game back, and in the Canadiens' two remaining regular season games he scored two points. In the playoffs, Koivu led the team to a first-round victory over Boston (the Canadiens then lost to Carolina in the conference semifinals). Koivu, who only months before could barely get out of bed, notched 10 points in 12 playoff games. Not surprisingly, at season's end he received the Bill Masterton Memorial Trophy for perseverance, sportsmanship, and dedication to hockey.

Koivu had always been well respected and active in the community, and his inspirational story made him a hero, especially to those battling cancer. He was also driven to fill a very specific and glaring need in Montreal. Amazingly, the city, home to several major hospitals and two medical schools, did not have a PET/CT scanner, an expensive and valuable imaging tool for diagnosing and monitoring cancer. When Koivu received the PET scan declaring him cancer-free, it was at a hospital in Sherbrooke, Quebec, 100 miles east of Montreal. Koivu told Canadiens team doctor David Mulder that he was embarrassed for him that he did not have a PET/CT scanner at the Montreal General Hospital, and so was born the Saku Koivu Foundation. The Foundation's first goal was to raise the millions needed to help purchase and install the PET/CT machine, and it was wildly successful in this effort. The hospital obtained the machine in 2004, enabling thousands of patients yearly to receive scans.

Until he was diagnosed with cancer, Koivu had led a charmed life. The elder of two boys (his younger brother, Mikko, would also go on to star in the NHL), Koivu was born in 1974 and grew up in a happy middle-class family in Turku, Finland. His father was a well-known hockey coach, and Koivu played three seasons for TPS in the Finnish Elite League, winning two championships. In his third season with TPS, he was the league's top scorer, season MVP, and playoff MVP. Pretty good for a player who many thought was too small (5-foot-10) to make it in the Finnish pro league, never mind the NHL. Drafted by the Canadiens in the first round in 1993, he scored 20 goals in his rookie season in 1995–96, finishing fourth in rookie of the year voting. In 1999 Koivu was named Habs captain, the first European-born player to receive this honor. He would go on to serve ten years in this capacity, tying him with Jean Béliveau as Montreal's longest-serving captain.

Prior to his battle with cancer, Koivu had suffered knee and shoulder injuries, causing him to miss major parts of several seasons. Still, as he returned to Montreal in early September 2001, Koivu was a handsome, wealthy twenty-six-year-old pro hockey player plying his trade in the game's Mecca. His personal life was also solid: he'd spent the summer in Finland, much of it with family members at a lakeside cottage, and had become engaged to Hanna, whom he would marry the following year. Koivu's goal for 2001–02 was to return the Canadiens to the playoffs. He had his challenges, but Koivu's life was by all measures an enviable one.

That all changed very quickly in early September 2001 when on the flight to Montreal for training camp, Koivu was stricken with severe abdominal pain and vomiting. Teammate Brian Savage and his wife, both of whom could tell that Koivu was very sick, met Saku and Hanna at the airport. Koivu initially dismissed his illness as food poisoning, but when the pain in his stomach spread to his lower back and he continued vomiting, Hanna urged him to seek medical attention. It didn't take long for Canadiens team doctor David Mulder to diagnose Koivu with cancer. Koivu had experienced occasional stomach pain while training over the summer in Finland, and now it made sense.

Koivu underwent an aggressive regimen of both chemo and radiation therapy, including forty injections into his spinal column. The cancer, and the treatments for it, waylaid him, and for long periods he just lay in a dim room, hardly able to move. The idea of returning to the NHL seemed not just remote, but irrelevant; Koivu was in a fight for his life. This was different than a knee injury that can certainly end a hockey career, but not kill a person.

Eventually, Koivu turned a corner in his treatment and his cancer went into remission. Once he got the news, he immediately began working on returning to the ice, and in eight weeks went from cancer patient to NHL player again. When the Habs' 2002 playoff run ended, Koivu went home to Finland and married Hanna. When he returned to Montreal the following September, a year after having been diagnosed with cancer, he was in excellent shape, and went on to have a stellar season—and an injury-free one—scoring 20 goals and 71 points in 82 contests.

Injuries had always been a problem for Koivu, and well before his battle with cancer, he had struggled with serious knee injuries as well as a separated shoulder. In 1995–96, a spectacular sophomore season was cut short and he wound up playing only 50 games (and scoring 56 points). In 1999–2000, Koivu suited up for a mere 24 contests, and in 2000–01 he missed 28 matches. There were also a number of other years in which the center would miss 10–15 games.

No doubt the scariest injury Koivu sustained was not to his chronically bad left knee, but to his eye. In 2006, coming off what had been an injury-free season in which he scored 75 points, Koivu nearly lost his eye to a high stick in a playoff game against Carolina. That summer was a grueling one for Koivu as he had surgery on a detached retina, and struggled to regain full vision. Once again, he found himself in a darkened room, able to do little except listen to (not watch) television. It was deemed doubtful that Koivu would return for the beginning of the following season, but once again he rose to the occasion, and ended up playing 77 games.

For a player who suffered as many injuries as he did, Koivu had a long NHL career—playing thirteen seasons with Montreal, then another five with Anaheim. He also had an additional year with his alma mater, TPS Turku, in 2004–05 during the strike year. One thing was certain with Koivu—regardless how many games he played in a given season, he was always full value. He possessed both skill and grit, and was a deft stick-handler and playmaker with a quick shot. Koivu was also an exceptional defensive player, not afraid to mix it up with larger opposition. Later in his career as a member of the Anaheim Ducks, Koivu's offensive powers had dimmed, but he was still dangerous with the puck, and a relentless forechecker.

Koivu's time in Montreal ended on something of a sour note, as he came under fire from Guy Bertrand, a prominent Québecois nationalist lawyer, for having failed to learn French during the many years he had spent in Montreal. This was the first time Koivu himself had been at the center of controversy. Since his arrival in Montreal there had been numerous changes in coaches, front office staff, and even ownership. Star goalie Patrick Roy was traded in a blow-up with then-coach Mario Tremblay during Koivu's rookie year (*see St. Patrick's Last Day, page 38*), and the following season the Habs left the Forum for a new building. Moreover, the turmoil in coaching and management was a reflection of the many mediocre teams—particularly in the late 1990s—Koivu played on.

Throughout his time in Montreal, Koivu's work ethic, his character, and the quality of his play were unassailable, and that left the captain's lack of ability to speak French as a sore point, less so among hockey fans than Québecois nationalists keen to score political points. Maybe the high bar that Koivu had set—becoming a first-round draft pick despite measuring only 5-foot-10, being named team captain in his mid-twenties, and beating cancer and helping those suffering from the disease—made people wonder, well, if he can do all that, surely he could learn to speak the language of Molière. And they were probably right; Koivu himself expressed regret that he hadn't learned the dominant language in the city he called home for over a dozen years.

Koivu's contract with the Canadiens expired at the end of the 2008–09 season, and both sides knew it was time for a change. A free agent, he signed with Anaheim during the off-season, joining fellow Finn Teemu Selanne for five years before retiring following the 2013–14 season. While not the offensive force he'd been earlier in his career, Koivu remained productive during his time in Southern California. Moreover, he was able to relax a bit as he moved from the constant scrutiny under which Montreal's players live, to an environment where hockey is a pleasant diversion, not life itself.

A proud Finn, Koivu is very popular in his homeland. He was wildly successful in the Finnish league and in representing his country in international play. In his third season playing for TPS Turku, Koivu was the league's top scorer, season MVP, and playoff MVP. Koivu also shone on the world stage, and scored 120 points in 102 games suiting up for Suomi in the Olympics, the World Cup of Hockey, and other tournaments. He was a member of Finland's silver medal team at the 2006 Olympics, and won bronze medals in 1994, 1998, and 2010. Koivu also led Finland to a silver medal at the 2004 World Cup of Hockey. He carried on a tradition of excellence by Finns in the NHL, ending his career with 832 points, trailing only superstars Teemu Selanne and Jari Kurri in points scored by Finnish-born players.

Saku Koivu remains a revered figure to many in Montreal: his service as captain for 10 years, his work in getting the Montreal General its PET/CT scanner, and, of course, his outstanding play and courage in battling cancer, secured him a permanent place in the hearts of Montreal fans. In 2011, in his first game back in Montreal as a member of the visiting Anaheim Ducks, he received a warm welcome, something that is not always the case for returning former players. Koivu's last game in front of Montreal fans was in 2013, and he was greeted with a standing ovation by Bell Centre fans.

In December 2014, the dust had settled on Koivu's NHL career and the Canadiens honored him in a half-hour ceremony before a game against the Ducks. Koivu, his wife and two children, and his parents joined the former captain on the ice for the honor.

Koivu, wearing his number 11 jersey emblazoned with its customary "C," thanked the city and its fans, in English and in French, for the love and support they had shown him. The ceremony came just one week after an emotional tribute to Canadiens legend Jean Béliveau, who had died two weeks earlier. Once again, the tribute to Koivu was emotional, and had special resonance for those who had been in the stands in 2002. In those intervening twelve years, Koivu had thrived as a dedicated and outstanding player, a devoted husband and father, and a survivor, leader, and inspirational figure.

TEAM CLINIC

Saku Koivu and his teammates kept team physician Dr. David Mulder and his colleagues on the Canadiens' medical staff very busy in the late 1990s and early 2000s.

The first serious incident of that period took place in Los Angeles on November 20, 1999, when Canadiens winger Brian Savage suffered a neck injury in a game against the Kings. As he wound up to take a slap shot in the Los Angeles zone, Savage was checked hard by rugged Kings forward Ian Laperrière, whose shoulder hit him flush on the chin. Savage fell to the ice, writhing in pain, and was tended to by the Kings' medical team before being carried off on a stretcher. At the hospital, he was diagnosed with two fractured vertebrae and ligament damage in his spinal column. Savage was out of the lineup for four months.

That same season, Canadiens forward Trent McCleary nearly died as a result of a throat injury sustained at the then-Molson Centre. On Saturday January 29, 2000, midway through the second period of an afternoon game against Philadelphia, McCleary slid awkwardly to block a slap shot by Flyers defenseman Chris Therien. The puck struck McCleary squarely in the throat, completely fracturing his larynx. McCleary lay on his stomach, kicking his skates frantically, and then got to his feet with the help of teammates and team trainers. Unable to breathe, he collapsed in the hallway seconds after leaving the ice. Members of the Canadiens' medical staff partially opened McCleary's airway and he was rushed to the Montreal General Hospital, where Mulder and head trauma surgeon Daniel Fleiszer performed an emergency tracheotomy on him while he was still in his full equipment, including his skates (which, according to rumour, were later stolen in the hospital). Mulder later said that McCleary, who had also suffered a collapsed lung, had come within minutes of dying. McCleary attempted a comeback in training camp the following season, but, unable to breathe sufficiently due to an air passage that was 15 percent more narrow than normal, he could not play a full shift and was forced to retire. McCleary, who the Canadiens then hired as a scout for Western Canada, needed several surgeries on his throat to restore his voice.

On December 1, 2001, only a few months after Saku Koivu was diagnosed with cancer and two weeks after coming to Montreal in a trade with the Buffalo Sabres, Canadiens forward Donald Audette had his left forearm stepped on by a skate after diving to make a play in a game at the Molson Centre against the New York Rangers. Audette immediately got to his feet, and with blood spouting from his arm, skated directly off the ice. He was rushed to hospital, where surgeons worked on his arm, which had suffered 10 lacerated tendons, for four hours.

On April 25, 2002, less than a month after Audette returned to action and only two weeks after Koivu's incredible return, Canadiens winger Richard Zednik was seriously injured in a first-round playoff game against the Boston Bruins. With 1:15 left to play in the third period of Game 4, less than 12 minutes after his second goal of the game had cut Boston's lead to 4–2, and only 34 seconds after a fight between Bruins agitator P. J. Stock and Montreal tough guy Gino Odjick, Zednik was knocked unconscious after taking a vicious forearm to the face from Boston defenseman Kyle McLaren. He suffered a concussion, a broken nose, a bruised throat, and a cut on his right eyelid. McLaren was suspended for one game, and the Canadiens won the next two to win the series, 4–2.

Celebrating a Centennial

24

When you are one of the oldest sports teams in the world and part of the fabric of your community, turning one hundred years old is worthy of a major celebration. And the Montreal Canadiens have always known how to celebrate in style.

In late September 2008, on the eve of the team's 100th season, the Canadiens announced a program of centennial events that would span parts of two seasons, with the finale scheduled for the anniversary date itself, December 4, 2009.

At the time of the announcement, the Canadiens were owned by American businessman George N. Gillett, whose purchase of the team from Molson Inc. in January 2001 was met with raised eyebrows in some quarters. Gillett's business past was a checkered one, which included a bankruptcy as recently as 1992, but it was his nationality that garnered the most attention, and there were even concerns that this outsider would one day move the team, which Gillett immediately defused. The Canadiens were a Canadian and Quebec institution; certainly local owners could be found to keep the team in Canadian hands, couldn't they? But the answer, according to Molson Inc. CEO Daniel O'Neil, was no. With the business of hockey on shaky ground, no Canadian buyers had stepped forward and Gillett acquired 80 percent of the hockey team and 100 percent of the Molson Centre for $275 million. The Molson Centre had been built only six years before, at a cost of $265 million. But the team had been losing millions of dollars per year, and Molson, a publicly owned company, could no longer justify the losses to its shareholders. George Gillett got a real bargain.

It was the end of an era for the Molson family, whose members had owned the Canadiens for most of the previous fifty years, going back to the 1957 purchase of the team and the Montreal Forum by brothers Hartland and Thomas Molson.

Gillett, for the most part, turned out to be a good owner with great respect for the team's history and traditions, and the controversy over his nationality eventually died down. Under his ownership, the planning of the team's centennial celebrations started several years in advance of the anniversary itself, and included jersey retirement ceremonies every year beginning with the 2005–06 season. In separate ceremonies, the number 12 was retired in honor of Dickie Moore and Yvan Cournoyer, followed by the raising to the rafters of the number 5 worn by Bernie "Boom Boom" Geoffrion. Ceremonies for Serge Savard (18) and Ken Dryden (29) took place in 2006–07, and were followed by events honoring Larry Robinson (19) and Bob Gainey (23), the team's general manager at the time, in 2007–08.

Among the major events scheduled to take place over the next sixteen months were the presentation of the 57th NHL All-Star Game on January 25, 2009, and the 2009 NHL Entry Draft, to be held at the Bell Centre June 26–27. The inauguration of a community rink initiative, a special concert by the Montreal Symphony Orchestra, and the premiere of a feature-length film on the team were also on the program. One of the most talked about initiatives was the Centennial Jersey Nights, 12 games in which the Canadiens would wear jerseys of historical significance from their past.

One of the most important of the centennial events, in the eyes of the team's fans, anyway, occurred early in the 2008–09 season, on November 22, when the team retired the number 33 jersey belonging to prodigal goaltender Patrick Roy, who left the team in controversy nearly thirteen years before (see *St. Patrick's Last Day, page 38*). The ceremony represented an official homecoming for the man largely responsible for the team's last two Stanley Cups. A few weeks later, the team inaugurated the Centennial Plaza, featuring historical plaques dedicated to the team's 24 Stanley Cup wins and retired jerseys. The Plaza's centerpieces were stunning bronze statues of Canadiens legends Howie Morenz, Maurice "Rocket" Richard, Jean Béliveau, and Guy Lafleur.

One of the most surprising events of the centennial period took place shortly after the end of the 2008–09 NHL season, and it was not part of the official program. On June 20, 2009, George Gillett, needing cash to help fund the purchase of the Liverpool FC soccer team in England, sold the Canadiens, the Bell Centre, and the Gillett Entertainment Group to brothers Geoff, Andrew, and Justin Molson, for an estimated $550 million. The team was back in the Molson family's hands.

The Big Night

The grand finale of the celebrations took place on December 4, 2009, one hundred years to the day the Club de Hockey Le Canadien was founded by J. Ambrose O'Brien. In that night's Centennial Game, which would be followed by a lavish gala, the Canadiens would play their archrivals, the Boston Bruins.

The night's program had not been made public, so there was a curious buzz in the air when the siren wailed and Bell Centre lights went dark well before game time. A cheer went up when the number 100 appeared on the scoreboard and began to count down: 99, 98, 97 . . . When it hit zero, the first of two short videos featuring some of the highlights of the past hundred years was played, followed by an introduction to the evening's program, which was described as a final tribute to the team's players, builders, and administrators.

In contrast to the pomp that had marked some of the other events, the next portion of the ceremonies was heartwarming in its simplicity. It started with sixty-nine-year-old Eddy Palchak, the beloved Canadiens trainer and equipment manager for thirty-one years, resplendent in the red satin team jacket he wore with pride for so long. Behind the home team's bench he came, toting a bucket of pucks, which he proceeded to dump on the ice, as he had so many times before prior to the pregame warm-up. The fans chanted, "Eddy, Eddy . . ."

Then they followed, the heart and soul of hockey's most legendary team, the players:

First out was forty-four-year-old Patrick Roy, in full goaltender's equipment, masked flipped up on his head, and wearing his famous number 33. The Bell Centre fans had not been expecting this, and roared with approval at the sight of St. Patrick in his old uniform again, striding hard around the ice.

Then they stepped out onto the ice, one by one, in no order particular order of chronology or importance, players from the 1960s and the very near present, scorers and checkers, defensemen and even fighters, each in full equipment and sporting a white Canadiens jersey with their name and number emblazoned across the back: Chris Nilan, Mats Naslund (The "Little Viking" who became the first European-born player to play for the team), Pierre Bouchard, Claude Lemieux, Guy Lafleur, Serge Savard, Eric Desjardins, Vincent Damphousse, Stéphane Richer, Guy Carbonneau, Steve Shutt, Mike Keane, Lyle Odelein, Patrice Brisebois (the youngest of the group at age thirty-seven, and only a few months into retirement), Larry Robinson, Réjean Houle, Yvan Cournoyer, Guy Lapointe, Yvon Lambert, Doug Jarvis, Pierre Turgeon, Frank Mahovlich (at almost seventy-one years of age, the oldest of the group), Pete Mahovlich, Bob Gainey (the general manager of the team), and finally, the evening's other goaltender, also in full equipment, Ken Dryden.

The whistling and cheering continued as the heroes of years gone by skated and stick-handled around the rink. Behind their bench, each wearing a Canadiens centennial tie, stood the surviving Stanley Cup winning coaches—Jacques Demers, Jean Perron, Claude Ruel, and Scotty Bowman, the latter two speaking animatedly, as if it was 1976 all over again and they were arguing about which drills to run. Bowman, who had seen it all in a hockey life that lasted more than a half-century, later mouthed a single word: "Wow."

Soon, Roy stepped into his goal, lowered his mask, and began kicking away shots. Dryden followed suit shortly after, playing barefaced as his mask would not fit over his

Elmer Lauch (left), Emile "Butch" Bouchard (middle), and Emile's son Pierre Bouchard prior to the jersey retirement ceremony that took place during the Centennial Game celebrations on December 4, 2009 (The Associated Press/THE CANADIAN PRESS/Paul Chiasson).

eyeglasses. But no game broke out, and the players gradually left the ice. Those that lingered picked up the pucks and tossed them to the still cheering fans. Many would never return to the ice, and a few would never lace up a pair of skates again. It was nothing more than an easy skate-around, a warm-up. But it was more than enough. It was perfect.

After a beautiful video tribute to the players, coaches, and builders who passed away, each of the players in uniform as well as Dickie Moore, Henri Richard, and Jean Béliveau, legends beyond their skating years, was formally introduced. Roy (introduced by Serge Savard) and Lafleur (introduced by actor and Canadiens fan Viggo Mortensen) and Béliveau (introduced by Detroit Red Wings legend Gordie Howe), delivered speeches.

The final pregame ceremony was a touching one indeed. In the last of the centennial jersey retirements, the Canadiens paid tribute to the two oldest Canadiens alumni—ninety-one-year-old Elmer Lach, whose number 16 was first retired in 1975 in honor of Henri Richard, and ninety-year-old Emile "Butch" Bouchard. After banners bearing Lach's number 16 and Bouchard's number 3 were raised to the rafters to raucous cheers and the tears of the family members accompanying the two legends, Canadiens defenseman Ryan O'Byrne peeled off his number 3 jersey to reveal another beneath it bearing the number 20.

The ceremony was completed by the taking of the most unique photo in team history, as the former Canadiens, in white, and the 2009–10 Canadiens, in red, posed alongside each other. The photographer needed to stand way back.

The evening would go down as being among the most memorable ever, as long as the current Canadiens, who had a losing record at the time, didn't screw things up. But the inspired team didn't disappoint, easily beating the Bruins 5–1 on the strength of a Mike Cammalleri hat trick. The team's biggest star, goaltender Carey Price, wearing a special mask paying tribute to legendry Canadiens netminders of the past, stopped 37 of the 38 shots he faced.

The last word on the night went to the always-thoughtful Ken Dryden. Still in his goalie equipment, while being interviewed alongside Roy and Lafleur on the *Hockey Night in Canada* telecast, he reflected on the past and also on the current and future Canadiens.

"They've got to write their own story. It's pretty hard to carry around a hundred-year-old story . . . that's pretty intimidating. Now it's the next hundred years, and now it's up to them to write their new story, and they can write that story of 24 Stanley Cups in a hundred years too. It's time now, for the second hundred years to begin."

ROOKIE GOALTENDER HALAK LEADS CUP RUN

After their Centennial Game win over Boston on December 4, 2009, the 2009–10 Canadiens had a record of 13–14–2. But a six-game winning streak in March helped get them in the playoff hunt. The team earned the eighth and final playoff spot by a single point and had to face the NHL's best team, the high-scoring Washington Capitals, in the first round.

The Canadiens took Game 1 on an overtime goal by Tomas Plekanec, and had a 4–1 lead in the second period of Game 2, but a late Washington goal sent the contest to overtime, where Washington's Nicklas Backstrom scored after only 31 seconds of play. The Canadiens trailed the series when goaltender Jaroslav Halak, who had taken over for an ineffective Carey Price, caught fire. He gave up one goal on 38 shots in Game 5, one goal on 54 shots in Game 6, and one goal on 42 shots in Game 7, which Montreal won, 2–1.

In the next round, the Canadiens faced the defending Stanley Cup champion Pittsburgh Penguins. Pittsburgh scored four power play goals in their 6–3 Game 1 win, but Halak bounced back in Game 2 with a 38-save effort in a 3–1 Montreal victory. The teams traded wins and forced a seventh game in Pittsburgh on May 12, when the underdog Canadiens silenced the 17,132 Penguins fans in what would prove to be the final game at Mellon Arena. Brian Gionta scored 32 seconds into the game and Travis Moen scored shorthanded 5:14 into the second to give Montreal a 4–0 lead. Halak made 37 saves in what would be a 5–2 Canadiens win.

For the first time since 1993, the Canadiens were headed to the Conference Finals. But the dream of a 25th Stanley Cup died there, as the exhausted team bowed out in five games to the Philadelphia Flyers.

The Canadiens returned to the Conference Finals again in 2014. After sweeping the Tampa Bay Lightning in the first round and eliminating the favored Boston Bruins in seven dramatic games, the Canadiens lost goaltender Carey Price to injury in Game 1 of their series against the New York Rangers. They subsequently lost the series in six games.

To paraphrase the U2 song that played over one of the tribute videos during the Centennial Game ceremonies, the Canadiens and their legion of passionate fans still haven't found what they're looking for.

3rd Period

ACKNOWLEDGMENTS

The biggest cliché in acknowledgments is the classic "I couldn't have done this without . . ." But in this case, it is completely true. To finish this book on time, I called on some writer friends who also happen to be knowledgeable hockey guys as well: Jim McRae, a friend first, and longtime colleague second, who still skates like the wind and who grew up a stone's throw from the Montreal Forum, contributed "The Greatest Season," about the Canadiens of 1976–77; Doug Sweet, a politics nut who became a friend while he was my boss at McGill University, did a great job explaining "The Richard Riot"; Tim Lehnert, an old friend, ex-Montrealer, and an all-around smart, funny, and great guy who now resides in Cranston, Rhode Island, delivered "Captain Courageous Conquers Cancer," the story of Saku Koivu's return from illness in 2001–02. And finally, someone I only got to know through this project, John McFetridge, another former Montrealer, who writes crime fiction from his new home of Toronto, came through with "Dryden Debuts as Canadiens Shock Bruins," the story of the Habs' 1971 Cup victory. Thank you so much guys. I owe you a debt of gratitude and a good meal the next time we meet.

More sincere thanks are due to Craig Campbell, Manager, Resource Centre & Archives at the Hockey Hall of Fame, for his patience and expertise; to Patricia Desjardins, Licensing Coordinator/Visual Researcher of Photo and Video Resales and the *Montreal Gazette*; and to Niels and Julie at Skyhorse for thinking of me when this project first came up. Also, special thanks go out to all the hockey writers out there, especially D'Arcy Jenish and Todd Denault, whose books are more than great resources, but sources of inspiration, too.

Finally, some personal thanks: To Jason and Sam and all the other kids I have coached and forced to listen to my crazy hockey stories, thanks for reminding me how fun this game is. You keep me young. To the great hockey families in our new home of Ithaca, New York, who made us feel at home after our big move from Montreal. I send you all a big hug . . . and some of you one of those awkward both cheeks, Montreal kisses. And finally, to Mary: you always encourage me and support me and never let me down. I owe you everything.

—JH